A Basic Course in GULF ARABIC

HAMDI A. QAFISHEH

LIBRAIRIE DU LIBAN

&

THE UNIVERSITY OF ARIZONA PRESS
Tucson, Arizona

About the Author

HAMDI A. QAFISHEH, member of the University of Arizona Oriental Studies facility, specializes in Arabic and linguistics. Holder of degrees from the University of Baghdad and the University of Michigan, he also has taught at universities and language schools throughout the Middle East. His numerous other publications include *A Reference Grammar of Gulf Arabic,* and *Gulf Arabic: Intermediate Level,* published by the University of Arizona Press, and *An Introduction to Gulf Arabic, A Course in Levantine Arabic* (with others), and *Beginning English: A Basic Course for Arab Students.*

The research reported herein was performed pursuant to a contract with the United States Office of Education, Department of Health, Education, and Welfare, under the provisions of Title VI, Section 602, NDEA.

Fourth Printing 1984

THE UNIVERSITY OF ARIZONA PRESS

Manufactured in the U.S.A.

I.S.B.N. 0-8165-0483-0

ACKNOWLEDGMENTS

I would like to express my thanks and appreciation to all those who helped in the preparation of this book. To Professor Ernest N. McCarus, Chairman of the Department of Near Eastern Languages and Literatures of the University of Michigan, goes my deepest appreciation for having carefully read the manuscript and made a number of corrections and invaluable suggestions; to Professor Wallace M. Erwin, Chairman of the Department of Arabic, Georgetown University, for his constructive criticism at the early stages of writing; to my students in Tucson and in Abu Dhabi for having used the first draft; to Mrs. Emily K. Lovell for her insightful suggestions, corrections, and a laborious typing job well done ; to Miss Carol Bridgewater for her typing and assistance in compiling the glossary; to the Chairman of the Department of Oriental Studies, the Dean of Liberal Arts, and the Vice President for Research of the University of Arizona, for having provided the use of adequate office facilities and certain administrative and secretarial support; and to the administrators of the Office of Education of the Department of Health, Education, and Welfare for the contract which made this book possible. I acknowledge with deep appreciation the invaluable assistance and encouragement I had from Dr. Ezzeddin Ibrahim of the Ministry of Cabinet Affairs, Abu Dhabi, U.A.E. I must not neglect to mention the kindness and generosity of the Ministry of Cabinet Affairs of Abu Dhabi for bearing a partial cost of the publication of this book. My thanks go also to the Qatari Ministry of Education, which arranged for me to meet many useful informants and helped in several other ways. Finally it remains for me to record my hearty thanks to my informants, Mr. and Mrs. Abdalla Kaddas, Mr. Mohammad Mijrin, and Mr. Salim Khamis of Abu Dhabi, Mr. Abdul Aziz Bin Turki and Mr. Ibrahim al-Sharif of Qatar, and Mr. Mahdi al-Tajir of Bahrain. Last, but not least, my hearty thanks go to Mr. Carl N. Hodges, Director of the Environmental Research Laboratory, the University of Arizona, and the resident staff members of the Arid Lands Research Center of Abu Dhabi for their steady interest and encouragement.

TABLE OF CONTENTS

UNIT 1

I. TEXT
II. TRANSLATION
III. VOCABULARY
IV. PRONUNCIATION
  1. Short and Long Vowels
  2. Stress
V. GRAMMAR
  1. Suffixed Pronouns
  2. Equational Sentences
  3. Vowel Elision
  4. The Conjunction w
VI. DRILLS

UNIT 2

I. TEXT
II. TRANSLATION
III. VOCABULARY
IV. PRONUNCIATION
  1. Short and Long Vowels
  2. Stress
V. GRAMMAR
VI. DRILLS

UNIT 3

I. TEXT
II. TRANSLATION
III. VOCABULARY
IV. PRONUNCIATION
  1. Doubled Consonants
     Velarized ḷ
  2. Stress
V. GRAMMAR
  1. Suffixed Pronouns
  2. Gender in Nouns and Pronouns
  3. Gender in Adjectives
  4. The Article Prefix
VI. DRILLS

UNIT 4

I. TEXT
II. TRANSLATION
III. VOCABULARY
IV. PRONUNCIATION
  1. ∂̄, ∂̣̄, and ġ
  2. Stress
V. GRAMMAR
  1. Equational Sentences
  2. Noun Constructs
  3. Vowel Elision
VI. DRILLS

UNIT 5

I. TEXT
II. TRANSLATION
III. VOCABULARY
IV. PRONUNCIATION: t and ṭ
V. GRAMMAR
  1. The Vocative Particle
  2. Demonstratives
VI. DRILLS

UNIT 6

I. TEXT
II. TRANSLATION

III. VOCABULARY
IV. PRONUNCIATION : s and ṣ
V. GRAMMAR
1. Proper Names
2. Nisba Adjectives
3. Suffixed Pronouns
VI. DRILLS

UNIT 7
I. TEXT
II. TRANSLATION
III. VOCABULARY
IV. PRONUNCIATION : 9
V. GRAMMAR: Suffixed Pronouns
VI. DRILLS

UNIT 8
I. TEXT
II. TRANSLATION
III. VOCABULARY
IV. ADDITIONAL VOCABULARY
V. PRONUNCIATION: h and 9
VI. GRAMMAR
1. 9ind as a Verb
2. Telling Time
VII. DRILLS

UNIT 9
I. TEXT
II. TRANSLATION
III. VOCABULARY
IV. PRONUNCIATION: H
V. GRAMMAR
1. Imperatives
2. Telling Time
VI. DRILLS

UNIT 10
I. TEXT
II. TRANSLATION
III. VOCABULARY
IV. ADDITIONAL VOCABULARY
V. PRONUNCIATION: h and H; x and H
VI. GRAMMAR
1. Proper Names
2. The Negative Particle muu(b)
3. The Intensifier waajid
VII. DRILLS

UNIT 11 REVIEW

UNIT 12
I. TEXT
II. TRANSLATION
III. VOCABULARY
IV. ADDITIONAL VOCABULARY
V. GRAMMAR
1. Verbs: Imperfect Tense
2. The Intensifier killiš
VI. DRILLS

UNIT 13
I. TEXT
II. TRANSLATION
III. VOCABULARY
IV. ADDITIONAL VOCABULARY
V. GRAMMAR
1. Verbs: Imperfect Tense
2. The Dual
3. Double Imperfect
4. Cardinal Numerals
5. čam (var. kam)
VI. DRILLS

UNIT 14
I. TEXT
II. TRANSLATION
III. VOCABULARY

IV. ADDITIONAL VOCABULARY
V. GRAMMAR
1. Verbs: Imperfect Tense
2. Ordinals
3. Special Constructions
VI. DRILLS

UNIT 15
I. TEXT
II. TRANSLATION
III. VOCABULARY
IV. ADDITIONAL VOCABULARY
V. GRAMMAR
1. Imperatives
2. Telling Time
3. Cardinal Numerals
VI. DRILLS

UNIT 16
I. TEXT
II. TRANSLATION
III. VOCABULARY
IV. ADDITIONAL VOCABULARY
V. GRAMMAR
1. Cardinal Numerals
2. Collective Nouns
3. Imperatives
4. The Negative Particle **maa**
VI. DRILLS

UNIT 17
I. TEXT
II. TRANSLATION
III. VOCABULARY
IV. ADDITIONAL VOCABULARY
V. GRAMMAR
1. Collective Nouns
2. Colors
3. The Conjunction **li'ann**
4. The verb **–gdar–**
5. Imperatives
VI. DRILLS

UNIT 18
I. TEXT
II. TRANSLATION
III. VOCABULARY
IV. ADDITIONAL VOCABULARY
V. GRAMMAR
1. Verbs: Imperfect Tense
2. Plurals of Nouns
3. Noun - Adjective Concord
4. **maHHad**
5. Object Pronouns
VI. DRILLS

UNIT 19
I. TEXT
II. TRANSLATION
III. VOCABULARY
IV. ADDITIONAL VOCABULARY
V. GRAMMAR
1. The Preposition **'ila**
2. Cardinal Numerals
VI. DRILLS

UNIT 20
I. TEXT
II. TRANSLATION
III. VOCABULARY
IV. ADDITIONAL VOCABULARY
V. GRAMMAR
1. Negative Commands
2. The Particle **Hagg**
3. **xaḷḷ–** (+imperfect)
VI. DRILLS

UNIT 21 REVIEW

UNIT 22

I. TEXT
II. TRANSALTION
III. VOCABULARY
IV. ADDITIONAL VOCABULARY
V. GRAMMAR
1. laazim
2. The Particle b–
3. Elative Adjectives
VI. DRILLS

UNIT 23

I. TEXT
II. TRANSLATION
III. VOCABULARY
IV. ADDITIONAL VOCABULARY
V. GRAMMAR
1. Elative Adjectives
2. The Conjunction **leen**
3. Verbs: Imperfect Tense
4. **raayiH**
VI. DRILLS

UNIT 24

I. TEXT
II. TRANSLATION
III. VOCABULARY
IV. ADDITIONAL VOCABULARY
V. GRAMMAR
1. Telling Ages
2. **maal**
3. Vowel Change
4. **fii**
5. Suffixed Pronouns
VI. DRILLS

UNIT 25

I. TEXT
II. TRANSLATION
III. VOCABULARY
IV. ADDITIONAL VOCABULARY
V. GRAMMAR
1. Collective Nouns
2. **Haaðir**
VI. DRILLS

UNIT 26

I. TEXT
II. TRANSLATION
III. VOCABULARY
IV. GRAMMAR
1. **şaarli**
2. **Hazza**
3. **Hawaali**
4. **ṣoob**
V. DRILLS

UNIT 27

I. TEXT
II. TRANSLATION
III. VOCABULARY
IV. ADDITIONAL VOCABULARY
V. GRAMMAR : θaani
VI. DRILLS

UNIT 28

I. TEXT
II. TRANSLATION
III. VOCABULARY
IV. ADDITIONAL VOCABULARY
V. GRAMMAR : Perfect Tense

UNIT 29
I. TEXT
II. TRANSLATION
III. VOCABULARY
IV. ADDITIONAL VOCABULARY
V. GRAMMAR
1. Perfect Tense
2. The Conjunction **lajil**
3. **kaan fii**
VI. DRILLS

UNIT 30
I. TEXT
II. TRANSLATION
III. VOCABULARY
IV. ADDITIONAL VOCABULARY
V. GRAMMAR
1. Perfect Tense
2. Perfect Tense with Suffixed Pronouns
VI. DRILLS

UNIT 31 REVIEW

UNIT 32
I. TEXT
II. TRANSLATION
III. VOCABULARY
IV. ADDITIONAL VOCABULARY
V. GRAMMAR : Perfect Tense
VI. DRILLS

UNIT 33
I. TEXT
II. TRANSLATION
III. VOCABULARY
IV. GRAMMAR
1. Perfect Tense
2. Relative **'illi**
V. DRILLS

UNIT 34
I. TEXT
II. TRANSLATION
III. VOCABULARY
IV. ADDITIONAL VOCABULARY
V. GRAMMAR
1. Perfect Tense
2. Relative Clauses
3. **ya9ni**
VI. DRILLS

UNIT 35
I. TEXT
II. TRANSLATION
III. VOCABULARY
IV. ADDITIONAL VOCABULARY
V. GRAMMAR
1. Perfect Tense
2. Verb Strings
3. Negative Particle **ma**
VI. DRILLS

UNIT 36
I. TEXT
II. TRANSLATION
III. VOCABULARY
IV. ADDITIONAL VOCABULARY
V. GRAMMAR : **ṣalla**

UNIT 37
I. TEXT
II. TRANSLATION
III. VOCABULARY
IV. ADDITIONAL VOCABULARY

V. GRAMMAR : ṣaad
VI. DRILLS

UNIT 38
I. TEXT
II. TRANSLATION
III. VOCABULARY
IV. ADDITIONAL VOCABULARY
V. DRILLS

UNIT 39
I. TEXT
II. TRANSLATION
III. VOCABULARY
IV. ADDITIONAL VOCABULARY
V. GRAMMAR :
9umur– ma + Perfect Tense
VI. DRILLS

UNIT 40
I. TEXT
II. TRANSLATION
III. VOCABULARY
IV. GRAMMAR : čaan + Imperfect
V. DRILLS

UNIT 41
I. TEXT
II. TRANSLATION
III. VOCABULARY
IV. ADDITIONAL VOCABULARY
V. GRAMMAR
1. Conditionals
2. 'illi

UNIT 42
I. TEXT
II. TRANSLATION
III. VOCABULARY

GLOSSARY : GULF ARABIC - ENGLISH
ENGLISH - GULF ARABIC

INDEX OF GRAMMATICAL TERMS

INTRODUCTION

1. The Arabic Language

In the Arab world, colloquial dialects vary not only from country to country and town to town, but even from village to village. Strictly speaking, we cannot speak of the colloquial dialect of a particular country or town or village, because speakers of a particular dialect differ among themselves, mainly due to their educational and cultural backgrounds. In addition to these colloquial dialects, there is a superposed standard language commonly referred to as Classical Arabic, the revered language of the Quran, pre-Islamic poetry, and the medieval classics of Arabic literature.[1] Modern Standard Arabic (MSA), as used nowadays, refers to the language learned by Arab students after their initial acquisition of a colloquial dialect of spoken Arabic. It is used on formal occasions —— speeches, discussions, debates, news broadcasts, and in schools and universities, being the medium of instruction. Furthermore, newspapers and textbooks all over the Arab world are written almost exclusively in MSA.[2]

Differences between MSA and the colloquials are apparent in phonology and morphology, for the most part a matter of deletion of MSA inflections; e.g., case inflections, dual forms for pronouns

---

1) For a more detailed introduction to this literary language, see "9arabiyya," **Encyclopedia of Islam**, New Edition, pp. 561 - 574.

2) Other names currently used are "Contemporary Arabic", "Modern Literary Arabic", "Modern Written Arabic", etc. The name abbreviated MSA: however, is intended to represent the literary language in both its spoken and written forms.

and verbs, and feminine plural inflections of personal pronouns and verbs of MSA are not present in most of the colloquials. Syntactic features of MSA and most colloquial dialects, however, are similar.

2. The Language of the Text

The language which this book utilizes is to be commonly known as Gulf Arabic (GA); it is the language used in informal situations by the educated indigenous populations of the United Arab Emirates. These territories have much in common. Geographically, they lie on the southern coast of the Arabian Gulf, and most of them are coastal settlements, although some, such as Ajman, are inland territorial enclaves which presumably originated from settlements around watering places and summer gathering centers of nomads. Historically, the whole area came into the orbit of European influence: the Portuguese, the Dutch, the French, and finally, the British. The most recent developments in the Gulf are the formation of the United Arab Emirates and the establishment of a U.S. naval base in Bahrain. Socially, the indigenous population of the Gulf states is made up of Arabs. Linguistically, a high degree of mutual intelligibility exists among the dialects of these states. There are differences, of course, but ...

> The fact that these differences exist, however, should not be allowed to obscure the fact of their essential unity as a dialect group. The coastal dialects from Kuwait to Khor Fakkan have many more features in common than differences, and can be clearly distinguished as a group from the dialects of Oman, S.W. Arabia ...[3]

---

3) T.M. Johnstone, Eastern Arabian Dialects, London: Oxford University Press, 1967, p. 18.

The native speakers ("informants") whose speech served as the basis for the language of this text are unsophisticated speakers of GA in Abu Dhabi, Qatar, and Bahrain. Initially, a frequency word list of about 3,000 items was compiled from the recordings of spontaneous, unprepared conversations of those informants in different situations, such as greetings, telephone conversations, comments, interviews, etc. There was a search for tales, fables, proverbs, and stories. In checking with the informants, the question of "How do you say...? " was avoided as much as possible for the sake of authenticity. Out of the 3,000 vocabulary items in the frequency word list, about 1,200 items were selected for this text.

It should be pointed out that all of these informants have come in direct contact with a great number of Arab immigrants working in the Gulf: Palestinians and Jordanians, Egyptians, Lebanese, Iraqis, Syrians, etc. The influence of the dialects of those immigrants on the local dialects has been so great that Gulf Arabs tend to emulate other dialects, especially Egyptian and Palestinian. The author has run across contrast of styles in the same speaker on different occasions.

4. Arrangement of the Materials

A typical unit in the textbook is divided into the following:

a. TEXT

There is a total of forty-two texts: thirty-two dialogs and ten narratives. The dialogs cover a wide variety of subjects of interest, such as greetings, getting acquainted, appointments, telephone conversations, shopping, education, mailing letters, telling time, directions, festivals, etc. The content of the dialogs is determined mainly by the word frequency list and the feedback the writer has obtained from prospective users of the book. The ten narratives are in the form of anecdotes and short stories suited to the particular needs of prospective students. The first ten lessons are short because emphasis in those lessons is placed on mastery of the phonological system of GA.

b. VOCABULARY

This section contains the new vocabulary items that occur in the text. The vocabulary items are arranged according to the order in which they occur in the text. The average number of vocabulary items in this section is about twenty.

c. ADDITIONAL VOCABULARY

Additional vocabulary items related to VOCABULARY are included in this section. The average number is about ten items per lesson. Students are held responsible for the meanings of these words. An attempt has been made to keep tight control over vocabulary items in both sections. Each new vocabulary item in a lesson is repeated at least five times in lessons thereafter.

d. PRONUNCIATION

Sounds that are similar in GA and American English are not presented. Those sounds are represented by the following symbols: **b, č, d, f, g, h, j, k, m, n, p, s, š, t, w, y, z,** *θ*, and **ð**. No lesson in the first ten lessons contains more than two difficult sounds. Stress patterns are described in the first three lessons and irregularities are pointed out as the need arises. Two detailed pronunciation lesson plans have been worked out in UNIT 1 and in UNIT 2. They are model plans; reference is made to them in the subsequent eight units.

e. GRAMMAR

An attempt has been made to present grammar in a systematic way, so that by the end of the book the student will have acquired a virtually complete description of the basic structures of GA. The new grammatical structures that occur in a TEXT are explained to students so that they might understand the particular structure involved. The student is warned against ungrammatical phrases or structures, which are starred. Examples illustrating new grammatical structures are cited from the lesson or previous lessons. There are not more than two major grammatical structures in any one unit.

f. DRILLS

In addition to providing practice in using the items in the lesson, drills illustrate the phonological and grammatical points. The drills are not limited in number or type. The average number in each lesson is ten. There are at least five types, the most frequent being substitution and transformation drills. There are three review units, the purpose of each of which is to review previous vocabulary, phonology, and grammar.

5. **How to Use the Materials**

In order to achieve the best results, it is suggested that the course be taught by a language specialist trained in contrastive analysis, preferably a native speaker of any variety of Arabic and an informant. Such a langauge specialist is cognizant of the implications of contrastive analysis for different types of teaching programs and is better equipped to better guide his students, for if an error is made, he will understand the cause, and will be able to construct illustrative examples, and present corrective drills, Lectures concerning the differences between the target language and the native language should not replace drill in the patterns or structures in the language. But the simplicity (or complexity) of the rules to be learned in the target language is an important factor. For example, a student coming from English, in which adjectival modifiers almost always precede the noun-head, will have some difficulty learning a language like Arabic where they always follow the noun-head, but he will have more difficulty learning the structure **Cardinal numeral + N** in MSA, where the cardinal changes according to the gender of the noun counted (switch gender) and the cardinal numeral is sometimes singular and sometimes plural, thereby creating a split in the branching properties of the modifiers. It has been found that a split, involving a part similarity between corresponding structures of the target language and the native language, is likely to be more difficult than a straightforward reversal where there is no similarity at all.

The following recommendations are offered to the teacher:

a. Read the TEXT slowly, clearly, and carefully twice. Students listen.

b. Break the passage into short phrases, and have students repeat after you. If the short phrase contains a new grammatical point, explain it and do the relevant drills. Encourage students to take turns and act the passage out. Do not spend too much time on the passage at this stage.

c. For the following day ask students to listen to the tape and try to commit the TEXT to memory. Memorization is very useful in foreign language learning.

d. In DRILLS, put the pattern sentence or phrase on the board. Draw students' attention to it. Explain the grammatical point involved. It is recommended that books be shut throughout. If a student makes an error, do not stop him but lead him to the correct answer.

e. At the beginning of each teaching period, **begin** the lesson by asking questions of a general nature. These questions can be taken from previously learned materials. Examples of such questions are: What's your name? How are you? What's today? What time is it? Do you study Arabic every day? ... etc. Beginning a lesson in this manner gives the students a sense of continuity in the lessons, organizes and enlivens the students' attitude to the whole subject, and gives the students further practice in many useful structures, words, and everyday expressions.

f. Do not use English unless needed. **Translation** is a means and not a method. While translation might be used only for some content-words, it should never be used for structures, which should be taught in context and practiced.

TRANSCRIPTION

The transcription adopted in this textbook is a modified version of the romanization system used by the Library of Congress for the cataloging of all Arabic writings.

CONSONANTS

Symbol	Approximate Sound		
ʼ	(glottal stop)	p	**p in pen**
b	**b in big**	q	— — — — —
č	**ch in church**	r	Spanish **r in caro**
d	**d in dog**	s	**s in sip**
f	**f in fat**	ṣ	**cs in Tucson**
g	**g in God**	š	**sh in ship**
ġ	Parisian **r in Paris**	t	**t in still**
h	**h in hat**	ṭ	**t in tot**
H	— — — — —	w	**w in win**
j	**j in jam**	x	German **ch in nacht**
k	**k in skim**	y	**y in yet**
l	**l in lathe**	z	**z in zeal**
ḷ	**l in bell**	θ	**th in thin**
m	**m in mat**	ð	**th in this**
n	**n in nap**	ð̣	— — — —
		9	— — — —

VOWELS

Short		Long	
i	i in sit	ii	ea in seat
a	– – – –	ee	a in maze
		aa	a in hat
			a in hard
u	u in put	uu	oo in food
o	British o in pot	oo	aw in gnaw

ABBREVIATIONS AND SYMBOLS

Abbreviation	Word	Abbreviation	Word
adj.	Adjective	ord.	ordinal
adv.	adverb	part.	particle
coll.	collective	p.	plural
conj.	conjunction	pred.	predicate
f.	feminine	pron.	pronoun
foll.	following	s.	singular
imp.	imperative	s.o.	someone
lit.	literally	s.th.	something
m.	masculine	subj.	subject
n.	noun	syn.	synonym
neg.	negative	var.	variant

Symbol	Meaning
C	consonant
C_1	first consonant
C_2	second consonant
MSA	Modern Standard Arabic
( )	item enclosed is optional or explanatory
*	indicates an ungrammatical utterance
GA	Gulf Arabic
S	student
T	teacher

UNIT 1

I. TEXT

yuusif : ʼasmi yuusif. šu smak ?
seef : ʼasmi seef.
yuusif : min ween inta ?
seef : ʼaana min dbayy. w inta mneen ?
yuusif : ʼaana min li-kweet.

II. TRANSLATION

Joseph : My name is Joseph. What's your name ?
Seif : My name is Seif.
Joseph : Where are you from ?
Seif : I'm from Dubai. And where are you from ?
Joseph : I'm from Kuwait.

III. VOCABULARY

yuusif	Joseph	ʼaana	I
ʼasim	name (m.)	dbayy	Dubai
seef	Seif	w	and
min	from	mneen ?	where from ?
ween ?	where ?	li-kweet	Kuwait
ʼinta	you (m.s.)		

IV. PRONUNCIATION

1. Short and Long Vowels

GA has in its sound system five short and five corresponding long vowels: **a – aa, i – ii, e – ee, u – uu, and o – oo,** A long vowel is twice as long as a short vowel. Long **aa** in GA is pronounced more or less like the **a** in English **bad**; short **a** is half as long.

In the following exercise exaggerate, for the time being, long **aa** and make short **a** short and abrupt in production; otherwise you will fall into the pitfall of confusing short and long vowels.

Drill 1

short **a** *and long* **aa**

a. Listen; do not repeat.

baab →	bab	waan →	wan	kaan →	kan
daan	dan	faat	fat	maad	mad
kaaf	kaf	faan	fan	baat	bat
gaas	gas	haam	ham	maan	man

b. Listen and repeat after the model: baab → bab, daan → dan, etc.

c. Teacher makes a random selection of words from the above. Students are asked to indicate under **aa** and **a** words that have those vowels, e.g., teacher says **baab**; students write 1 under **aa**; teacher says **ban**; students write 2 under **a**, etc.

d. Teacher says, e.g., a word with long **aa**; individual students give the corresponding word with short **a**, etc.

e. Listen and repeat. Do the same words again in pairs.

Drill 2

short **i** *and long* **ii**

GA short **i** is similar to English **i** in **sit**. The long vowel **ii** is not similar to English **ea** in **seat**. In the English word seat,

ea is a little shorter and has a glide quality; GA **ii** is a monophthong and does not have any glide quality.

min	→	miin	sif	→	siif	zin	→	ziin
kif		kiif	sin		siin	ri		rii
lif		liif	jin		jiin	fi		fii

Follow the same procedure in Drill 1 above.

Drill 3

short **e** *and long* **ee**

GA short **e** is similar to English **e** in **pen; ee** is twice as long as **e**. Keep in mind that **ee** does not have any glide quality.

bet	→	beet	def	→	deef	šek	→	šeek
kef		keef	det		deet	zen		zeen
wen		ween	mes		mees	ben		been
fen		feen	wet		weet	sed		seed

Follow the same procedure in Drill 1 above.

2. Stress

A stressed syllable in any given word is the one that is pronounced the loudest. In GA stress is generally predictable, i.e., you can deduce which syllable in a word is stressed from the consonant-vowel sequence in that word. (There are some exceptions, which will be pointed out as they arise.) You should note the following general comments on syllable structure in GA :

1. Every syllable should have a vowel, short or long.

2. Every syllable begins with a consonant. The first syllable may have one, two, or three consonants initially.

3. If a word has two consonants or a doubled consonant (identical consonants) in the middle, syllable division is between these two consonants.

Each word in UNIT 1 has either one or two syllables. A syllable with a long vowel (long syllable) is stressed whether it is the first or the second syllable in a word. A word with two short syllables has the first syllable stressed.

Drill 4

Listen and repeat :

⟶

ʼásmi	yúusif	šúsmak	ʼínta
ʼásmak	li-kwéet	mnéen	ʼáana
ʼásim	wínta	wána	šúsmi

V. GRAMMAR

1. Suffixed Pronouns

Nouns in GA can have pronominal suffixes attached to them. These pronominal suffixes or, as they are sometimes called, suffixed pronouns, indicate possession :

ʼasmi (–i) ʼmy nameʼ ʼasmak (–ak) ʼyour (m.s.) nameʼ

Other suffixed pronouns will be presented later. (Drills 1,2,3,4)

2. Equational Sentences

'asmi seef.	'My name is Seif.'
'aana min dbayy.	'I am from Dubai.'

The two sentences above are examples of equational sentences, containing a subject and a predicate. The subject in the first sentence is the phrase **'asmi** 'my name' and in the second sentence, the pronoun **'aana** 'I'. The predicate is either a proper noun or a prepositional phrase: **seef** 'Seif' and **min dbayy** 'from Dubai'. (Drills 1,2,3,4).

3. Note that **'asim** 'name', the form of this word when it stands alone, becomes **'asm–** when the pronominal suffixes **–i** and **–ak** are added :

'asim + –i → 'asmi	'my name'
'asim + –ak → 'asmak	'your (m.s.) name'

4. The Conjunction w

w is a coordinating conjunction corresponding to English 'and'. It has four forms, depending upon the environment in which it is used and the rate of speech :

a) either **w** or **'u** is used at the beginning of a sentence or a phrase :

w 'inta mneen?	'And where are you (m.s.) from? '
'u yuusif	'and Joseph'

b) **w** is usually used before a word that begins with a vowel and after a word that ends with a vowel :

w ismi	'and my name'
karaama w yuusif	'Karama and Joseph'

c) **u** is usually used after a word that ends with a consonant:

yuusif u karaama	'Joseph and Karama'
dbayy u li-kweet	'Dubai and Kuwait'

d) **wa** is used in phrases that are primarily borrowed from Modern Standard Arabic or Classical Arabic, e.g.:

'ahlan wa sahlan 'Welcome ! ' (See UNIT 2.)

VI. DRILLS

Drill 1 *Chain*

Each student repeats the sentence: **'asmi (seef)** 'My name is (Seif)' in turn, substituting his (her) own name for the name in parenthesis.

Example : 'asmi seef. 'asmi naansi, etc. .....

'My name is Seif. My name is Nancy, etc.'

Drill 2 *Chain*

Repeat **Drill 1** by making a statement and then asking a question. (Male students only).

Example : 'asmi seef. šu smak?

'My name is Seif. What is your name? '

Drill 3 *Chain*

Repeat **Drill 2** by making a statement and then asking a question. (Male students only).

Example : ʹaana min dbayy. w inta mneen?

ʹI am from Dubai. And where are you from?ʹ

Drill 4 *Chain*

Each male student gives two statements and then asks a question.

Example : ʹasmi seef. ʹaana min dbayy. w inta?

ʹMy name is Seif. I am from Dubai. And you?ʹ

Drill 5 *Translation*

Use the correct form of **w** ʹandʹ with the following:

1. Linda and Salwa
2. and Joseph
3. Karim and Sami
4. I and you
5. Joseph and Salim
6. And where are you (f.s.) from?
7. Amina and Laila
8. Dubai and Kuwait

UNIT 2

I. TEXT

jaasim :	ʼasmi jaasim. ʼaana min iš-šaarja.
karaama:	ʼasmi karaama. ʼaana min dbayy.
jaasim :	ʼahlan wa sahlan. šloonak?
karaama:	zeen. w inta?
jaasim :	bxeer maškuur.

II. TRANSLATION

Jasim :	My name is Jasim. I 'm from Sharja.
Karama:	My name is Karama. I 'm from Dubai.
Jasim :	Nice meeting you. How are you?
Karama:	Fine. And you?
Jasim :	Fine. Thank you.

III. VOCABULARY

jaasim	Jasim
ʼiš-šaarja	Sharja
ʼahlan wa sahlan!	Nice meeting you!
šloonak?	How are you (m.s.)?
zeen	fine, good (m.)
bxeer	fine
maškuur	Thank you. (lit. ʼYou are thanked.ʼ)

IV. PRONUNCIATION

1. Short and Long Vowels

Drill 1

short **u** *and long* **uu**

GA **u** and English **u** as in **put** are similar. GA **uu** as in **yuusif** 'Joseph' is a monophthong. In the production of this long vowel the lips are rounded throughout. In the English word **food,** however, the position of the lips changes to a more rounded position. Again, in GA it is vowel length as opposed to vowel quality in English.

šuf	→	šuuf	bus	→	buus	ru	→	ruu
kur		kuur	tub		tuub	zu		zuu
bud		buud	gum		guum	šu		šuu
mub		muub	zur		zuur	nu		nuu

Follow the same procedure in UNIT 1, Pronunciation Drill 1.

Drill 2

long **oo**

GA long **oo** and American English **aw** or **ow** in **law** and **low,** respectively, are markedly different. GA **oo** as in **šloonak** 'How are you (m.s.)? ' is a monophthong and, thus, does not have the off-glide quality that the American or British **ow** does as in **low** and **hoe**. GA **oo** is close to the American English sound **oo** in **door**.

↓ yoom	↓ doob	↓ joor	↓ loof	↓ mooz
loomi	booy	šool	noom	foog
loon	koom	toor	mool	booš
ðool	soot	joof	θoor	looz

Follow the same procedure in UNIT 1, Pronunciation Drill 1, a, b.

Drill 3

r

GA **r** is not like American English **r**; the former is a consonant, while the latter is more of a vowel than a consonant. For the production of **r**, most Americans curl the tongue up toward the roof of the mouth as in **car**, **far**, etc., and round their lips when the **r** is word-initial or syllable-initial, as in **ream, rock, marry**, etc. GA **r** is a tongue-flap. It is produced by striking the tip of the tongue against the roof of the mouth. It is like the **r** in Spanish or Italian **caro** 'dear.' In the speech of some Americans intervocalic **t** sounds like GA **r**: **city, Betty, pity**, etc.

In the following exercise the first word in each pair is a meaningful English word, and the second one is an approximation of the pronunciation of that same English word by a native speaker of GA. Pay special attention to this second pronunciation.

a. Listen: donot repeat :

ream →	riim	berry →	beri	bar →	baar
rub	rub	Arizona	'arizoona	four	foor
rough	raf	marry	mari	bear	beer
run	ran	carry	kari	beer	biir

b. Listen and repeat after the model : ream – riim, rub – rub, etc.

c. Teacher makes a random selection of words from the above. Students indicate under English **r** and GA **r** words that have those sounds, e.g., teacher says **ream**; students write 1 under English **r**; teacher says **mari**; students write 2 under GA **r**, etc.

d. Teacher gives, e.g., a word with English **r**; students give the corresponding word with GA **r**.

e. Listen and repeat. Do the same words again in pairs.

Drill 4

k *versus* **x**

GA **k** and American English **k** are similar. GA **x** is different and needs a little practice to master. It is a voiceless fricative and it is velar. It is like Scottish **ch** in **loch** and German **ch** in **nacht**. For the production of **x**, put your tongue in the same position as for **k** and move it down just a little bit in order to let the air pass through. A helpful hint: try clearing your throat to spit :

keer →	xeer	daktar →	daxtar	baak →	baax
kaas	xaas	bakbak	baxbax	šeek	šeex
keema	xeema	'ilkeema	'ilxeema	daak	daax
kiis	xiis	sikan	sixan	šiik	šiix

2. Stress

In UNIT 1 stress rules for two-syllable words were given. In this UNIT we have two three-syllable words with a long vowel in each: 'iš-šáarja 'Sharja' and **karáama** 'Karama'. That long vowel should be stressed.

Drill 1

Divide the following words into syllables and stress mark them:

jaasim	'asmi	'aana	karaama
'iš-šaarja	'inta	'ahlan	sahlan
šloonak	maškuur	'il-xeema	li-kweet

Drill 2

Listen and repeat :

→

'áana	'ínta	šúsmak	'ásmi
sáhlan	'áhlan	'ásim	'ásmak
jáasim	karáama	šlóonak	yúusif
li-kwéet	'iš-šáarja	'il-xéema	maškúur

V. GRAMMAR

There are no new grammatical points in this lesson.

NOTES ON TEXT

1. **šloonak** literally means 'What color are you (m.s.)?' and corresponds in meaning and use to 'How are you?'

2. **'ahlan wa sahlan** is a useful polite formula. Its general literal meaning is 'You (m. or f.) are among your folks and you tread upon plane (i.e., not bumpy) land.' It is used on the following occasions :

a. As a courtesy expression, as in this lesson.

b. As a welcoming expression in the context of a host greeting a guest, e.g., at home or in the office. It is used by the host only.

c. As a response, especially in some other Arab countries, to **maškuur** 'Thank you'.

d. As a response after someone has been introduced to you, in which case it is used for 'Nice meeting you!'

VI. DRILLS

Drill 1 *Chain*

Example: šloonak? zeen. 'How are you (m.s.)?' 'Fine (m.s.).'

Drill 2 *Chain*

Repeat **Drill** 1 with the following :

šloonak? zeen bxeer. 'How are you (m.s.)?' 'Fine (m.s.).'

Drill 3 *Chain*

Repeat **Drill** 1 with the following :

šloonak? zeen bxeer. w inta? bxeer maškuur

'How are you?' 'Fine.' 'And you?' 'Fine, thanks.'

Drill 4 *Chain*

Repeat **Drill** 1 with the following :

S_1 : 'asmi karaama. 'aana min iš-šaarja.
'My name is Karama. I'm from Sharja.'

S_2 : 'ahlan wa sahlan! šloonak?
'You are welcome ! How are you (m.s.)?'

S_1 : bxeer maškuur. 'Fine, thanks.'

Drill 5 *Translation*

1. My name is Karama.
2. I'm from Sharja.
3. Jasim is from Dubai.
4. How are you (m.s.)?
5. You are welcome (m.s.).
6. My name is Linda.
7. I'm from Kuwait.
8. Seif is from Arizona.
9. What's your name?
10. Are you from Sharja?
11. Is Jasim from Dubai?
12. I'm fine, thanks.
13. Thank you.
14. What's your (m.s.) name?
15. Where are you (m.s.) from?
16. What are you (m.s.)?

UNIT 3

I. TEXT

maryam :	massaač aḷḷa bi l-xeer!
šeexa :	massaač aḷḷa bi l-xeer! ʼahlan wa sahlan!
maryam :	čeef inti?
šeexa :	zeena bxeer. w inti?
maryam :	zeena. šloon il– ʼahil?
šeexa :	killana bxeer. maškuura.
maryam :	fi maan illaa.

II. TRANSLATION

Mary :	Good afternoon (evening)!
Shaikha :	Good afternoon (evening)! You're welcome!
Mary :	How are you?
Shaikha :	I ' m fine. And you?
Mary :	Fine. How are the folks?
Shaikha :	We are all fine, thanks.
Mary :	Good-bye!

III. VOCABULARY

maryam	Mary, Miriam	ʼahil	folks, family
šeexa	Shaikha	kill	(foll. by definite noun or pron.

masa	evening, night (m.)		suffix) all of the
'aḷḷa	God		the whole of the
čeef?	how?	fi	in
'inti	you (f.s.)	maškuura	Thank you (f.)

IV. PRONUNCIATION

1. Doubled Consonants

Clusters of two identical consonants, traditionally known as geminates, occur frequently in GA. Doubled consonants in English occur across word boundaries, e.g., **straight to, hot tea, guess so,** etc., and occasionally within compound words and words with prefixes or suffixes, e.g., **cattail, unnamed, thinness,** etc. Doubled consonants in GA occur medially and finally and, in a few cases, initially. Native speakers of English encounter no difficulty in producing doubled consonants as in **hot tea, cattail, thinness,** etc., but they fail to produce doubled consonants that are differently distributed in Arabic. They either prolong the vowel following the doubled consonants or, simply, produce the word with one consonant, especially if the following vowel is short.

The following drill compares and contrasts words with single and doubled consonants. In order to help you pronounce words with doubled consonants correctly, think of the word that has doubled consonants as being made up of two words, thus :

massaač : mas-saač

killana : kil-lana

Keep in mind that doubled consonants mark syllable boundaries.

Drill 1

masaač	→	massaač	θamar	→	θammar
kilana		killana	salaam		sallaam
mara		marra	xasa		xassa
sita		sitta	rawi		rawwi
daras		darras	saba		sabba

The procedure in UNIT 1, Pronunciation Drill 1, is followed.

Drill 2

Velarized ḷ

GA velarized ḷ is relatively easy, compared to the plain GA l, which was described and drilled in UNIT 1. ḷ is similar to the American English dark l in **peel, tell, ball,** etc. ḷ occurs more frequently in GA than in other dialects of Arabic.

Listen and repeat :

ʼaḷḷa	waḷḷa	baḷḷa	yaḷḷa	gaḷa
gaaḷ	xaaḷi	xaḷḷa	magḷi	gḷaaṣ

2. Stress

In this lesson we have more examples of three-syllable words. These words are: **ʼil-ʼahil** ʼthe folksʼ, **maškuura** ʼthank you (f.)', and **killana** 'all of us'. The following rule applies to three-syllable words :

If a three-syllable word contains a long vowel (VV) or a consonant-vowel-consonant-consonant (CVCC) sequence, the syllable containing that vowel nearest the end of the word is stressed. If all the three syllables are short, the second one is stressed. Examples :

V́V :	maškúura	'il-xéema	mithaawšíin
CVCC :	yam9áwwad	yam9ázzba	kíllana
short syllables :	madrása	maktába	'adrísha

V. GRAMMAR

1. Suffixed Pronouns

–**ič** and –**ana** (sometimes –**na**) when added to nouns signal possession: **'asmič** 'your (f.) name', **'asmana** 'our name'.

Suffixed pronouns can also be added to particles, e.g., **kill** 'all of; the whole of': **killana** 'all of us'.

2. Gender in Nouns and Pronouns

Nouns in GA have gender, either masculine or feminine. Nouns, including personal names, that refer to males are masculine, and those referring to females are feminine. Thus, **yuusif, jaasim, karaama, seef,** and **'aḷḷa** are masculine, while **šeexa** and **maryam** are feminine. This distinction is important in grammar, since the choice of pronoun depends on the gender of the noun or person involved: **'inta** for masculine and **'inti** for feminine.

Nouns referring to non-living things also have gender. As a rule nouns ending in **–a** are feminine, e.g., **'iš-šaarja** 'Sharja', while all others are masculine, e.g., **'asim** 'name'. An exception is **masa** 'evening, night', which is masculine even though it ends in **–a**. Gender of nouns will be identified in the VOCABULARY section through UNIT 10. Thereafter, only the gender of nouns like **masa** will be identified.

3. Gender in Adjectives

Adjectives in GA, as in most other dialects, agree with the nouns they modify in gender (masculine or feminine), number (singular or plural), and definiteness. Gender will be dealt with here; the other items will be discussed in later lessons. Note :

jaasim zeen.	but	maryam zeena.
'Jasim is well.'		'Mary is well.'

If the adjective modifies a masculine noun, it also is masculine, e.g., **zeen** 'good, fine' and **maškuur** 'thank you' (lit. 'You are thanked.') If the noun is feminine, the modifying adjective should also be feminine, e.g., **zeena, maškuura.**

4. The Article Prefix 'il–

The article prefix **'il–** 'the' in GA, as well as in any other form of Arabic, is a prefix. It defines nouns, adjectives, and other parts of speech. While its basic form is **'il–**, it has other forms, depending upon its environment, i.e., the words that precede it and follow it :

a. If the word to which the article is prefixed begins with any of the following consonants: ', b, j, H, x, 9, ġ, f, q, k, m, h, w, then its form is 'il–. Examples :

'ahil	'folks'	'il-'ahil	'the folks'
'asim	'name'	'il-'asim	'the name'
xeer	'good thing'	'il-xeer	'the good thing'
masa	'evening'	'il-masa	'the evening'

b. If the word begins with any of the following consonants (These are the rest of the consonants of GA.), the article prefix is assimilated, i.e., the l changes to the same consonant as the initial consonant of the word to which it is prefixed: t, θ, d, đ, r, z, s, š, ṣ, ṭ, đ̣, l, n, č.

Examples :

zeen	'good, fine (one)'	'iz-zeen	'the good, fine (one)'
šeexa	'Shaikha'	'iš-šeexa	'the Shaikha'
đ̣abi	'deer, gazelle'	'iđ̣-đ̣abi	'the deer, gazelle'

c. If the word begins with a consonant cluster, 'il– changes into li–: **'il-kweet → li-kweet** 'Kuwait'. Note: In the speeches of most Gulf Arabs, the article prefix is reduced to l–. However, throughout this beginning course it will be written 'il–.

d. If the word preceding 'il– ends with a consonant, the ' sound is dropped. If it ends with a vowel, 'i is dropped.

Examples :

šloon il-'ahil?	'How are the folks? '
kill il-xeer	'all of the good things'
min iš-šeexa	'from the Shaikha'
massaač aḷḷa bi l-xeer!	'Good afternoon (evening)!'
fi š-šaarja	'in Sharja'

NOTES ON TEXT

1. Arabs, especially Gulf Arabs, are prolific in their use of greetings and polite formulas on social occasions. On meeting someone such greetings as "Welcome!", "How are you? ", "How is the family? ", and "I hope you are all fine" are practically indispensable polite expressions. It is difficult, sometimes impossible, to give a literal translation of a polite formula. It is important, however, to know what the polite formula corresponds to in English and how it is used, as well as the expected response. In this lesson **massaač aḷḷa b il-xeer** corresponds to English 'Good evening!' said to a female and **massaak aḷḷa b il-xeer** to a male. It literally means "God wished you (= may God wish you) a good evening." Note that the response is the same.

2. **fi maan illaa**! 'in God's safety (protection)' is a leave-taking polite formula for leave-taking, the response to which is the same. It is similar to English 'Good-bye! bye!'

VI. DRILLS

Drill 1 *Chain*

S_1 (f.): massaač aḷḷa bi l-xeer! 'Good afternoon (evening)!'

S_2 (f.): massaač aḷḷa bi l-xeer! 'Good afternoon (evening)!'

Drill 2 *Chain*

S_1 (f.):	čeef inti?	'How are you?'
S_2 (f.):	zeena bxeer.	'Fine.'

Drill 3 *Chain*

S_1 (f.):	čeef inta?	'How are you (m.)?'
S_2 (m.):	zeen maškuura.	'Fine, thanks.'
S_1 :	šloon il-'ahil?	'How is the family?'
S_2 :	killana bxeer maškuura.	'We are all fine, thanks.'

Drill 4 *Transformation:* m. → f.

1. šu smak?
2. šloon 'ahlak
3. zeen maškuur.
4. massaak alla bi l-xeer!
5. min ween inta?
6. čeef inta?

Drill 5 *Translation*

1. How is the family?
2. How are you (f.s.)?
3. Is your (f.s.) name Shaikha?
4. Where are you (f.s.) from?
5. We are all fine, thanks.
6. Good evening (m.s.)!
7. We are all fine.
8. I'm fine, thanks (m.s.).
9. You (f.s.) are welcome!
10. Salim is in Sharja.
11. I'm fine, thanks (f.s.).
12. Good evening (f.s.)!

UNIT 4

I. TEXT

Kariim min beruut fi libnaan. huwa daxtar fi l-mustašfa. ʹaana muhandis min ʹabu đ̣abi. šuġli fi wazaarat il-batrool. ʹuxti sikirteera fi bank ʹabu đ̣abi.

II. TRANSLATION

Ḳarim is from Beirut in Lebanon. He is a doctor in the hospital. I am an engineer from Abu Dhabi. My work is in the Ministry of Petroleum. My sister is a secretary in the Bank of Abu Dhabi.

III. VOCABULARY

beruut	Beirut (f.)	šuġul	work, job (m.)
libnaan	Lebanon	wazaara	ministry (f.)
huwa	he	batrool	petroleum, gasoline (m.)
daxtar	doctor (m.)	ʹuxut	sister (f.)
mustašfa	hospital (m.)	bank	bank (m.)
muhandis	engineer (m.)	sikirteera	secretary (f.)
ʹabu đ̣abi	Abu Dhabi		

IV. PRONUNCIATION

1. Consonants đ and đ̣

đ should cause no problem since it is similar to the English sound **th** in **this**. It is a voiced interdental spirant.

The dot under ð̣ represents velarization, traditionally known as "emphasis". A velarized sound (e.g., ḷ in UNIT 3, Pronunciation Drill 2) is pronounced with the tongue farther back and farther down in the mouth; the lips are rounded or protruded slightly. In producing the plain non-velarized ð, the tongue is relaxed and its tip protrudes a little beyond the edges of the upper and the lower teeth. For the velarized ð̣, on the other hand, the tongue is tense, lower in the middle, and more raised toward the back part. Note that this will change the quality of adjacent vowels, especially a and aa, and give a 'hollow' or 'backed' effect. (The **aa** sound in **ðaak**, for instance, is similar to the **a** sound in **that**; but in **ð̣aak** it changes to a sound similar to **a** in **hard.**)

In the following drill listen carefully to the pronunciation of ð̣ (as well as the quality of the vowel) and imitate as faithfully as possible.

baað	→	baað̣	ðabb	→	ð̣abb	haaða	→	haað̣a
laað		laað̣	ðamm		ð̣amm	yðiim		yð̣imm
beeð		beeð̣	ðabi		ð̣abi	muwaððaf		muwað̣ð̣af
biið		biið̣	ðeel		ð̣eel	naðiif		nað̣iif
buuð		buuð̣	ðuul		ð̣uul	buuði		buuð̣i

Follow the same procedure in UNIT 1, Pronunciation Drill 1.

Drill 2

ġ

If you have mastered the production of **x** in UNIT 2, Pronunciation Drill 4, it will be easy for you to produce GA **ġ** (which is a voiced velar spirant) since the only difference between the two is that **x** is voiceless while **ġ** is voiced. Note that this sound is produced when gargling. **ġ** is close in quality to the Parisian **r**, as in **Paris, rien,** etc. Practice this sound in the following :

xxxxxxx → ġġġġġġġ	ġġġġġġġ → xxxxxxx

xaa xaa xaa	ġaa ġaa ġaa	xoo xoo xoo	ġoo ġoo ġoo
xuu xuu xuu	ġuu ġuu ġuu	xee xee xee	ġee ġee ġee
xii xii xii	ġii ġii ġii	xuxuxux	ġuxġuxġux

Contrast between **x** *and* **ġ**

xaali	→	ġaali	naxal →	naġal	saayix →	saayiġ
xooš		ġooš	taxayyar	taġayyar	xoox	ġooġ
xiib		ġiib	laxxa	laġġa	liix	liiġ
xuub		ġuub	baxeet	baġeet	suux	suuġ

2. Stress

The following are general rules for the placement of stress in GA:

a. A long vowel (–VV–) or a consonant-vowel-consonant-consonant sequence (–CVCC–) nearest the end of the word is stressed. Practice the following :

maškúur	'il-xéema	mithaawšíin	šlóonak
massáak	massáač	yúusif	li-kwéet
kíllana	yam9áwwad	yam9ázzba	dáxtar
mustášfa	muhándis	wannasátni	ktabátli

b. In words with no long vowels or –CVCC– sequences stress is penultimate, i.e., it falls on the next to the last syllable. Practice the following:

katába šjára ḍ̄arába kabáti darása ġasála

V. GRAMMAR

1. Equational Sentences

In UNIT 1 it was pointed out that the subject of an equational sentence could be a personal pronoun, e.g., **'aana** 'I', **'inta** 'you (m.s.)' or a noun with a suffix, e.g., **'asmi** 'my name' and the predicate could be a personal noun, e.g., **saalim** 'Salim' or a prepositional phrase, e.g., **min dbayy** 'from Dubai'. In this lesson we learn that the predicate of an equational sentence can also be a common noun. Examples :

huwa daxtar. 'He is a doctor.'

'uxti sikirteera. 'My sister is a secretary.'

'aana muhandis. 'I am an engineer (m.).'

2. Noun Constructs

A noun construct in Arabic is a construction composed of two nouns or noun phrases syntactically bound together. The first element consists of a noun which must always be indefinite in form, i.e., it can never take the article prefix **'il–** 'the'. The entire construction is definite or indefinite in accordance with the second element. The second element can be a single noun or a noun phrase. Thus :

daxtar mustašfa	'a hospital doctor'
daxtar il-mustašfa	'the hospital doctor'
'asim bank	'the name of a bank'
'asm is-sikirteer	'the secretary's (m.) name'

The second element can itself be a phrase :

bank 'abu ð̣abi	'the Bank of Abu Dhabi'
'ahil sadiigi	'my friend's family'
sikirteer bank 'abu ð̣abi	'the Abu Dhabi Bank secretary'
'asim daxtar il-mustašfa	'the hospital doctor's name'

If the first element of a noun construct has the feminine ending –a, –t must be added to it :

sikirteerat il-bank	'the bank secretary (f.)'
sikirteerat bank	'a bank secretary (f.)'

***daxtoora il-mustašfa** would mean 'a doctor is the hospital,' and so is ungrammatical.

The noun construct, i.e., N + ('il–) N, is equivalent in meaning to any of the following English constructions:

a. NN : 'the hospital doctor' **daxtar il-mustašfa**

b. N's N : 'Jasim's sister' **'uxut jaasim**

c. N of N : 'the Ministry of Petroleum' **wazaarat il-batrool** (Drill 5).

3. Vowel Elision

In UNIT 1 you noticed that words like **'asim** 'name' become **'asm–** before the suffixes **–i** and **–ak** are added. The rule that governs this feature of GA is this :

A word that ends with –**VC**, where –**V**– is any unstressed vowel except –**a**–, drops its –**V**– when any vowel-initial suffix is added to it. Examples :

šuġul	+	**–i** ---	šuġli	'my work'
'uxut	+	**–ak** ---	'uxtak	'your (m.s.) sister'
'ahil	+	**–ana** ---	'ahlana	'our folks'
'asim	+	**–ič** ---	'asmič	'your (f.s.) name' (Drill 4)

4. Note that **daxtoora** is the feminine form of **daxtar** 'doctor' and not ***daxtara**. Although **mustašfa** 'hospital' ends with **–a**, it is masculine, not feminine.

VI. DRILLS

Drill 1 *Chain*

Each student is asked to say: **'aana min __ fi __.** 'I am from __ in __', supplying the names of the city and state (country) he (she) comes from.

Drill 2 *Substitution*

Base Question: čeef jaasim? 'How is Jasim? '

Substitute for **jaasim** the following :

1.	yuusif	9.	dbayy
2.	karaama	10.	šeexa
3.	'il-'ahil	11.	beruut
4.	'abu ḏ̣abi	12.	šuġlič
5.	seef	13.	raas il-xeema
6.	maryam	14.	'iš-šaarja
7.	'iš-šuġul	15.	'uxtič
8.	šuġlak	16.	libnaan

Drill 3 *Variable Substitution*

Base Sentence : 'aana muhandis min libnaan.
'I am an engineer from Lebanon.'

1.	'inta	9.	'uxti
2.	huwa	10.	šeexa
3.	daxtar	11.	sikirteera
4.	'inti	12.	'aana
5.	kariim	13.	'inti
6.	maryam	14.	'abu ḏ̣abi
7.	'iš-šaarja	15.	muhandis
8.	daxtoora	16.	'uxti

Drill 4 *Substitution*

Attach the suffixed pronouns: **–i**, **–ak**, **–ič**, **–ana** to the following nouns. Make the necessary changes.

1.	ʹasim	5.	daxtoora
2.	muhandis	6.	sikirteera
3.	ʹahil	7.	daxtar
4.	ʹuxut	8.	šuġul

Drill 5 *Repetition*

1.	wazaarat il-batrool	6.	bank ʹabu ḏ̣abi
2.	bank dbayy	7.	bank iš-šaarja
3.	bank beruut	8.	sikirteerat il-bank
4.	sikirteerat il-wazaara	9.	sikirteerat il-mustašfa
5.	daxtoorat il-mustašfa	10.	daxtoorat jaasim

Drill 6 *Transformation:* indefinite → definite

Example : bank ʹbankʹ → ʹil-bank ʹthe bankʹ

1.	ʹasim	7.	ʹahil
2.	sikirteer	8.	mustašfa
3.	šuġul	9.	sikirteera
4.	masa	10.	kill
5.	daxtar	11.	muhandis
6.	wazaara	12.	daxtoora

Drill 7 *Question → Answer*

1.	šu smak?	5.	min ween inta?
2.	ween beruut?	6.	šloonak?
3.	čeef il-ʹahil?	7.	ween šuġlak?
4.	ween is-sikirteer?	8.	ʹinti daxtoora?

Drill 8 *Translation*

1. My work is in the bank.
2. Your (f.s.) doctor is from Lebanon.
3. Your (m.s.) sister is a secretary in Abu Dhabi Bank.
4. Our work is in the Ministry of Petroleum.
5. Good afternoon (evening)! (said to a female).
6. Good afternoon (evening)! (said to a male).
7. How are you (f.s.)?
8. How is the family?
9. We are all fine, thank you.
10. Good-bye.

UNIT 5

I. TEXT

xamiis : massaak aḷḷa bi l-xeer ya yuusif!

yuusif : massaak aḷḷa bi l-xeer.

xamiis : haaða ṭaam. huwa mudiir šarika hini, ʹu haaði faaṭma. hiya mumarrið̣a fi mustašfa giṭar. hum min amriika.

yuusif : ʹahlan wa sahlan. ʹintum mneen f amriika?

faaṭma : min ʹarizoona. w inta min hini?

yuusif : ʹii. ʹaana min hini, min giṭar.

II. TRANSLATION

Khamis : Good afternoon (evening), Joseph!

Joseph : Good afternoon (evening).

Khamis : This is Tom. He is a company manager here. This is Fatima. She is a nurse in Qatar Hospital. They are from America.

Joseph : Nice meeting you! Where are you from in America?

Fatima : From Arizona. And are you from here?

Joseph : Yes. I'm from here, from Qatar.

III. VOCABULARY

haaðа	this (m.)	giṭar	Qatar
mudiir	director, manager, principal (m.)	hum	they (m.)
		'amriika	America
šarika	company, firm (f.)	'intum	you (m.p.)
		mumarriḍa	nurse (f.)
haaði	this (f.)	hini	here
		'ii	yes

IV. PRONUNCIATION

Drill 1

t *and* ṭ

t and ṭ constitute the third pair of plain and velarized consonants. The first two were l – ḷ and ð – ḍ. t is similar to English **t**, as in **tin**. In the production of **t**, the tip of the tongue touches the upper teeth; for the velarized **ṭ**, the tongue, instead of remaining relaxed for plain **t**, is tense and a little retracted. **t** is a little aspirated, i.e., pronounced with a little burst of air, while **ṭ** is unaspirated. English **t** in some words has a quality fairly close to the GA **ṭ** sound, e.g., **Tom, tot, bought, caught,** etc. Keep in mind that **ṭ**, like any other velarized consonant, takes the backed pronunciation of adjacent vowels, while **t** takes the fronted variety: **taam** vs. **ṭaam.**

Contrast between initial and medial t and ṭ.

taam →	ṭaam	watan →	waṭan
tayyaar	ṭayyaar	fatar	faṭar
tibbi	ṭibbi	batiin	baṭiin
tiin	ṭiin	watees	waṭees
tees	ṭees	maatoor	maaṭoor
tuub	ṭuub	rutab	ruṭab

Follow the procedure in UNIT 1, Pronunciation Drill 1.

Drill 2

Contrast between medial tt -- ṭṭ and final t -- ṭ

fattan →	faṭṭan	xabat →	xabaṭ
batti	baṭṭi	xaat	xaaṭ
fatteet	faṭṭeet	baxiit	baxiiṭ
buttuu	buṭṭuu	ġeet	ġeeṭ
xuttaar	xuṭṭaar	tuut	ṭuuṭ

The same procedure in UNIT 1, Pronunciation Drill 1, is to be followed.

V. GRAMMAR

1. The Vocative Particle ya

The vocative particle **ya** is used in direct address before nouns, names, and titles in GA, as in **massaak aḻḻa bi l-xeer ya yuusif!** 'Good afternoon (evening), Joseph!' Examples:

ya daxtar xamiis!	'Dr. Khamis!'
ya daxtar jaasim!	'Dr. Jasim!'
šloonak ya jaasim?	'How are you, Jasim?'

ya sikirteer! 'Secretary (m.)!' is grammatically correct but socially discourteous, but **ya xamiis** 'Khamis' is normal.

2. Demonstratives

haaðа 'this (m.)' and **haaði** 'this (f.)' are demonstrative pronouns. In this lesson they are used as subjects:

haaða ṭaam.	'This is Tom.'
haaði 'uxti faaṭma.	'This is my sister, Fatima.'

The predicate of a demonstrative pronoun can be an indefinite noun :

haaða muhandis.	'This is an engineer (m.).'
haaði sikirteera.	'This is a secretary (f.).'

This structure poses a problem for native speakers of English, as they tend to equate **haaða muhandis** with the phrase 'this engineer (m.) ... .'

If the noun following the demonstrative pronoun is definite, then the demonstrative functions either as the entire subject or part of the subject of the sentence or clause.

haaða l-mudiir.	'This is the director.'
haaða l-mudiir	'this director .....'
haaða l-mudiir zeen.	'This director is good.'

Titles like **'id-daxtar** 'Dr. (m.)', **'is-sikirteer** 'Secretary (m.)', etc., should always take the article prefix in Arabic when not used in direct address :

haaða d-daxtar yuusif.	'This is Dr. Joseph.'
haaði s-sikirteera faaṭma.	'This is Secretary Fatima.'
mneen id-daxtar saliim?	'Where is Dr. Salim from? '
*haaði sikirteera faaṭma	(Drill 2)

3. Note that in normal speech **fi 'amriika** 'in America' becomes **f amriika** and **'abu ḍ̄abi** 'Abu Dhabi' is usually shortened to **bu ḍ̄abi.** (TEXT)

VI. DRILLS

Drill 1 *Transformation:* noun → pronoun

Example: T : mooza 'Moza'

S : hiya 'she'

1. maryam	7. yuusif
2. šuġul	8. šarika
3. daxtoora	9. saalim
4. xamiis	10. šeexa
5. mumarriḍ̄a	11. mustašfa
6. mudiir	12. sadiiga

Drill 2 *Substitution*

Substitute the demonstrative pronoun that stands for the proper name.

Example :	T :	xamiis	'Khamis'
	S :	haađa xamiis.	'This is Khamis.'
	T :	maryam	'Mary'
	S :	haađi maryam	'This is Mary.'

1. šeexa
2. faaṭma
3. maryam
4. naansi
5. mooza
6. 'amiina
7. yuusif
8. karaama
9. 'amiin
10. jaasim
11. seef
12. saalim

Drill 3 *Chain*

Each student repeats the phrase **massaak (massaač) aḷḷa** bi l-xeer ya 'amiin ('amiina) 'Good afternoon (evening), Amin (Amina)!'

Drill 4 *Transformation:* masculine → feminine

1. haađa daxtar
2. haađa mumarriđ̣.
3. massaak aḷḷa bi l-xeer!
4. ween šuġlak?
5. min ween inta?
6. haađa fariid.
7. čeef inta?
8. haađa mudiir.
9. haađa muhandis.
10. ween mudiirak?
11. šu smak?
12. haađa 'amiin.
13. šloonak?
14. šu šuġlak?

15. huwa mudiir.
16. ʼaana min hini.
17. ʼinta min giṭar?
18. huwa daxtar.
19. šuġlak hini?
20. huwa mumarriḏ̣.

Drill 5 *Double substitution*

yuusif mudiir u **faaṭma** mudiira.

'Joseph is a director (manager), and Fatima is a director (manager).'

1. kariim – kariima
2. ʼamiin – ʼamiina
3. samiir – samiira
4. xamiis – šeexa
5. karaama – faaṭma
6. seef – mooza
7. jaasim – kalθam
8. saalim – xadiija
9. byaat – meesa
10. muršid – ʼaamna
11. saliim – saliima
12. yuusif – salma

Substitute **daxtar, mumarriḏ̣, muhandis** and their feminine forms for **mudiir** and **mudiira.**

Drill 6 *Variable Substitution*

Base Sentence: haaḏa mudiir min giṭar.

'This is a director (manager) from Qatar.'

1. muhandis
2. ʼaana
3. daxtar
4. iš-šaarja
5. huwa
6. bu ḏ̣abi
7. sikirteera
8. giṭar

9. dbayy
10. hiya
11. haađi
12. libnaan
13. 'inta
14. mumarriđ̣
15. fi
16. mudiir

Drill 7 *Chain*

Example :

T : mudiir — wazaara 'director — ministry'

S_1 : ween il-mudiir? 'Where is the director?'

S_2 : il-mudiir fi l-wazaara. 'The director is in the ministry.'

1. mudiir – bank
2. daxtar – mustašfa
3. muhandis – giṭar
4. sikirteera – šarika
5. šarika – dbayy
6. mumarriđ̣a – mustašfa
7. muhandis – šarika
8. mudiira – bank
9. sikirteer – wazaara
10. maryam – giṭar
11. xamiis – bank giṭar
12. šeexa – wazaarat il-batrool

Drill 8 *Translation*

1. Bank of Qatar
2. Bank of America
3. The company manager
4. They are all here.
5. You're (f.s.) welcome.
6. Abu Dhabi Bank
7. The Ministry of Petroleum
8. The petroleum company
9. Are you (m.p.) from America?
10. Yes, we are all from here.

UNIT 6

I. TEXT

sadiigi ṭaam ʹamrikaani min kalifoornya. huwa min madiinat los ʹanjiles fi wilaayat kalifoornya. huwa mudiir šarikat filibs fi giṭar. faaṭma zawjat ṭaam. hiya maṣriyya. šuġulha mumarriđ̄a fi l-mustašfa fi giṭar. binthum ṣaara muwađ̄đ̄afa fi l-bank u waladhum ʹasma saalim. huwa ṭaalib fi l-madrasa.

II. TRANSLATION

My friend Tom is an American from California. He is from the city of Los Angeles in the State of California. He is the director of the Phillips Company in Qatar. Fatima is Tom's wife. She is Egyptian. She works as a nurse in the hospital in Qatar. Their daughter, Sara, is an employee in the bank, and their son's name is Salim. He is a student at school.

III. VOCABULARY

ʹamrikaani	American (m.)	maṣriyya	Egyptian (f.)
madiina	city (f.)	bint	daughter; girl (f.)
wilaaya	state (f.) district, region	walad	boy; son (m.)
zawja	wife (f.)	ṭaalib	student, pupil (m.)

IV. PRONUNCIATION

Drill 1

s *and* ṣ

s and ṣ constitute the fourth pair of plain and velarized consonants. s is similar to English s, as in **sit.** ṣ, on the other hand, sounds different and is pronounced differently. For the production of ṣ, the front part of the tongue is in the same position as for s, but the central part is depressed and the back part raised toward the velum. Velarized ṣ has a lower pitch than plain s. English s, on the other hand, has a lower pitch in the vicinity of backed vowels as in **Tucson, sauce, sod,** etc., which will help you produce a satisfactory velarized ṣ.

GA velarized consonants are ḷ, ð̣, ṭ, and ṣ. You have noticed that in the production of these consonants the tongue is tense and its back part is raised toward the velum. You may have noticed that the most striking characteristic of velarization to native speakers of English is the change in the quality of adjacent vowels. To an Arab, the difference is in the velarized consonant, and it is this velarized consonant that affects adjacent vowels.

Contrast between initial and medial s — ṣ

saar →	ṣaar	basal →	baṣal
saada	ṣaada	xasa	xaṣa
saff	ṣaff	'asiir	'aṣiir
sbayy	ṣbayy	wasoob	waṣoob
seef	ṣeef	nasuub	naṣuub

The same procedure in UNIT 1, Pronunciation Drill 1, is to be followed.

Drill 2

Contrast between medial ss — ṣṣ and final s — ṣ

xassa →	xaṣṣa	baas →	baaṣ
bassaam	baṣṣaam	labas	labaṣ
xasseet	xaṣṣeet	mallaas	maḷḷaaṣ
hassoob	haṣṣoob	ġoos	ġooṣ
'issiin	'iṣṣiin	suus	ṣuuṣ

Follow the same procedure in UNIT 1, Pronunciation Drill 1.

V. GRAMMAR

1. Proper Names

Proper names include the names of people, places, books, films, newspapers, etc. They do not need any marking for definiteness, for they are definite by virtue of being proper nouns. Whether they appear with the article prefix or not is a matter of lexical etymology, and not a realization of two different states of definiteness. Learn the following names of countries :

libnaan	'Lebanon'	giṭar	'Qatar
kanada	'Canada'	maṣir	'Egypt'
'abu ḏ̣abi	'Abu Dhabi'	suuriyya	'Syria'

tuunis	'Tunis'	maṣkat	'Muscat'
liibya	'Libya'	dbayy	'Dubai'
faṛansa	'France'	'ingiltara	'England'
'il-baakistaan	'Pakistan'	'is-suudaan	'the Sudan'
'il-'ardun	'Jordan'	'iš-šaarja	'Sharja'
'amriika	'America'	ṛaas il-xeema	'Ras al-Khaima'
'iiraan	'Iran'	'il-hind	'India'
'umm il-giween	'Umm al-Qaiwain'		

2. Nisba Adjectives

Nisba adjectives are relative adjectives which indicate something characteristic of, or having to do with, the words from which they are derived. Most nisba adjectives are derived from nouns; a few are derived from words other than nouns. In this section we are concerned with nisba adjectives that are derived from names of countries. Note the following rules:

a. Most nisba adjectives are formed by suffixing –i to a noun. The following are masculine singular forms:

libnaan	'Lebanon'	→	libnaani	'Lebanese'
tuunis	'Tunis'		tuunisi	'Tunisian'
giṭar	'Qatar'		giṭari	'Qatari'
maṣir	'Egypt'		maṣri	'Egyptian'
maṣkat	'Muscat'		maṣkati	'Muscati'
'iiraan	'Iran'		'iirani	'Iranian'

b. Nouns with the article prefix **'il–** lose this prefix when **–i** is added. Examples :

'il-baakistaan	'Pakistan'	→	baakistaani	'Pakistani'
'is-suudaan	'The Sudan'		suudaani	'Sudanese'
'il-'ardun	'Jordan'		'arduni	'Jordanian'
'il-hind	'India'		hindi	'Indian'

c. Nouns ending with **–a** drop this **–a** when **–i** is added.

Examples :

kanada	'Canada'	→	kanadi	'Canadian'
faṛansa	'France'		faṛansi	'French'
'iš-šaarja	'Sharja'		šaarji	(relating to Sharja)

Note that **–iyya** or **–ya** are dropped when **–i** is added :

suuriyya	'Syria'	→	suuri	'Syrian'
liibya	'Libya'		liibi	'Libyan'

d. A few formations are irregular :

'amriika	'America'	→	'amrikaani	'American'
'ingiltara	'England'		'ingiliizi	'English'

Compound nouns in GA, e.g., **raas il-xeema, 'umm il-giween,** etc., and nouns like **'abu ḏ̣abi, dbayy,** do not usually have nisba adjectives derived from them, though **ḏ̣ibyaani,** 'someone from (or something characteristic of)

Abu Dhabi' and **giweeni** 'someone from (or something relating to) Umm al-Qaiwain' might be heard. The phrase "min 'fom' + country" is usually used instead of the nisba adjective.

The feminine singular forms of the nisba adjectives in this lesson are derived by suffixing **–yya** to the masculine forms. Examples :

libnaani	'Lebanese (m.s.)'	→	libnaaniyya	'Lebanese (f.s.)'
hindi	'Indian (m.s.)'		hindiyya	'Indian (f.s.)'
'amrikaani	'American (m.s.)'		'amrikaaniyya	'American (f.s.)'
'ingiliizi	'English (m.s.)'		'ingiliiziyya	'English (f.s.)'

(Drills 1, 2, 8)

3. Suffixed Pronouns

In the preceding lessons we have had four pronominal suffixes, –i 'my', **–ak** 'your (m.s.)', **–ič** 'your (f.s.)', and **–ana** 'our'. In this lesson four more pronominal suffixes are presented :

'asim**ha**	(–ha)	'her name'
'asm**a**	(–a)	'his name'
'asim**hum**	(–hum)	'their (m.) name'
'asim**kum**	(–kum)	'your (m.p.) name'

(Note that 'asim + a → 'asma 'his name'. See UNIT 4, GRAMMAR, 3.)

Feminine nouns with the –**a** ending add **t** when a suffixed pronoun is added :

madiina	'city' - - - - -	madiinati	'my city'
		madiinatha	'her city'
		madiinat**kum**	'your (m.p.) city'

(Drills 5, 6, 8)

VI. DRILLS

Drill 1 *Transformation :*

prep. phrase → nisba adjective (m.)

Examples: ṭaam min 'amriika. → ṭaam 'amrikaani.

'Tom is from America. → Tom is (an) American.'

1. karaama min bu ðabi.
2. seef min 'iiraan.
3. mbaaṛak min suuriyya.
4. joorj min 'ingiltara.
5. yuusif min maṣir.
6. hanri min faṛansa.
7. ṣulṭaan min il-baakistaan.
8. rašiid min liibya.
9. 'ibraahiim min li-kweet.
10. xamiis min libnaan.
11. 'idward min kanada.
12. 'amiin min tuunis.
13. saalim min is-suudaan.
14. rafiig min il-hind
15. byaat min giṭar.
16. saami min 'amriika.

Drill 2 *Transformation :*

prep. phrase → nisba adjective (f.)

Repeat Drill 1 with the following feminine personal names :

1. faaṭma
2. 'aamna
3. šeexa
4. ṣaara
5. maryam
6. naansi
7. linda
8. 'amiina
9. kalθuum
10. nuura
11. mišel
12. salma
13. xaalida
14. rooḏ̣a
15. xadiija
16. noora

Drill 3 *Double substitution*

jim min madiinat **los 'anjiles** fi wilaayat **kalifoornya.**

'Jim is from the city of Los Angeles in the state of California.

1. tuuṣaan – 'arizoona
2. nyuu yoork – nyuu yoork
3. ditroyt – mišigan
4. šikaaġu – 'ilinoy
5. kolombos – 'ohaayo
6. fiiniks – 'arizoona
7. san fransisko – kalifoornya
8. poortland – 'origon
9. 'ostin – teksas
10. denvar – koloraado

Drill 4 *Repetition*

1. mudiir šarikat filibs
2. zawjat mudiir iš-šarika
3. bint sikirteer il-wazaara
4. bint mudiirat il-mustašfa
5. walad muhandis iš-šarika
6. sikirteer wazaarat il-batrool
7. muhandis šarikat B P
8. mudiir mustašfa giṭar
9. muwaððaf šarikat ADMA
10. mudiir madrasat zaayid

Drill 5 *Substitution*

Attach the suffixed pronouns: –**i**, –**ak**, –**ič**, –**a**, –**ha**, –**hum** and –**kum** to the following nouns. Make the necessary changes.

1. bint
2. walad
3. madiina
4. šuġul
5. šarika
6. ʼuxut
7. ʼahil
8. ʼasim
9. wilaaya
10. sadiig

Drill 6 *Substitution*

a. Attach to the noun given in the base sentence the proper suffixed pronoun that corresponds to the personal pronoun.

Example : ʼaana: šuġli zeen. ʼI : My work is good.ʼ

ʼinti: šuġlič zeen. ʼYou (f.s.): Your work is good.ʼ

1. huwa
2. ʼinta
3. ʼinti
4. ʼaana

5. hum
6. hiya
7. 'intum
8. 'inta
9. huwa
10. 'inta

b. *Repeat a. with the following :*

1. 'aana : byaat sadiigi.
'I : Byat is my friend.'
2. 'aana : binti 'asimha muna.
'I : My daughter's name is Muna.'

Drill 7 *Transformation :* statement → question

Ask questions to which the following are the answers. Use the question words: **čeef** 'how', **šu** 'what', **ween** 'where', and **mneen** 'where from'.

1. bxeer maškuur.
2. 'asma saalim.
3. bint sikirteer il-wazaara
4. 'ii, 'aana min hini.
5. 'ii, 'il-mudiir hini.
6. beruut fi libnaan.
7. 'il-walad fi l-madrasa.
8. binthum 'asimha mooza.
9. 'id-daxtar fi l-mustašfa.
10. hum min maṣir.
11. zeen maškuur.
12. haaða mustašfa.
13. hiya min giṭar.
14. killana bxeer.
15. šuġli zeen.
16. 'ii, huwa 'amrikaani.

Drill 8 *Translation*

1. Good evening, Salim!
2. This is my friend, George.
3. You are welcome, George.
4. My son is an employee here.

5. She is a student in Zayid's school.
6. She is an American from Tucson.
7. He is English from London.
8. Yes, I'm from here, from Qatar.
9. My friend is an engineer.
10. She is a nurse in the hospital.
11. What is your work?
12. I am in the Ministry of Petroleum.
13. Their son is a student.
14. Dukhan is a city in Qatar.
15. The Director of BP is here.
16. Her sister is my friend.

UNIT 7

I. TEXT

9ali : 'is-salaamu 9aleekum!

ṣulṭaan : wa 9aleekum is-salaam.

9ali : čeef inta ?

ṣulṭaan : waḷḷa zeen. w inta?

9ali : ṭayyib. čeef il-9aayla? killkum bxeer nšaaḷḷa?

ṣulṭaan : killna bxeer maškuur.

9ali : fi maan illaa!

ṣulṭaan : ma9 is-salaama.

9ali : 'aḷḷa ysallimk.

II. TRANSLATION

Ali : Peace be upon you!

Sultan : And peace be upon you!

Ali : How are you?

Sultan : I'm fine. And you?

Ali : Fine. How is the family? I hope you are all fine?

Sultan : We are all fine, thanks.

Ali : Good-bye!

Sultan : Bye.

Ali : God protect you.

III. VOCABULARY

salaam	peace (m.)	9aayla	family (f.)
9ala (9alee–)	on	nšaaḷḷa	(lit. 'If God wills') hope–
9aleekum	on you (m.p.)		fully; I hope
waḷḷa	(lit. 'by God')	ma9	with
ṭayyib	fine, good (m.)	salaama	safety (f.)

IV. ADDITIONAL VOCABULARY

hin	they (f.)	'intin	you (f.p.)

V. PRONUNCIATION

Drill 1

9

Arabic 9, technically known as a voiced pharyngeal fricative, is a relatively difficult sound; there is nothing in the English sound system that is similar or even close to it. For the production of 9, the muscles in the throat become very tense and the passageway at the back of the throat becomes constricted. Several ways have been suggested for a satisfactory production of the 9sound. As a first exercise, say "ah," and then tense up the muscles of your throat as in gagging. Another exercise is to try to imitate the bleating of a sheep "baa". Tighten your neck and throat muscles as if someone were choking you. The result would be a strangled or a squeezed sound, which is an approximation of the Arabic **9een** sound

Initial and medial 9

↓	9aam	9eeš	jamaa9a	ʼil-9een
	9aad	9een	saa9a	ʼil-9eeš
	9aayla	9iid	na9am	ʼil-9ooda
	9aṛab	9ooda	sim9aw	ʼil-9oora
	9aleek	9oora	tisma9iin	s9uud
	9indi	9uud	ba9iid	ʼil-9uud
	9ugub	9uum	ma9i	maa9uun

Medial –9C– and final 9

↓	ba9ð̣a	jaa9	loo9	rafa9
	sa9di	ð̣aa9	noo9	šaari9
	ba9deen	baa9	juu9	tisi9
	si9ra	bee9	kuu9	jaami9
	li9baw	ð̣ii9	zara9	jarii9
	ti9baw	bii9	ṭala9	muzaari9

Drill 2

Contrast between ʼ *and* 9

ʼadil	→	9adil	ʼeen	→	9een
ʼaadi		9aadi	ʼooda		9ooda
ʼajiib		9ajiib	naʼam		na9am
ʼiida		9iida	jariiʼ		jarii9
ʼeeš		9eeš	saʼal		sa9al

VI. GRAMMAR

1. Suffixed Pronouns

a. Below is a list of all the personal pronouns and the corresponding suffixed pronouns in GA :

Personal Pronoun		Suffixed Pronoun	Example
huwa	'he'	– a	šuġla 'his work'
hum	'they (m.)'	– hum	šuġúlhum 'their (m.) work
hiya	'she'	– ha	šuġúlha 'her work'
hin	'they (f.)'	– hin	šuġúlhin 'their (f.) work'
'inta	'you (m.s.)'	– ak	šuġlak 'your (m.s.) work'
'intum	'you (m.p.)'	– kum	šuġúlkum 'your (m.p.) work'
'inti	'you (f.s.)'	– ič	šuġlič 'your (f.s.) work'
'intin	'you (f.p.)'	– kin	šuġúlkin 'your (f.p.) work'
'aana	'I'	– i	šuġli 'my work'

b. It was pointed out in UNIT 1 that suffixed pronouns indicate possession when they are attached to nouns, as in the examples above. Suffixed pronouns can also be attached to prepositions, in which case they become objects governed by those prepositions. Examples :

ma9a	'with him'	ma9**kum**	'with you (m.p.)'
ma9**hum**	'with them (m.)'	ma9**ič**	'with you (f.s.)'
ma9**ha**	'with her'	ma9**kin**	'with you (f.p.)'
ma9**hin**	'with them (f.p.)'	ma9i	'with me'
ma9**ak**	'with you (m.s.)'	ma9**na**	'with us'

9ala 'on' and **min** 'from' have the following special forms:

9ala : (9alee–) **9alee, 9aleehum, 9aleeha, 9aleehin, 9aleek, 9aleekum, 9aleeč, 9aleekin, 9alayy, 9aleena**

min : (minn–) (+ vowel) **minna, minhum, minha, minhin, minnak, minkum, minnič, minkin, minni, minna.**

(Drills 3, 6, 7)

NOTES ON TEXT

Note that upon meeting or leaving someone or a group of people (regardless of gender or number), you bid them **'is-salaamu 9aleekum** 'Peace be upon you!' The response is **(wa) 9aleekum is-salaam** '(And) peace be upon you!' The response to **ma9 is-salaama** 'with safety' is **'aḷḷa ysallimk** 'God keep you (m.s.) safe, protect you', which should be learned as a formula.

VII. DRILLS

Drill 1 *Chain*

a. S_1 : 'is-salaamu 9aleekum! 'Peace be upon you!'

S_2 : wa 9aleekum is-salaam! 'And peace be upon you!'

b. S_1 : fi maan illaa! 'Good-bye!'

S_2 : ma9 is-salaama 'Good-bye!'

S_1 : 'aḷḷa ysallimk! 'God protect you!'

Drill 2 *Chain*

S_1 : čeef inta (inti)? 'How are you (m., f.)? '

S_2 : waḷḷa zeen. w inta (inti)?' 'I'm fine. And you (m., f.)? '

S_1 : ṭayyib (ṭayyba) 'I'm fine (m., f.).'

Drill 3 *Substitution*

a. Attach to the noun in the base sentence the proper suffixed pronoun that corresponds to the personal pronoun given.

Base Sentence : **'aana:** waladi 'asma 9ali.

'I : My son's name is Ali.'

1. huwa
2. hum
3. hiya
4. hin
5. 'inta
6. 'inti
7. 'intum
8. 'intin
9. niHin
10. 'aana

b. Repeat a. with the following :

1. **'aana** : 9aayilti hini 'My family is here.'
2. **'aana** : mudiiri hini 'My director is here.'

Drill 4 *Repetition*

1. 'il-9een fi 'abu ḏ̣abi.
2. 'il-qaahira fi maṣir.
3. 'il-xarṭuum fi s-suudaan.
4. beruut fi libnaan.
5. banġaazi fi liibya.
6. 9ammaan fi l-'ardun.
7. duxaan fi giṭar.
8. landan fi ngiltara.

Drill 5 *Transformation :* prep. phrase → nisba adjective

Example : ṭaam min 'arizoona f amriika. → ṭaam 'amrikaani min 'arizoona.

'Tom is from Arizona in America. → Tom is an American from Arizona.'

1. 9afṛa min duxaan fi giṭar.
2. 9ali min tuunis fi tuunis.
3. seef min ṭahraan fi 'iiraan.
4. sa9iid min iḷ-xarṭuum fi s-suudaan.
5. suha min dbayy fi dbayy.
6. kalθuum min il-qaahira fi maṣir.
7. jorj min landan fi ngiltara.
8. nuura min bu ḏ̣abi fi bu ḏ̣abi.
9. liisa min baariis fi faṛansa.
10. 9eeša min 9ammaan fi l-'ardun.
11. 'amiin min il-qaahira fi maṣir.
12. rooḏ̣a min li-kweet fi l-kweet.
13. rafiig min bombey fi l-hind.

14. xaadim min karaači fi l-baakistaan.
15. byaat min id-dooHa fi giṭar.
16. xadiija min banġaazi fi liibya.
17. saami min 'otawa fi kanada.
18. salwa min beruut fi libnaan.
19. saam min 'arizoona f amriika.
20. linda min nyuu yoork f amriika.

Drill 6 *Substitution*

Attach to the preposition given in the base sentence the suffixed pronoun that corresponds to the personal pronoun.

a. Base Sentence : **'aana** : huwa ma9i. **'I** : He is with me.'

1. hum	6. 'inti
2. hiya	7. 'intin
3. hin	8. 'aana
4. 'inta	9. niHin
5. 'intum	10. hum

b. Base Sentence: **'inta**: 'is-salaamu 9aleek! **'You**: Peace be upon you!

1. hum	6. 'inti
2. hiya	7. 'intin
3. hin	8. 'inta
4. 'inta	9. 'inti
5. 'intum	10. 'intum

c. Base Sentence: **huwa: haađa minna.** 'He: This is from **him.**'

1. 'inta	6. hum
2. 'inti	7. hin
3. 'intum	8. niHin
4. 'intin	9. 'aana
5. huwa	10. 'inta

Drill 7 *Substitution.*

Example : killana min giṭar. 'We are all from Qatar.'

hum: killahum min giṭar. 'They are all from Qatar.'

1. hin	6. 'intum
2. 'intum	7. 'intin
3. 'intin	8. hum
4. niHin	9. hin
5. hum	10. niHin

Drill 8 *Transformation :* masculine → feminine

1. 'is-salaamu 9aleekum!	9. 'inta min hini?
2. čeef inta?	10. huwa maṣri min il-qaahira.
3. ṭayyib. maškuur.	11. 'intum bxeer?
4. killakum bxeer nšaaḷḷa?	12. hum min wilaayat kalifoornya.
5. šuġla daxtar fi l-mustašfa.	13. haađa mumarriđ̣ hini.
6. sadiigi 'amrikaani.	14. haađa mudiir iš-šarika.
7. waladi fi l-madrasa.	15. haađa sikirteer iš-šarika.
8. šloonak?	16. 'inta muwađ̣đ̣af?

Drill 9 *Question – Answer*

1. šloonak?
2. čeef il-9aayla?
3. killakum bxeer nšaaḷḷa?
4. ʼinti sikirteera?
5. ʼinta muwaḍ̄ḍ̄af hini?
6. ʼintum fi madrasat jaasim?
7. hin mneen?
8. ween šuġlak?
9. šu šuġlak?
10. hiya ʼamrikaaniyya?
11. haaḏ̄a mudiir bank bu ḍ̄abi?
12. ween il-qaahira?
13. ween 9ammaan?
14. dbayy fi giṭar?
15. zawjatak ween šuġlaha?
16. zawjič šu sma?

UNIT 8

I. TEXT

9abdaḷḷa :	'is-salaamu 9aleekum!
jum9a :	wa 9aleekum is-salaam.
9abdaḷḷa :	'asmi 9abdaḷḷa bin turki. 9indi maw9id ma9 il-mudiir.
jum9a :	zeen tfaḏ̣ḏ̣al yamm is-sikirteer!
9abdaḷḷa	(to the Secretary): 9indi maw9id wiyya l-mudiir il-yoom.
'is-sikirteer:	mata? 'ay saa9a?
9abdaḷḷa :	'is-saa9a 9ašir. 'il-mudiir hini?
'is-sikirteer:	'ii na9am. 'il-mudiir hini. tfaḏ̣ḏ̣al!

II. TRANSLATION

Abdalla :	Peace be upon you!
Jum'a :	And peace be upon you !
Abdalla :	My name is Abdalla bin Turki. I have an appointment with the director.
Jum'a :	Fine. Please go to the secretary.
Abdalla :	(to the Secretary): I have an appointment with the director today.
Secretary :	When? What time?
Abdalla :	At ten o'clock. Is the director here?
Secretary :	Yes. The director is here. Please sit down!

III. VOCABULARY

bin	bin (lit. 'the son of')
9ind—	to have; to own, possess
maw9id	appointment (m.)
tfaḍḍal!	please (m.) ...; go ahead!
'il-yoom	today (m.)
yamm	close to, by
wiyya	with
saa9a	hour; clock; watch (f.)
na9am	yes
mata?	when?
'ay	what? which?
'ii na9am	yes, indeed, certainly

IV. ADDITIONAL VOCABULARY

xamsa	five	yoom	day (m.)
sitta	six	baačir	tomorrow
sab9a	seven	'ams	yesterday
θamaanya	eight	'il-jum9a	Friday (f.)
tis9a	nine	'is-sabt	Saturday (m.)
9ašara	ten	la	no
		maktab	office (m.)

V. PRONUNCIATION

Drill 1

Contrast between **h** *and* 9

hala →	9ala	haayla →	9aayla	hoon →	9oon
haal	9aal	hayal	9ayal	heeba	9eeba
hamm	9amm	heela	9eela	hooda	9ooda
hindi	9indi	saheet	sa9eet	huud	9uud

Drill 2

Mark the following words for stress, and then read them, being careful to stress them as you have marked them:

maw9id	tfaḏ̣ḏ̣al	ʼil-yoom	mata
saa9a	9ašir	na9am	sitta
θamaanya	baačir	ʼis-sabt	ʼil-jum9a
9aleekum	ysallmak	nšaal̤l̤a	maṣriyya

Practicing 9

Read the following :

→

9abdal̤l̤a	jum9a	9aleekum	9indi	9indak
maw9id	mas9uud	9ašara	9ašir	saa9a
na9am	sab9a	tis9a	ʼil-jum9a	9ali

VI. GRAMMAR

1. 9ind– as a Verb

9ind is used with suffixed pronouns to form a verb-like expression meaning approximately 'to have', e.g., **9indi 9aayla** 'I have a family'. **9indi** without suffixed pronouns is generally a preposition meaning 'at, close to; in the possession of; at the house of or place (e.g., store, building, etc.) of'. Examples of this latter use will be given later on.

This preposition **9indi** has two forms, depending on the suffix: **9ind–** if the suffix begins with a vowel, and **9inda–** if the suffix begins with a consonant. Examples:

9indi	'I have'	9indana	'we have'
9indak	'you (m.s.) have'	9indahum	'they (m.) have'
9indič	'you (f.s.) have'	9indahin	'they (f.) have'

(The –a– in the examples on the right is a sort of a helping vowel inserted between two consonants for ease in pronunciation.)

(Drills 1, 2, 6)

2. Telling Time

Note that in GA when you count (e.g., 5–10) you keep the –a ending of the numerals: **xamsa** 'five', **sitta** 'six', **sab9a** 'seven', **θamaanya** 'eight', **tis9a** 'nine', and **9ašara** 'ten'. When you tell time (e.g., 'It's five o'clock'), you usually drop the –a ending from the numerals.

Examples :

'is-saa9a xams.	'It's five o'clock.'
'is-saa9a sitt.	'It's six o'clock.'

Note the following changes: **sab9a** 'seven' changes into **sabi9** in **'is-saa9a sabi9** 'It's seven o'oclock'; **θamaanya** 'eight' into **θamaan**; **tis9a** 'nine' into **tisi9**; and **9ašara** 'ten' into **9ašir**.

(Drills 5, 9)

3. Note that the short vowel **–a** in **wiyya** 'with' changes into a long vowel **–aa** with suffixed pronouns. Examples :

wiyyaak	'with you (m.s.)'	wiyyaaha	'with her'
wiyyaakum	'with you (m.p.)'	wiyyaahin	'with them (f.)'

Note the shift in stress : **wíyya** but **wiyyáak.**

ma9 and **wiyya** 'with' are used almost interchangeably.

4. *Note the following :*

'il-yoom il-jum9a.	'Today is Friday.' (subject and predicate)
yoom il-jum9a	'on Friday' (noun construct)

NOTE ON TEXT

tfaḍḍal is the imperative form of the verb **tfaḍḍal** 'to be so good as to do something'. As an imperative it means 'please ..... !' You say it when you offer someone something (e.g., coffee, food, etc.), or a seat (as in the TEXT) or when urging someone to go first, for example, through a door. The other forms of **tfađ̣đ̣al** are :

tfađ̣đ̣ali	'said to a female'
tfađ̣đ̣alu	'said to two or more males'
tfađ̣đ̣alin	'said to two or more females'

VII. DRILLS

Drill 1 *Substitution*

9indi maw9id wiyya l-**mudiir**. 'I have an appointment with the director.'

1. doctor (m.)
2. doctor (f.)
3. engineer (m.)
4. secretary
5. secretary (m.)
6. employee (m.)
7. employee (f.)
8. nurse (f.)
9. nurse (m.)
10. manager
11. bank manager
12. boy
13. girl
14. 9eeša
15. ṣaara
16. 9ali

Drill 2 *Double Substitution*

9indi maw9id wiyya l-**mudiir**. 'I have an appointment with the director.'

'inta – employee (m.)
'intum – secretary (m.)
hiya – nurse (f.)
niHin – employee (m.)

hum – manager (m.) 'aana – engineer (m.)

hin – doctor (f.) 'intin – director (f.)

'inti – secretary (f.) huwa – secretary (m.)

Drill 3 *Substitution*

tfaḍ̄ḍ̄al yamm is-**sikirteer**. 'Please go to the secretary (m.).' Use the substitutions from Drill 1, above.

Drill 4 *a. Repetition*

xamsa sitta sab9a θamaanya tis9a 9ašara

b. T. asks individual students to count from **xamsa** 'five' through **9ašara** 'ten'.

c. T. writes, e.g., the numeral 7 on the board; students are asked to give the GA word for **seven**.

Drill 5 *a. Repetition*

↓ 'is-saa9a xams. 'is-saa9a θamaan.

'is-saa9a sitt. 'is-saa9a tisi9.

'is-saa9a sabi9. 'is-saa9a 9ašir.

b. T. asks individual students to tell the time, starting with: **'is-saa9a xams.** 'It's five o'clock,' through: **'is-saa9a 9ašir.'** 'It's ten o'clock.'

Drill 6 *Variable Substitution*

Base Sentence : 9indi maw9id wiyya l-mudiir il-yoom.

'I have an appointment with the manager today.'

1. 'inta	8. 'intin	15. 'is-saa9a xams
2. 'inti	9. sikirteer	16. 'is-saa9a sitt
3. baačir	10. mumarriḏ̣a	17. 'is-saa9a sabi9
4. mudiira	11. huwa	18. 'is-saa9a θamaan
5. muhandis	12. 'aana	19. 'is-saa9a tisi9
6. niHin	13. 'intum	20. 'is-saa9a 9ašir
7. hum	14. hiya	21. baačir

Drill 7 *Chain*

T :	muhandis –– mudiir	'engineer –– director'
S_1 :	ween il-muhandis?	'Where is the engineer? '
S_2 :	'il-muhandis yamm il-mudiir.	'The engineer is with the director.'

1. mudiir – muhandis	8. bint – sikirteera
2. daxtar – mumarriḏ̣	9. daxtoora – mumarriḏ̣a
3. mudiir – daxtar	10. mudiira – muwaḏ̣ḏ̣af
4. muwaḏ̣ḏ̣af – mudiir	11. muwaḏ̣ḏ̣afa – mudiir
5. muhandis – sikirteer	12. walad – bint
6. sikirteer – muhandis	13. zawja – zawijha
7. walad – mudiir	14. mudiir – muhandis

Drill 8 *Chain*

T :	byaat	'Byat'
S_1 :	huwa byaat?	'Is he Byat?'
S_2 :	'ii na9am. huwa byaat.	'Yes, indeed. He is Byat.'

1. jum9a	5. muršid	9. mudiir
2. xamiis	6. nuura	10. daxtoora
3. 'aamna	7. yuusif	11. muwaḏ̣ḏ̣af
4. šeexa	8. maryam	12. sikirteera

Drill 9 *Question – Answer*

T :	'is-saa9a xams?	'Is it five o'clock?'
S :	'ii na9am 'is-saa9a xams.	'Yes, it's five o'clock.'

1. 'is-saa9a sitt?	8. 'il-yoom il-jum9a?
2. 'is-saa9a sabi9?	9. 'il-yoom is-sabt?
3. 'is-saa9a θamaan?	10. 'ams il-jum9a?
4. 'is-saa9a tisi9?	11. 'ams is-sabt?
5. 'is-saa9a 9ašir?	12. 9indak maw9id?
6. 'is-saa9a xams?	13. 'il-mudiir hini?
7. 'is-saa9a θamaan?	14. haaḏi madrasa?

Drill 10 *Repetition*

9indi maw9id wiyyaa.	9indi maw9id wiyyaak.
9indi maw9id wiyyaahum.	9indi maw9id wiyyaakum.
9indi maw9id wiyyaaha.	9indi maw9id wiyyaač.
9indi maw9id wiyyaahin.	9indi maw9id wiyyaakin.

Drill 11 *Translation*

1. What's today?
2. Today is Friday.
3. What was yesterday?
4. Yesterday was Saturday.
5. I have an appointment.
6. At what time?
7. At ten o'clock.
8. The office is here.
9. We are all fine, thanks.
10. Good-bye!
11. Good-bye (with safety)!
12. God protect you!
13. You are welcome.
14. He is from Arizona.
15. I have a boy and a girl.
16. The director (m.) is in the office.

UNIT 9

I. TEXT

ʼaamna :	ṣabbaHč aḷḷa bi l-xeer ya layla!
layla :	ya hala w marHaba.
ʼaamna :	9indi maw9id ma9 il-waziir is-saa9a waHda. ʼil-waziir hini?
layla :	ʼii na9am hini, bas mašġuul šwayy halHiin. tfaḓḓali stariiHi!
ʼaamna :	maškuura.

layla (to servant): gahwa ya xamiis!

II. TRANSLATION

Amna :	Good morning, Layla!
Layla :	Hello! Hi!
Amna :	I have an appointment with the Minister at one. Is the Minister here?
Layla :	Yes. He is here, but he is a little busy now. Please sit down!
Amna :	Thank you.

Layla (to servant): Khamis! Coffee!

III. VOCABULARY

hala	hi, helo	šwayy	little (bit)
marHaba	hello, hi	halHiin	now

waziir	minister (m.)	tfað̣ð̣ali ... !	please (f.) ... !
waHda	one (f.)	stariiHi!	rest (f.) !
bas	but; only	gahwa	coffee (f.)
mašġuul	busy (m.)		

IV. ADDITIONAL VOCABULARY

waaHid	one (m.)	'il-aHad	Sunday (m.)
'aθneen	two (m.)	'il-'aθneen	Monday (m.)
θalaaθa	three	'iθ-θalaaθ	Tuesday (f.)
'arba9a	four	'il-'arba9	Wednesday (f.)
θinteen	two (f.)	'il-xamiis	Thursday (m.)
niHin	we	stariiH!	rest (m.) !

V. PRONUNCIATION

H

From the writer's own experience in teaching Arabic, **H** and 9 are the most difficult sounds for native speakers of English. **H** shares all the features of 9 except that it is voiceless while 9 is voiced. In both of these sounds the muscles of the throat become tense and the passageway at the back of the throat becomes constricted. If you have mastered the production of the voiced 9, you will be able to produce an acceptable GA **H** if you devoice 9. However, it will take some practice to learn to recognize and produce **H**. Try the following :

a. Whisper and repeat the phrase 'Hey you!' as loudly and as deep in your throat as you can; then say only 'Hey', elongating the initial **h** sound, 'Hhhhhhhhhhhey'. Repeat this with the muscles used in gagging (as in the case with 9) tensed up. This would be an acceptable approximation of **H.**

b. An alternative suggestion is to start with 'ah!', whispering it as loudly as you can. Now repeat it and narrow the pharynx by moving the root of the tongue back, and raising the larynx.

Drill 1

Initial **H**

↓ Haal	Hamd	Haṭṭ	Hurma
Haaff	Hamad	Hawwal	Huṭṭ
Haakim	Habb	Hazza	Hukk
Haarr	Hammaam	Hijra	Hoos
Haamiθ̣̄	Hariim	Hinna	Hool
Haliib	Harraan	Hukuuma	Huum
Hamar	Haṣṣal	Hummoṣ	Huux

Drill 2

Medial **H**

↓ marHaba	fitHaw	waaHid	ṣaHiiH
laHam	ṣiHHa	stariiHi	taruuHiin
'il-aHad	siHab	'aHibb	niHin
baḢar	baHaθ	halHiin	riHt
tiffaaHa	'isHab	ruuHi	'aHsan

Drill 3

Final **H**

↓ ṣabaaH	'iftaH	ṣaHiiH	truuH
raaH	maaliH	maliiH	'aruuH
staraaH	miliH	stariiH	ruuH
tiffaaH	jiHH	muriiH	nuuH
fitaH	yiHH	looH	masmuuH

VI. GRAMMAR

1. Imperatives

The imperative verb **stariiH**! 'Sit down!', like tfaḏ̣ḏ̣al! (UNIT 8) has four different forms, reflecting differences in gender and number. **tfaḏ̣ḏ̣al** is often used with other imperatives, e.g. :

tfaḏ̣ḏ̣al stariiH	'Please sit down, rest (m.s.)!'
tfaḏ̣ḏ̣ali stariiHi	'Please sit down, rest (f.s.)!'
tfaḏ̣ḏ̣alu stariiHu	'Please sit down, rest (m.p.)!'
tfaḏ̣ḏ̣alin stariiHin	'Please sit down, rest (f.p.)!'

2. Telling Time

Note that since **saa9a** 'hour; clock; watch' is feminine, you should use the feminine form of **one** and **two** to agree with it :

'is-saa9a waHda.	'It is one o'clock.'
'is-saa9a θinteen.	'It is two o'clock.'
*'is-saa9a waaHid.	* 'is-saa9a θneen.

(Drills 4, 5, 7)

VII. DRILLS

Drill 1 *Chain*

S_1 (f.) : ṣabbaHč aḷḷa bi l-xeer ya layla!
'Good morning, Layla!'

S_2 (f.) : ya hala w marHaba! 'Hello! Hi!'

Drill 2 *Chain*

Repeat **Drill 1** with male students.

Drill 3 *a. Repetition*

waaHid	'aθneen	θalaaθa	'arba9a	xamsa
sitta	sab9a	θamanya	tis9a	9ašara

b. T. asks individual students to count from **waaHid** through **9ašara.**

c. T. writes, e.g., 9 on the board; students give the GA word for **nine.**

Drill 4 *Repetition*

1. 'is-saa9a waHda.
2. 'is-saa9a θinteen.
3. 'is-saa9a θalaaθ.
4. 'is-saa9a 'arba9.
5. 'is-saa9a xams.
6. 'is-saa9a sitt.
7. 'is-saa9a sabi9.
8. 'is-saa9a θamaan.
9. 'is-saa9a tisi9.
10. 'is-saa9a 9ašir.

Drill 5 *Question – Answer*

Example : T : 'is-saa9a waHda halHiin?
'Is it one o'clock now?'

S : 'ii na9am. 'is-saa9a waHda halHiin.
'Yes, indeed. It's one o'clock now.'

Drill 6 *Chain*

T. writes, e.g., 9 on the board; an individual student says: **'is-saa9a tisi9 halHiin.** 'It's nine o'clock now.'

Drill 7 *Variable Substitution*

Base Sentence : 9indi maw9id wiyya l-waziir 'is-saa9a xams.
'I have an appointment with the minister at five o'clock.'

1. you (m.)
2. you (f.)
3. she
4. secretary (m.)
5. manager (m.)
6. daxtar (m.)
7. they (m.)
8. you (m.p.)
9. they (f.)

10.	you (f.p.)	15.	1 o'clock	20.	1 o'clock
11.	niHin	16.	10 o'clock	21.	today
12.	he	17.	7 o'clock	22.	now
13.	'aana	18.	8 o'clock	23.	3 o'clock
14.	4 o'clock	19.	2 o'clock	24.	2 o'clock

Drill 8 *Substitution*

'il-waziir mašġuul šwayy. 'The minister is a little busy.'

1. 'il-mudiir
2. 'is-sikirteera
3. 'id-daxtar
4. 'id-daxtoora
5. 'il-muhandis
6. 'il-mudiira
7. 'is-sikirteer
8. 'il-waziir
9. 'iš-šeex
10. mHammad
11. ṣaaliH
12. Hamad
13. 'il-bint
14. 'il-walad
15. sadiigi
16. 'uxti
17. 'il-mumarriḓ̣a
18. 'il-muwaḓ̣ḓ̣af

Drill 9 *Repetition*

1. 'il-yoom is-sabt.
2. 'il-yoom il-'aHad.
3. 'il-yoom il-'aθneen.
4. 'il-yoom iθ-θalaaθ.
5. 'il-yoom il-'arba9.
6. 'il-yoom il-xamiis.
7. 'il-yoom il-jum9a.
8. 'il-yoom is-sabt.

Drill 10 *Chain*

T :	'il-jum9a	'Friday'
S_1 :	yoom il-jum9a	'on Friday'
S_2 :	'il-yoom il-jum9a.	'Today is Friday.'

Drill 11 *Transformation:* masculine → feminine

1. 'aana libnaani min beruut.
2. huwa maṣri min il-qaahira.
3. 'inta 9iṛaaqi min baġdaad?
4. tfaḏ̣ḏ̣al stariiH!
5. 9inda maw9id il-yoom.
6. ṣabbaHk aḷḷa bi l-xeer!
7. massaak aḷḷa bi l-xeer!
8. šloonak ?
9. čeef intum?
10. čeef inta?
11. ṭayyib maškuur.
12. huwa mašġuul halHiin.
13. haaḏa mudiir zeen.
14. waladhum 'asma 'amiin.
15. tfaḏ̣ḏ̣al yamm il-waziir.
16. huwa liibi w 'aana 'arduni.

Drill 12 *Translation*

1. I have an appointment with the doctor today at two o'clock.
2. The minister is a little busy now. Please sit down. Coffee?
3. What's today? Today is Wednesday.
4. What time do you (f.s.) have an appointment with the director (f.)?
5. Today at 1 o'clock. I hope the director is in the office.
6. How is the family? We are all fine, thank you.

7. Good-bye!Good-bye (with safety)!May God protect you!
8. She is an American from the city of Detroit in Michigan.
9. I am a little busy now. Tomorrow is Friday.
10. He is Qatari from the city of Umm Said.

UNIT 10

I. TEXT

ʼasmi 9abdaḷḷa. ʼaana min il-baHreen. ʼaana mitzawwij u 9indi walad u bint. ʼil-walad ʼasma jum9a w il-bint ʼasimha šeexa. hum fi l-madrasa. ʼaana kuuli fi wazaarat iṣ-ṣiHHa.

ʼil-hawa fi l-baHreen waajid zeen fi š-šita. muub Haarr u muub baarid, walaakin fi l-geeḏ̣ il-hawa Haarr u raṭib.

II. TRANSLATION

My name is Abdalla. I am from Bahrain. I am married, and I have a boy and a girl. The boy's name is Jum'a, and the girl's name is Shaikha. They are at school. I am a workman in the Ministry of Health.

The weather in Bahrain is very good in the winter. It's neither hot nor cold, but in the summer it is hot and humid.

III. VOCABULARY

ʼil-baHreen	Bahrain (f.)
mitzawwij	married (m.)
kuuli	coolie, workman (m.)
ṣiHHa	health (f.)
hawa (hawaa–)	weather; air, atmosphere (m.)
waajid	very; much; many (var. kaθiir)
šita (šitaa–)	winter (m.)

muub	(neg. particle) not
Haarr	hot (m.)
baarid	cold; cool (m.)
walaakin	but
geeḏ̣	summer (m.)
raṭib	humid, wet (m.)

IV. ADDITIONAL VOCABULARY

jaami9a	university (f.)	9ajmaan	Ajman
mu9allim	teacher (m.)	9umaan	Oman
kaatib	clerk (m.)	ʼis-su9uudiyya	Saudi Arabia (f.)
bariid	post, mail (m.)	li-9raag	Iraq
Hukuuma	government (m.)		

V. PRONUNCIATION

Drill 1

Contrast between **h** *and* **H**

haal →	Haal	hamar →	Hamar	laham →	laHam
haajj	Haajj	haṭṭ	Haṭṭ	bahhaar	baHHaar
haar	Haarr	harram	Harram	sahar	saHar
haaff	Haaff	hazza	Hazza	šaah	šaaH
haamil	Haamil	hanna	Hanna	nabah	nabaH

Drill 2

Contrast between **x** *and* **H**

xaal →	Haal	xammaam →	Hammaam	xooš →	Hooš
xaali	Haali	xaass	Hass	xoof	Hoof
xazza	Hazza	xasiis	Hasiis	xumma	Humma
xaaf	Haaff	xafiif	Hafiif	xđ̣eeri	Hđ̣eeri
xaayis	Haayis	xaliij	Haliij	tixayyar	tiHayyar
xaṭṭ	Haṭṭ	xeel	Heel	baxar	baHar
xaḷḷa	Haḷḷa	xeeṭ	Heeṭ	yxiis	yHiis

VI. GRAMMAR

1. Proper Names

Names of towns, cities, etc., and most countries, states, etc., are feminine. The names of a few countries and regions, however, may be masculine or feminine, e.g., **libnaan** 'Lebanon', **'il-yaman** 'Yemen', **li-9raag** 'Iraq', **'il-'ardun** 'Jordan', etc. Names that end with **–a** are feminine only, e.g., **faṛansa** 'France', **kanada** 'Canada', **suuriyya** 'Syria', **liibya** 'Libya', **'is-su9uudiyya** 'Saudi Arabia', **'ingiltara** 'England', etc.

Learn the following names of countries and cities:

'il-fijeera 'Fujaira', **'il-jazaa'ir** 'Algeria', **'il-maġrib** 'Morocco', **dimašq** 'Damascus', **'il-qaahiṛa** 'Cairo', **baġdaad** 'Baghdad', **9ammaan** 'Amman', **'il-manaama** 'Manama', **'id-dooHa** 'Doha'.

(Drill 4)

2. The Negative Particle **muub**

muub (sometimes **muu**) is a negative particle which should always precede a noun, an adjective, an adverb, or a phrase :

huwa muub muhandis.	'He is not an engineer.'
'il-hawa muub Haarr.	'The weather is not hot.'
hiya muub hini.	'She is not here.'
hum muub fi l-madrasa.	'They (m.) are not in (at) school.'

muub ... u muub ... means 'neither ... nor ...', as in the TEXT.

3. The Intensifier **waajid**

waajid 'very; very much; a lot' is an intensifier and can be used to modify nouns, adjectives, or verbs. It, like other particles of degree, can either precede or follow the word it modifies :

9indi waajid gahwa.	'I have a lot of coffee.'
'il-hawa Haarr waajid.	'The weather is very hot.'
'il-hawa waajid Haarr.	'The weather is very hot.'
9indak gahwa?	'Do you (m.s.) have (any) coffee?'
'ii na9am, waajid.	'Yes, indeed. (I have) a lot.'
9indi šwayy gahwa.	'I have a little coffee.'

VII. DRILLS

Drill 1 *Substitution*

9indi walad u bint. 'I have a boy and a girl.'

1. 'inta	11. hiya
2. 'inti	12. hum
3. hiya	13. 'inta
4. hum	14. 'inti
5. hin	15. 'intum
6. 'intin	16. 'intin
7. 'intum	17. 'aana
8. niHin	18. huwa
9. huwa	19. hin
10. 'aana	20. 'inta

Drill 2 *Double Substitution*

'il-walad 'asma jum9a w il-bint 'asimha šeexa.

'The boy's name is Jum'a, and the girl's name is Shaikha.'

Example : T : mudiir 'manager'

S : 'il-mudiir 'asma jum9a w il-mudiira 'asimha šeexa.

1. minister	4. manager
2. secretary	5. student
3. engineer	6. American

7. Bahraini	12. nurse
8. clerk	13. doctor
9. husband	14. director
10. this	15. minister
11. he	16. teacher

Drill 3 *Repetition*

1. čeef il-hawa l-yoom? ʼil-hawa zeen il-yoom.

   ʼHow is the weather today? The weather is nice today.ʼ
2. čeef il-hawa l-yoom? ʼil-hawa baarid il-yoom.
3. čeef il-hawa l-yoom? ʼil-hawa Haarr il-yoom.
4. čeef il-hawa l-yoom? ʼil-hawa zeen il-yoom.
5. čeef il-hawa l-yoom? ʼil-hawa muub baarid il-yoom.
6. čeef il-hawa l-yoom? ʼil-hawa muub Haarr il-yoom.
7. čeef il-hawa l-yoom? ʼil-hawa raṭib il-yoom.
8. čeef il-hawa l-yoom? ʼil-hawa muub raṭib il-yoom.
9. čeef il-hawa l-yoom? ʼil-hawa waajid zeen il-yoom.
10. čeef il-hawa l-yoom? ʼil-hawa Haarr u raṭib il-yoom.

Drill 4 *Double Substitution*

čeef il-hawa fi giṭar fi š-šita?

ʼHow is the weather in Qatar in the winter? ʼ

1. ʼabu ðabi – ʼiš-šita	4. 9umaan – ʼil-geeð
2. raas il-xeema – ʼiš-šita	5. 9ajmaan – ʼil-geeð
3. il-baHreen – ʼil-geeð	6. ʼiš-šaarja – ʼiš-šita

7. giṭar – 'iš-šita
8. li-kweet – 'il-geeđ̣
9. 'is-su9uudiyya – 'il-geeđ̣
10. 'umm il-giween – 'il-geeđ̣
11. li-9raag – 'il-geeđ̣
12. li-9raag – 'iš-šita
13. 'arizoona – 'iš-šita
14. wašinṭon – iš-šita

Drill 5 *Double Substitution*

'aana **kuuli** fi **wazaarat** iṣ-ṣiHHa.

'I am a coolie in the Ministry of Health.'

1. engineer – Ministry of Petroleum
2. secretary – Bank of Qatar
3. coolie – ADMA Company
4. manager – BP
5. Clerk – Phillips Company
6. secretary – Bank of Abu Dhabi
7. teacher – university
8. nurse – Qatar Hospital
9. doctor – Ministry of Health
10. director – Ministry of Health
11. coolie – BP
12. Clerk – Shell Company
13. employee – ADMA Company
14. teacher – school

Drill 6 *Transformation :* positive → negative

1. 'il-hawa waajid zeen il-yoom.
2. fi l-geeḏ il-hawa baarid.
3. 'il-walad 'asma ṣaaliH.
4. 'il-mu9allim min suuriyya.
5. 'il-yoom il-hawa Haarr.
6. 'il-mu9allim mitzawwij.
7. 'il-gahwa Haarra waajid.
8. 'il-kaatib fi l-maktab.
9. halHiin is-saa9a xams.
10. 'il-waziir mašġuul.
11. hum fi l-jaami9a.
12. 'il-mu9allim min il-baHreen.
13. 'aana zeen il-yoom.
14. hiya 'amrikaaniyya.

Drill 7 *Variable Substitution*

Base Sentence : 9indi maw9id il-yoom is-saa9a sitt.
'I have an appointment today at six o'clock.'

1. he
2. she
3. they (m.)
4. you (f.)
5. you (m.)
6. tomorrow
7. one o'clock
8. two o'clock
9. ten o'clock
10. with the minister

11. I
12. you (p.)
13. we
14. three o'clock
15. five o'clock
16. we
17. today
18. he
19. 2 o'clock
20. I
21. she
22. 7 o'clock
23. 1 o'clock
24. with the teacher

Drill 8 *Transformation :* masculine → feminine

1. huwa suuri min dimašq.
2. 'inta mu9allim hini?
3. 'aana mašġuul il-yoom.
4. tfađ̣đ̣al stariiH !
5. ṣabbaHk aḷḷa bi l-xeer.
6. 'inta mitzawwij?
7. 9inda maw9id wiyya l-mu9allim.
8. šuġlak hini?
9. massaak aḷḷa bi l-xeer !
10. čeef inta?
11. huwa maṣri min il-qaahira.
12. 'inta muub mitzawwij?
13. hum fi l-madrasa.
14. 'intum fi l-jaami9a?
15. 'inta mašġuul il-yoom?
16. 9indak walad fi l-madrasa?

Drill 9 *Substitution*

haađa l-hawa waajid zeen. 'This weather is very good.'

1. mu9allim
2. mu9allima
3. kuuli
4. gahwa
5. maktab
6. waziir
7. sikirteera
8. muh'andis
9. walad
10. bint
11. yoom
12. saa9a
13. 'ingiliizi
14. jaami9a
15. ṭaalib
16. mudiir
17. šarika
18. daxtar
19. mumarriđ̣
20. 'amrikaani

Drill 10 *Questions* (based on Text)

1. šu smi?
2. mneen 'aana?
3. 'aana mitzawwij?
4. 9indi walad u bint?
5. šu 'asm il-walad?
6. šu 'asm il-bint?
7. 'il-walad fi l-madrasa?
8. šu šuġlak?
9. ween šuġlak?
10. čeef il-hawa fi l-baHreen?
11. 'il-hawa baarid fi š-šita?
12. 'il-hawa Haarr fi l-geeđ̣?
13. 'il-hawa raṭib fi l-geeđ̣?
14. čeef il-hawa l-yoom?

UNIT 11

REVIEW

Drill 1 *Question – Answer*

1. šu smak?
2. mneen inta?
3. šloonak?
4. čeef il-'ahil?
5. massaak aḷḷa bi l-xeer!
6. 'inta baHreeni?
7. ween šuġlak
8. 'inta mitzawwij?
9. šu l-yoom?
10. 9indak šuġul il-yoom?
11. 9aayiltak hini?
12. 'inta mašġuul il-yoom?
13. 'ay saa9a 9indak šuġul?
14. 'is-saa9a sitt halHiin?
15. čeef il-hawa l-yoom?
16. 'il-hawa Haarr waajid il-yoom?

Drill 2 *Transformation :* non-definite → definite

1. huwa mudiir šarika.
2. haađi mumarriđ̣a.
3. hiya sikirteera fi bank.
4. daxtar fi mustašfa
5. waziir batrool
6. daxtar wazaarat ṣiHHa
7. maktab bariid
8. mudiir šarika 'amrikaaniyya
9. ṭaalib fi madrasa
10. šuġul waajid zeen
11. sikirteerat bank 'iiraani
12. muwađ̣đ̣af Hukuuma

Drill 3 *Variable Substitution*

Base Sentence : ʼil-yoom il-jum9a. 'Today is Friday.'

1. yesterday
2. Saturday
3. Monday
4. tomorrow
5. Tuesday
6. Wednesday
7. Thursday
8. today
9. Friday
10. Saturday
11. Sunday
12. Monday
13. yesterday
14. Tuesday
15. Wednesday
16. Thursday
17. Friday
18. hot
19. cold
20. humid

Drill 4 *Transformation :* statement → question

Use question words.

1. ʼasmi jaasim bin Hamad.
2. ʼil-yoom il-hawa waajid zeen.
3. killana bxeer, maškuur.
4. hiya min il-baHreen.
5. 9indi maw9id is-saa9a 9ašir.
6. hum min madiinat beruut.
7. ʼii na9am. ʼil-mudiir hini.
8. ʼil-hawa waajid zeen il-yoom.
9. landan fi ngiltara.

10. ʼil-mudiir yamm il-waziir.
11. ʼil-gahwa Haarra.
12. hum min wilaayat ʼarizoona.
13. šuġli fi wazaarat iṣ-ṣiHHa.
14. ʼii na9am. ʼis-saa9a xams halHiin.

Drill 5 *Transformation :* masculine → feminine

1. ʼaana sikirteer.
2. huwa ʼingiliizi.
3. ʼinta ʼamrikaani?
4. ʼil-walad fi l-madrasa.
5. ʼasma ṣaaliH.
6. šloonak?
7. ṣabbaHk aḷḷa bi l-xeer!
8. ween šuġlak?
9. tfaθ̣θ̣al stariiH!
10. šu smak?
11. ʼaḷḷa ysallimk!
12. hum min is-su9uudiyya.
13. ʼintum min giṭar?
14. haaδa d-daxtar waajid zeen.
15. haaδa s-sikirteer maṣri.
16. tfaθ̣θ̣al yamm is-sikirteer!

Drill 6 *Variable Substitution*

Base Sentence : 9indi maw9id wiyya l-waziir.

ʼI have an appointment with the minister.ʼ

1. director (m.)
2. doctor (f.)
3. secretary (f.)
4. manager (f.)
5. engineer (m.)
6. employee (m.)
7. today
8. at 10:00
9. he
10. they (m.)

11. tomorrow
12. doctor (f.)
13. they (f.)
14. at 7:00
15. we
16. today
17. you (m.s.)
18. you (f.s.)

Drill 7 *Transformation :* statement → negative

1. 'il-hawa Haarr il-yoom.
2. 'il-mudiir hini.
3. 'is-saa9a θalaaθ halHiin.
4. 'il-gahwa Haarra?
5. 'il-hawa zeen fi š-šita.
6. 'il-mu9allim fi l-madrasa.
7. haaδ̄a l-mudiir waajid zeen.
8. haaδ̄i š-šarika zeena.
9. 'aana mašġuul il-yoom.
10. baačir il-jum9a.
11. il-yoom il-xamiis.
12. 'ams il-'aHad.
13. 'inta su9uudi.
14. haaδ̄a 'iiraani.

Drill 8 *Substitution*

'il-hawa **baarid** il-yoom. 'The weather is cold today.'

1. hot
2. not hot
3. fine
4. not fine
5. wet
6. very wet
7. very hot
8. very cold
9. very good
10. cold and fine
11. hot but fine
12. not very hot
13. not very cold
14. not very wet
15. hot and humid

Drill 9 *Transformation :*

prepositional phrase → nisba adjective

Example : huwa min tuunis → huwa tuunisi.

'He is from Tunis. → He is Tunisian.'

1. 'aana min giṭar.
2. šeexa min il-baHreen.
3. 9abdaḷḷa min bu ḓabi.
4. nuura min libnaan.
5. linda min 'amriika.
6. joorj min 'ingiltara.
7. saalim min li-kweet.
8. 9ali min li-9raag.
9. mHammad min is-su9uudiyya.
10. 'ibraahiim min liibya.
11. kalθuum min maṣir.
12. karaama min il-'ardun.
13. xamiis min is-suudaan.
14. maryam min libnaan.
15. mišeel min faṛansa.
16. ṣaara min 'ingiltara.

Drill 10 *Translation*

1. We have an appointment with the minister today at ten o'clock.
2. He is from the city of Tucson in the State of Arizona.
3. It is seven o'clock now. I have work at the Ministry.
4. Yes, the Minister is here. Please sit down! He is a little busy.
5. I work as a coolie in the Ministry of Petroleum.
6. I work for (with) the government. My work is very good.
7. The weather is very good today. It is a little hot but good.
8. What is the name of the director of the Shell Company in Qatar?
9. In the summer the weather is very hot and very humid.
10. Do you (m.s.) have work tomorrow? Yes, at four o'clock.

UNIT 12

I. TEXT

9abdaḷḷa :	ʹis-salaamu 9aleekum!
fred :	wa 9aleek is-salaam.
9abdaḷḷa :	šu smak?
fred :	ʹasmi fred
9abdaḷḷa :	keef Haalak?
fred :	ṭayyib. ʹil-Hamdu lillaah.
9abdaḷḷa :	ʹinta min ween?
fred :	ʹaana min ʹamriika.
9abdaḷḷa :	min ween f amriika?
fred :	min tuuṣaan fi ʹarizoona.
9abdaḷḷa :	ʹinta titkallam 9aṛabi zeen waḷḷa !
fred :	la. muub zeen waajid. ʹaana ʹatkallam šwayy 9aṛabi.
9abdaḷḷa :	keef iṭ-ṭaqs fi tuuṣaan fi š-šita?
fred :	baarid u zeen fi š-šita.
9abdaḷḷa :	fi l-geeϑ̣̄ il-hawa Haarr?
fred :	ʹii waḷḷa killiš Haarr walaakin Haaff. hini l-hawa Haarr u raṭib fi ṣ-ṣeef.

II. TRANSLATION

Abdalla :	Peace be upon you!
Fred :	And peace be upon you!

Abdalla :	What's your name?
Fred :	My name's Fred.
Abdalla :	How are you?
Fred :	Fine. Praise be to God.
Abdalla :	Where are you from?
Fred :	I'm from America.
Abdalla :	Where from in America?
Fred :	From Tucson in Arizona.
Abdalla :	Gee, you speak Arabic well!
Fred :	No, not very well. I speak a little Arabic.
Abdalla :	How's the weather in Tucson in the winter?
Fred :	Cold and nice in the winter.
Abdalla :	Is it hot in the summer?
Fred :	Yes, indeed. It's very hot but dry. Here it is hot and humid in the summer.

III. VOCABULARY

keef?	how?
Haal	condition
Hamd	praise; thanks
tuuṣaan	Tucson
titkallam	you (m.s.) speak, are speaking
9aṛabi	Arabic
′atkallam	I speak
ṭaqs	weather (var. **hawa**)

killiš	very
Haaff	dry
ṣeef	summer (var. **geeð̣**)

IV. ADDITIONAL VOCABULARY

'adris	I study, am studying
'at9allam	I learn, am learning
'aktib	I write, am writing

V. GRAMMAR

1. Verbs – Imperfect Tense

The two-verb tenses in GA, imperfect and perfect, roughly correspond to the English present and past tenses. The verb **'atkallam** 'I speak' is made up of a subject-marker **'a–**, referring to 'I' and a stem **–tkallam–** corresponding to the English infinitive 'to speak.' Below is a sample conjugation of the verb **–tkallam–**:

PRONOUN	**VERB**	**AFFIX**
huwa	yitkallam	y–
hiya	titkallam	t–
'inta	titkallam	t–
'inti	titkallamiin	t–iin
'aana	'atkallam	'a–
hum	yitkallamuun	y–uun

hin	yitkallamin	y–in
'intum	titkallamuuun	t–uun
'intin	titkallamin	t–in
niHin	nitkallam	n–

Note that the –i–, inserted between the stem **–tkallam–** and the subject markers (except for **'atkallam**), is a helping vowel. Its occurrence before the consonant cluster **tk–** is compulsory, as the initial clusters **vtk–** and **ttk–** do not occur in GA. It has more than one form, depending upon the initial consonant(s) of the stem and the speakers of GA. The other forms will be pointed out as they arise.

The imperfect tense in GA has the following meanings:

a. habitual: 'atkallam 9aṛabi kill yoom. 'I speak Arabic every day.'

b. general truth value ("generic", "dispositional," etc.): 'atkallam 9aṛabi zeen. 'I speak Arabic well.'

c. progressive: yitkallam 9aṛabi halHiin. 'He is speaking Arabic now.'

d. future: yitkallam baačir? 'Will he, is he going to, speak tomorrow?'

(Drills 2, 12)

Note : The verb normally occurs without an independent pronoun, but the latter may be expressed for emphasis.

2. The Intensifier **killiš**

killiš 'very' is used only as an adverb to modify adjectives. It can precede or follow the adjective :

haaᵭa zeen killiš.	'This is very good.'
haaᵭa killiš zeen.	'This is very good.'

waajid 'very; very much; a lot (of)' (UNIT 10) can be used as an adjective or as an adverb :

9indi gahwa waajid.	'I have a lot of coffee.'
huwa yitkallam waajid.	'He speaks a lot.'
* huwa yitkallam killiš.	(Drills 6, 11)

NOTES ON TEXT

1. **wal̤l̤a** 'honestly, really' (lit. 'by God, honest to God') is frequently used before or after words, phrases, and sentences for emphasis :

'il-hawa Haar̤r̤ il-yoom?	'Is it hot today? '
ʾii wal̤l̤a killiš Haarr.	'Yes, indeed. It's very hot.'
wal̤l̤a mašġuul waajid.	'Honestly, I'm very busy.'
wal̤l̤a 9indi gahwa.	'Certainly, I have coffee.'

2. **'al-Hamdu lillaah** 'fine, good' is a response to **keef Haalak?** 'How are you (m.s.)? ' It literally means 'Praise, thanks be to God.' Other responses are: **ṭayyib, zeen, wal̤l̤a zeen,** etc.

VI. DRILLS

Drill 1 *Chain*

S_1: 'is-salaamu 9aleekum! 'Peace be upon you!'

S_2: wa 9aleekum is-salaam. 'And peace be upon you.'

S_1: keef Haalak? 'How are you (m.s.)?'

S_2: ṭayyib. 'il-Hamdu lillaah. 'Fine (m.s.). Praise be to God.'

Drill 2 *Substitution*

'inta titkallam wiyyà l-**mudiir**. 'You are speaking (speak) with the manager.'

1. engineer (m.)
2. minister (m.)
3. secretary (f.)
4. director (f.)
5. employee (m.)
6. doctor (m.)
7. nurse (f.)
8. coolie (m.)
9. teacher (m.)
10. 9ali
11. mHammad
12. faaṭma
13. 9abdaḷḷa
14. teacher (f.)
15. doctor (f.)
16. secretary (m.)
17. employee (f.)
18. nurse (m.)
19. šeexa
20. clerk (m.)

Drill 3 *Substitution*

'atkallam wiyya l-mudiir. 'I am speaking (speak) with the manager.'

Use substitutions from **Drill 2** above.

Drill 4 *Repetition*

1. huwa yitkallam 9aṛabi zeen.
2. hum yitkallamuun 9aṛabi zeen.
3. hiya titkallam 9aṛabi zeen.
4. hin yitkallamin 9aṛabi zeen.
5. 'inta titkallam 9aṛabi zeen.
6. 'intum titkallamuun 9aṛabi zeen.
7. 'inti titkallamiin 9aṛabi zeen.
8. 'intin titkallamin 9aṛabi zeen.
9. 'aana 'atkallam 9aṛabi zeen.
10. niHin nitkallam 9aṛabi zeen.

Drill 5 *Repetition*

Repeat the sentences in **Drill 4** above with the verb **yiktib** 'he is writing (writes).'

Drill 6 *Transformation :* Conjugation

huwa yitkallam 9aṛabi waajid zeen. 'He speaks Arabic very well.'

1. hum
2. hiya
3. hin
4. 'inta
5. 'intum
6. 'inti
7. 'intin
8. 'aana
9. niHin
10. huwa
11. hiya
12. 'inta
13. 'inti
14. 'intin
15. 'intum
16. hum

Drill 7 *Transformation :* Conjugation

yitkallam šwayy 9aṛabi. 'He speaks Arabic a little.'

1. 'inta	11. 'aana
2. 'aana	12. niHin
3. hum	13. hum
4. hin	14. hin
5. 'inti	15. 'inta
6. huwa	16. 'inta
7. hiya	17. hiya
8. 'inta	18. 'inta
9. 'intum	19. huwa
10. 'intin	20. 'aana

Drill 8 *Chain*

T_1 : keef il-hawa l-yoom? 'How is the weather today? '

T_2 : waḷḷa baarid. 'It's very cold.'

Use the following in the answer :

1. hot and humid	7. very good
2. cold but nice	8. very hot and wet
3. cold and nice	9. very hot but dry
4. hot but dry	10. not very good
5. cold and wet	11. not very hot
6. hot and dry	12. neither cold nor hot

Drill 9 *Transformation :* Conjugation

wal̤l̤a huwa yidris 9aṛabi. 'He is studying (studies) Arabic.'

Use substitutions from **Drill 7** above.

Drill 10 *Transformation :* Conjugation

huwa yit9allam fi l-madrasa. 'He is learning (learns) at school.'

Use substitutions from **Drill 7** above.

Drill 11 *Variable Substitution*

Base Sentence : yitkallam 9aṛabi. 'He is speaking (speaks) Arabic.'

1. hiya
2. 'aana
3. hum
4. yiktibuun
5. 'inta
6. 'inti
7. zeen
8. killiš zeen
9. 'intum
10. muub zeen
11. huwa
12. 'intum
13. niHin
14. zeen
15. nidris
16. 'aana
17. hiya
18. tit9allam
19. 'inta
20. huwa

Drill 12 *Translation*

1. I don't speak Arabic very well. I speak only a little Arabic.
2. They are studying Arabic at the University of Arizona.
3. Do you (f.s.) speak Arabic well? No, not very well.
4. Are you (m.s.) learning Arabic in Abu Dhabi now?
5. Is it hot in Bahrain in the summer?
6. Yes, indeed. It is very hot and very humid in the summer.
7. Here, it is neither hot nor cold in the summer.
8. He is writing his name in Arabic. Do you (f.s.) write Arabic well?

UNIT 13

I. TEXT

ʼibraahiim :	taksi!
Taxi Driver :	ween tabi truuH?
ʼibraahiim :	ʼabi ʼaruuH ʼuteel il-hilton. čam triid?
Taxi Driver :	θalaaθa dirhim.
ʼibraahiim :	la. θalaaθa dirhim kaθiir. ʼadfa9 dirhimeen bas.
Taxi Driver :	zeen. tfað̣ð̣al.
ʼibraahiim :	tfað̣ð̣al haaða 9ašara dirhim.
Taxi Driver :	tfað̣ð̣al il-baagi θamaanimyat fils.
ʼibraahiim :	maškuur. fi maan illaa!
Taxi Driver :	ma9 is-salaama.

II. TRANSLATION

Ibrahim :	Taxi!
Taxi Driver :	Where do you want to go?
Ibrahim :	I want to go to the Hilton Hotel. How much do you want?
Taxi Driver :	Three dirhams.
Ibrahim :	No, three dirhams is a lot. I'll pay two dirhams only.
Taxi Driver :	O.K. Hop in.
Ibrahim :	Here you are! Ten dirhams.

Taxi Driver :	Here you are! The remainder is 800 fils.
Ibrahim :	Thank you. Good-bye!
Taxi Driver :	With safety.

III. VOCABULARY

taksi	taxi
tabi	you (m.s.) want, like
truuH	you (m.s.) go, are going
'abi	I want, like
'uteel	hotel
čam ?	how much (many)? (var. **kam**)
triid	you (m.s.) want, like
dirhim	dirham (100 fils)
'adfa9	I (will) pay
dirhimeen	two dirhams
bas	only
baagi	remainder; change
fils	fils (1/100 dirham)
θamaanimiya	800

IV. ADDITIONAL VOCABULARY

'imya	100	xamsimya	500
miteen	200	sittimya	600
θalaaθimya	300	sabi9imya	700
'arba9imya	400	θamaanimiya	800

tisi9imya	900	ryaal	riyal
'alf	1,000	diinaar	dinar
'alfeen	2,000	fundug	hotel

V. GRAMMAR

1. Verbs –– Imperfect Tense

The imperfect stems –**abi**– 'to want, (would) like to', –**ruuH**– 'to go', and –**riid**– 'to want, wish', do not take any helping vowels with the subject-markers. –**abi**–, however, has some irregular forms, since it ends with a vowel:

huwa yabi	hum yabuun
hiya tabi	hin yabin
'inta tabi	'intum tabuun
'inti tabiin	'intin tabin
'aana 'abi	niHin nabi

Note the following :

yabi + uun - - - - - yabuun 'they (m.p.) want'

tabi + uun - - - - - tabuun 'you (m.p.) want'

The stem –**dfa9**– 'to pay' takes the helping vowel –i– or –a– with the subject-markers: '**inta tidfa9** or **tadfa9** 'you (m.s.) pay', **hum yidfa9uun** or **yadfa9uun** 'they (m.p.) pay', etc.

(Drills 1, 2, 8)

2. The Dual

In English nouns are either singular or plural; in GA they are singular, dual, or plural. The dual in GA is formed by adding the suffix **–een** to a masculine noun and **–teen** to a feminine noun ending with **–a**:

diinar 'one dinar' ----- diinaareen 'two dinars'

dirhim 'one dirham' ----- dirhimeen 'two dirhams'

madrasa 'one school' ----- madrasateen 'two schools'

Remember that nouns ending with **–VC**, where **–V–** is any vowel except **–a–**, drop their **–V–** when the dual suffix **–een** is added.

Example :

'uxut 'sister' ----- 'uxteen 'two sisters'

'asim 'name' ----- 'asmeen 'two names'

Note the shift in stress: **'úxut** but **'uxtéen.**

Masculine nouns with the **–a** ending take **–yeen** as a dual suffix:

mustašfa 'one hospital' ----- mustašfayeen 'two hospitals'

šita 'one winter' ----- šitayeen 'two winters'

(Drill 6)

3. The Double Imperfect Construction

Note that double imperfect tenses of two verbs are used in GA for the **Verb + Infinitive** construction in English:

'ariid 'aruuH.	'I want, would like to, go.'
yabuun yruuHuun.	'They (m.) want to go.'
nriid nidris 9arabi.	'We want to study Arabic.'

Each form of the imperfect should agree with the subject, i.e., each form takes the same affixes :

yabuun yruuHuun.	'They (m.) want to go.'
*yabuun yruuH	(Drill 6)

4. Cardinal Numerals

a. The numerals for both 'one' and 'two' have two forms each, a masculine form and a feminine form, depending upon the noun they modify or refer to:

9indi walad waaHid.	'I have one boy (son).'
9indi bint waHda.	'I have one girl (daughter).'
'aθneen hini w θinteen fi l-madrasa.	'Two (boys) are here and two (girls) are in school.'

waaHid and **'aθneen** and their feminine forms follow the noun they modify: **walad waaHid** 'one boy', **waladeen 'aθneen** 'two boys'.

b. **θalaaθa – 9ašara.** The numerals for 'three' through 'ten' precede the noun they modify: if that noun is a unit of money, it is left in the singular :

xamsa dirhim	'five dirhams'
tis9a ryaal	'nine riyals'

Note that the feminine numeral is used with these nouns.

c. The hundreds, except for **'imya** 'one hundred' and **miteen** 'two hundred', consit of the numerals **θalaaθa** 'three' through **tis9a** 'nine' (the **–a** ending is dropped) and **'imya** :

xamsimya	'500'	θamaanimya	'800'

Exceptions : sab9a 'seven' ---- sabi9imya '700'

θamaanya 'eight' ---- θamaanimya '800'

tis9a 'nine' ---- tisi9imya '900'

If the noun counted is expressed, **'imya** changes to **'imyat.** The noun counted is singular, not plural :

xamsimyat diinaar	'500 dinars'	*xamsimya diinaar
'imyat ryaal	'100 riyals'	*miya ryaal

(Drills 3, 4, 5, 7)

5. **čam** (var. **kam**) **'how many, how much'**

čam is used with a countable noun, e.g., **book, man,** etc., or a noncountable noun, e.g., **money, food, water,** etc. The noun following **čam** should be singular, not plural as in English :

čam walad 9indak?	'How many boys (children) do you (m.s.) have?
čam gahwa tabi?	'How much coffee do you (m.s.) want?'

čam can also be used with a verb :

čam triid? 'How much do you (m.s.) want?'

(Drills 5, 9, 10)

NOTE ON TEXT

The basic unit of money in the U. A. E. is the dirham (DH) which is divided into 100 equal units, each of which is called a fils. Dirham notes are in denominations of 1, 5, 10, 50, 100, and 1000. Fils coins are in denominations of 1, 5, 10, 25, 50, and 100. In Qatar the basic unit of money is the Qatari riyal, which is 100 fils. In Bahrain the basic unit is the Bahraini dinar, which is divided into 1000 fils. The U. A.E. dirham (100 fils) has the same value as a Qatari riyal or 1/10 of a Bahraini dinar. At the time of this writing, a U. S. dollar has the value of DH 3.90.

VI. DRILLS

Drill 1 *Substitution*

a. 'abi 'aruuH **'uteel il-hilton.** 'I want to go to the Hilton Hotel.'

1. 'il-'uteel
2. 'il-fundug
3. 'uteel il-9een
4. 'uteel il-hilton
5. fundug il-beeč
6. 'il-madrasa
7. 'il-jaami9a
8. 'il-baHreen
9. 'is-su9uudiyya
10. dbayy
11. waziir iṣ-ṣiHHa
12. mudiir iš-šarika
13. mustašfa l-Hukuuma
14. jaami9at 'arizoona
15. madiinat nyuu yoork

b. huwa yabi yruuH 'ila 'uteel il-waaHa.

'He wants to go to the Oasis Hotel.'

Use substitutions from a, above.

Drill 2 *Variable Substitution*

Base Sentence : 'ariid 'aruuH 'ila l-fundug.

'I want to go to the hotel.'

1. sikirteer iš-šarika
2. mudiir il-bank
3. 'inta
4. 'inti
5. huwa
6. yabi
7. 'il-'uteel
8. 'il-mustašfa
9. hiya
10. baačir
11. 'aana
12. 'abi
13. hum
14. 'is-saa9a xams
15. 'intum
16. niHin
17. 'il-yoom
18. 'is-saa9a 9ašir
19. 'il-wazaara
20. 'il-bank
21. huwa

Drill 3 *a. Repetition*

'imya	miteen	θalaaθimya
'arba9imya	xamsimya	sittimya
sabi9imya	θamaanimya	tisi9imya
'alf		

b. T. writes, e.g., **700** on the board; individual students are asked to give the GA words for 700; i.e., **sabi9imya.**

Drill 4 *Identification*

Students give the GA words for the following:

300	600	900	400	1,000
100	200	10	7	1
2	200	3	300	100
500	700	800	200	900
8	3	700	500	2,000

Drill 5 *Chain*

S_1: kam triid? 'How much do you want?'

T : three dirhams.

S_2: θalaaθa dirhim bas.

1. 5 dirhams
2. 10 dirhams
3. 2 dirhams
4. 2 dinars
5. 8 dinars
6. 500 fils
7. 300 fils
8. 200 fils
9. 900 fils
10. 2 fils
11. 1,000 dinars
12. 2,000 riyals
13. 400 fils
14. 100 dinars
15. 100 fils

Drill 6 *Transformation :* singular → dual

1. diinaar
2. fils
3. dirhim
4. mustašfa

5. bint
6. madrasa
7. jaami9a
8. daxtoora
9. 'uteel
10. 'imya
11. fundug
12. sadiig
13. kaatib
14. mu9allima
15. mudiir
16. waziir
17. marHaba
18. gahwa
19. xamsa
20. 9aayla

Drill 7 *Substitution*

'il-baagi **xamsimyat fils.** 'The remainder is 500 fils.'

1. one dinar
2. two dinars
3. six dinars
4. 300 fils
5. 100 fils
6. 200 dinars
7. two dirhams
8. 1,000 dirhams
9. 2,000 dinars
10. eight riyals
11. one riyal
12. two fils
13. 200 fils
14. 100 dinars
15. seven dinars

Drill 8 *Variable Substitution*

Base Sentence : 'aana 'abi šwayy gahwa. 'I want a little coffee.'

1. hiya
2. 'inta
3. hum
4. niHin
5. 'intum
6. 'intin
7. triidin
8. 'aana
9. 'inta
10. hiya

11. 'inti
12. hum
13. niHin
14. hin
15. 'intum
16. kaθiir
17. 'aana
18. 'abi
19. hiya
20. huwa

Drill 9 *Question – Answer*

1. keef Haalak ya (xamiis)?
2. čam is-saa9a halHiin?
3. čam tabi?
4. ween tabi truuH?
5. šu tabi?
6. kam tidfa9?
7. čam walad 9indak?
8. čam diinaar tabi?
9. kam walad fi l-madrasa?
10. čam mustašfa fi giṭar?
11. čam ryaal tabi?
12. ween tidris 9aṛabi?
13. 'inta tiktib 9aṛabi?
14. tabi tidṛis 9aṛabi?
15. tabi tiktib 'asmak hini?
16. čeef iṭ-ṭaqs il-yoom?

Drill 10 *Translation*

1. Thank you very much. Good-bye! Good-bye (with safety)!
2. I have five dirhams. I pay only two dirhams.
3. Five dinars is a lot! How much do you want to pay?
4. He wants to go to the Hilton Hotel. How much?
5. All right. Hop in.
6. How many children do you (f.s.) have?

7. How much coffee do you (m.p.) want?
8. How many hospitals are there in Abu Dhabi?
9. How many dinars do you (m.s.) want to pay?
10. How much coffee does she want?

UNIT 14

I. TEXT

9ali :	ʼariid aruuH wazaarat it-tarbiya.
Taxi Driver :	zeen tfað̣ð̣al.
9ali :	kam tabi?
Taxi Driver :	rubbiteen. Si9r il-Hukuuma.
9ali :	zeen.
Taxi Driver :	ʼinta min giṭar?
9ali :	laa. min is-su9uudiyya.
Taxi Driver :	haaði ʼawwal marra taji d-dooHa?
9ali :	laa. haaði θaaliθ marra.
Taxi Driver :	čam ṣaarlak hini?
9ali :	min zamaan. ṣaarli 9ašir siniin.
Taxi Driver :	ween tištaġil?
9ali :	fi wazaarat it-tarbiya.
Taxi Driver :	nšaaḷḷa ʼa9jabatk id-dooHa?
9ali :	ʼii. ʼa9jabatni waajid. ʼaana killiš mistaanis hini.

II. TRANSLATION

Ali :	I want to go to the Ministry of Education.
Taxi Driver :	Fine. Hop in.
Ali :	How much do you want?
Taxi Driver :	Two rupees. (This is) the government tariff.

Ali :	O. K.
Taxi Driver :	Are you from Qatar?
Ali :	No, I'm from Saudi Arabia.
Taxi Driver :	Is this the first time you (have) come to Doha?
Ali :	No. This is the third time.
Taxi Driver :	How long have you been here?
Ali :	A long time. I've been here for ten years.
Taxi Driver :	Where do you work?
Ali :	In the Ministry of Education.
Taxi Driver :	I hope you like Doha.
Ali :	Yes, I like it very much. I am having a very good time here.

III. VOCABULARY

tarbiya	education
wazaarat it-tarbiya	the Ministry of Education
rubbiteen	two rupees
si9r	price
'awwal	first
marra	time
taji	you (m.s.) come, are coming
θaaliθ	third
ṣaarlak	you (m.s.) have been
zamaan	time
min zamaan	for a long time; a long time ago

siniin	(s. **sana**) years
tištaġil	you (m.s.) work, are working
nšaaḷḷa	(I) hope that (lit. 'if God wills')
'a9jabatk	you (m.s.) liked [lit. 'it (f.) pleased you (m.s.)]
mistaanis	happy, pleased

IV. ADDITIONAL VOCABULARY

θaani	second	θaamin	eighth
raabi9	fourth	taasi9	ninth
xaamis	fifth	9aašir	tenth
saadis	sixth	rubbiyya	rupee
saabi9	seventh	sana	year

V. GRAMMAR

1. Verbs – – Imperfect Tense

The imperfect verb stem **–ji–** 'to come' takes either **–a–** or **–i–** as a helping vowel, while **–štaġil–** 'to work' usually takes **–i–**:

'inta taji d-dooHa. 'You (m.s.) come to Doha.'

'inta taji d-dooHa.

huwa yištaġil il-yoom. 'He is working today.'

The stem **–ji–** (See UNIT 13) drops the **–i–** when the suffixes **–in, –iin** or **–uun** are added :

'inti tajiin.	'You (f.s.) come (are coming).'
'intum tajuun.	'You (m.p.) come (are coming).'
hum yajuun.	'They (m.p.) come (are coming).'

taji + iin ----- tajiin

yaji + uun ----- yajuun

–**štaġil**– 'to work' becomes –**štaġl**– when the suffixes –**in**, –**iin**, or –**uun** are added. (See UNIT 4, GRAMMAR 3.)

'inti tištaġliin	'You (f.s.) are working.'
'intum tištaġluun	'You (m.p.) are working.'
'intin tištaġlin	'You (f.p.) are working.'

(Drills 5, 6, 7)

2. Ordinals

Ordinals are derived from cardinals. The derivations of **'awwal** 'the first' and **θaani** 'the second' from **waaHid** 'one' and **'aθneen** 'two' are irregular. **θaaliθ** 'the third' through **9aašir** 'the tenth', derived from **θalaaθa** 'three' and **9ašir** 'ten', are fairly regular. They are formed according to the pattern C_1 aaC_2 iC_3, except for **saadis** 'the sixth' from **sitta** 'six' :

Cardinal		**Ordinal**	
θalaaθa	'three'	θaaliθ	'the third'
xamsa	'Five'	xaamis	'the fifth'
sitta	'six'	saadis	'the sixth'
θamaanya	'eight'	θaamin	'the eighth'

Ordinals can either precede or follow the nouns they modify. In this lesson they precede singular nouns, in which case they are not inflected for gender :

'awwal mu9allim	'the first teacher (m.s.)'
'awwal mu9allima	'the first teacher (f.s.)'
'awwal mu9allimateen	'the first two teachers (f.)'
'awwal waladeen	'the first two boys.'

(Drills 1, 2, 3, 4)

3. Special Constructions

a. **nšaal̤l̤a** literally means 'if God wills'. It is frequently used in the speech of Gulf Arabs. It generally means: 'I hope (that); I hope so; probably; it is to be hoped (that)':

nšaal̤l̤a 'a9jabatk il-balad.	'I hope you (m.s.) liked the country.'
nšaal̤l̤a l-mudiir hini.	'I hope the director is here.'
taji baačir?	'Will you come, are you coming, tomorrow? '
nšaal̤l̤a	'I hope so; probably.'

b. **'a9jab** is a perfect tense verb. It literally means 'to please or be pleasing'. **' a9jabatak** or **'a9jabatk il-bint** 'The girl pleased you (m.s.)' is equivalent to 'You (m.s.) liked the girl' in polished English. The suffix **–ak** (or **–k**) is the object of the verb **'a9jab** and it refers to the subject of the polished English sentence, i.e., **you**. So, instead of saying, e.g., **I liked the coffee**, say **The coffee pleased me**: **'il-gahwa 'a9jabatni** or **'a9jabatni l-gahwa**. If the subject that did the pleasing is masculine singular, say **'a9jabni..** for 'I liked'; if it is feminine singular, say **'a9jabatni**:

'a9jabni l-hawa. 'I liked the weather.'

'a9jabatni l-gahwa. 'I liked the coffee.'

The rest of the object pronouns suffixed to **'a9jab** are the same as those suffixed to nouns :

'a9jabhum 'They (m.) liked'

'a9jabna 'We liked'

'a9jabkin 'You (f.p.) liked'

(Drills 8, 9)

c. Learn **čam ṣaarlak hini?** 'How long have you (m.s.) been here? ' as a formula for the time being. Other forms are:

čam ṣaarlič hini? 'How long have you (f.s.) been here? '

čam ṣaarlakum hini? 'How long have you (m.p.) been here? '

čam ṣaarlaha hini? 'How long has she been here? '

(Drill 4)

VI. DRILLS

Drill 1 *Repetition*

'awwal	θaani	θaaliθ	raabi9	xaamis
saadis	saabi9	θaamin	taasi9	9aašir

Drill 2 *Transformation:* cardinal → ordinal

T : sana waHda 'one year'

S : 'awwal sana 'the first year'

1. walad waaHid	10. sana waHda
2. binteen	11. mustašfa waaHid
3. xams siniin	12. mu9allimeen
4. 'arba9 siniin	13. sanateen
5. bint waHda	14. sabi9 siniin
6. marra waHda	15. θamaan siniin
7. marrateen	16. taksi waaHid
8. θalaaθ siniin	17. jaami9a waHda
9. sitt siniin	18. 9ašir siniin

Drill 3 *a. Repetition*

1. haaði 'awwal marra 'aji giṭar. 'This is the first time I come to Qatar.'
2. haaði θaani marra 'aji giṭar.
3. haaði θaaliθ marra 'aji giṭar.
4. haaði raabi9 marra 'aji giṭar.
5. haaði xaamis marra 'aji giṭar.
6. haaði saadis marra 'aji giṭar.
7. haaði saabi9 marra 'aji giṭar.
8. haaði θaamin marra 'aji giṭar.
9. haaði taasi9 marra 'aji giṭar.
10. haaði 9aašir marra 'aji giṭar.

b . Chain

T : three

S : haaði θaaliθ marra 'aji bu ḍ̄abi.

'This is the third time I come to Abu Dhabi.'

Drill 4 *Chain*

S_1 : čam ṣaarlak hini? 'How long have you (m.s.) been here?'

T : θalaaθ siniin 'Three years'

S_2 : ṣaarli θalaaθ siniin hini bas.

'I have been here for three years only.'

1. sanateen
2. 'arba9 siniin
3. xams siniin
4. min zamaan
5. sabi9 siniin
6. θamaan siniin
7. tisi9 siniin
8. 9ašir siniin
9. sana waHda
10. yoom waaHid
11. yoomeen
12. sanateen
13. sitt siniin
14. xams siniin
15. min zamaan

Drill 5 *Variable Substitution*

Base Sentence : huwa yaji min il-madrasa s-saa9a θalaaθ.

'He comes (back) from school at 3 o'clock.'

1. hiya
2. 'inta
3. 'aana
4. niHin
5. two o'clock
6. one o'clock
7. four o'clock
8. hum
9. hin
10. five o'clock
11. 'intum
12. 'intin
13. 'aana
14. il-wazaara
15. il-mustašfa
16. il-'uteel
17. one o'clock
18. 'il-fundug
19. two o'clock
20. hiya
21. huwa

Drill 6 *Repetition*

1. huwa yištaġil fi wazaarat it-tarbiya.
   'He works in the Ministry of Education.'
2. hum yištaġluun fi wazaarat it-tarbiya.
3. hiya tištaġil fi wazaarat it-tarbiya.
4. hin yištaġlin fi wazaarat it-tarbiya.
5. 'inta tištaġil fi wazaarat it-tarbiya.
6. 'intum tištaġluun fi wazaarat it-tarbiya.
7. 'inti tištaġliin fi wazaarat it-tarbiya.
8. 'intin tištaġlin fi wazaarat it-tarbiya.
9. 'aana 'aštaġil fi wazaarat it-tarbiya.
10. niHin ništaġil fi wazaarat it-tarbiya.

Drill 7 *Variable Substitution*

Base Sentence : yištaġil fi wazaarat it-tarbiya.
'He works in the Ministry of Education.'

1. hum
2. hiya
3. 'inta
4. 'intum
5. wazaarat il-batrool
6. 'aana
7. 'il-mustašfa
8. bank giṭar
9. 'inti
10. 'intin
11. wazaarat iṣ-ṣiHHa
12. niHin
13. huwa
14. 'uteel il-9een

15. 'uteel il-hilton
16. 'il-'uteel
17. 'il-madrasa
18. hiya
19. 'inti
20. 'inta
21. hum

Drill 8 *Repetition*

a. 'il-baHreen 'a9jabatni waajid.
'I liked Bahrain very much.'

'il-baHreen 'a9jabatna waajid.
'We liked Bahrain very much.'

'il-baHreen 'a9jabatha waajid.
'She liked Bahrain very much.'

'il-baHreen 'a9jabathin waajid.
'They (f.) liked Bahrain very much.

'il-baHreen 'a9jabata waajid.
'He liked Bahrain very much.'

'il-baHreen 'a9jabathum waajid.
'They (m.) liked Bahrain very much.'

'il-baHreen 'a9jabatk waajid.
'You (m.s.) liked Bahrain very much.'

'il-baHreen 'a9jabatkum waajid.
'You (m.p.) liked Bahrain very much.'

'il-baHreen 'a9jabatič waajid.
'You (f.s.) liked Bahrain very much.'

'il-baHreen 'a9jabatkin waajid.
'You (f.p.) liked Bahrain very much.'

b. Substitute **'il-mu9allim** 'the teacher' for **'il-baHreen** 'Bahrain' in a, above.

Drill 9 *Substitution*

'a9jabni **id-daxtar.** 'I liked the doctor.'

1. the weather
2. the hotel
3. the Hilton Hotel
4. Beirut
5. the University
6. the teacher (m.)
7. the secretary (f.)
8. the clerk (m.)
9. Dubai
10. the coffee
11. the minister (m.)
12. the hospital
13. the work
14. the watch
15. the girl

Drill 10 *Chain*

T : 'inta min zamaan hini? 'Have you been here long? '
S : 'ii walla . 'aana killiš mistaanis hini.
'Yes, indeed . I am very happy here.'

Drill 11 *Question – Answer*

1. mneen 'inta?
2. 'inta min is-su9uudiyya?
3. haaði 'awwal marra taji hini?

4. čam ṣaarlak hini?
5. ṣaarlak hini min zamaan?
6. ween tištaġil?
7. kam saa9a tištaġil kill yoom?
8. nšaaḷḷa šuġlak zeen?
9. nšaaḷḷa 'a9jabatk il-madiina?
10. nšaaḷḷa mistaanis hini?

Drill 12 *Translation*

1. I liked Abu Dhabi a lot. I am having a good time here.
2. The first hospital here is the Government Hospital.
3. She has been here for two years only. She works as a secretary for the Ministry of Education.
4. Two dirhams isn't much. Five dirhams.
5. Here you are! The remainder is 700 fils.
6. You are an American, but you speak Arabic well. Are you studying Arabic here? '
7. Yes, indeed. I am studying Arabic here. I have been studying Arabic for five years.
8. Did you like the weather here in the summer?
9. To tell the truth, it is very hot and very humid here in the summer. The winter is very nice.
10. Are you married? Is the family with you? How many children do you have?

UNIT 15

I. TEXT

Hamad : ṣabbaHk aḷḷa bi l-xeer ya mbaarak!

mbaarak : ʼahlan wa sahlan. tfaḏ̣ḏ̣al stariiH!

Hamad : maškuur.

mbaarak : tišrab šayy? gahwa, čaay, baarid...?

Hamad : čaay min faḏ̣lak.

mbaarak : čeef Haalak? čeef il-ʼahil?

Hamad : waḷḷa muub zeen il-yoom. mariiḏ̣ u mṣaxxan.

mbaarak : ruuH id-daxtar.

Hamad : ʼil-yoom 9indi maw9id ma9 id-daxtar saami s-saa9a θinteen illa rub9 9ugb iḏ̣- ḏ̣uhur.

II. TRANSLATION

Hamad : Good morning, Mubarak!

Mubarak : Hello! Hi! Please sit down!

Hamad : Thank you.

Mubarak : Would you like to drink something ? Coffee, tea, something cold... ?

Hamad : Tea, please.

Mubarak : How are you? How is the family?

Hamad : Not very well today. (I am) sick and running a temperature.

Mubarak : Go to the doctor.

Hamad : Today I have an appointment with Dr. Sami at 1:45 p.m.

III. VOCABULARY

tišrab	you drink, are drinking
šayy	something, anything
čaay	tea
faẓ̄il	grace, favor
baarid	cold drink, beverage
mariiẓ̄	sick, ill
mṣaxxan	running a temperature
'illa	to (e.g., quarter of five)
rub9	quarter (time)
9ugub	(prep.) after
ẓ̄uhur	noon, noontime

IV. ADDITIONAL VOCABULARY

Haliib	milk	Hda9aš	eleven
biira	beer	θna9aš	twelve
šakar	sugar	θalatta9aš	thirteen
mayy	water	'arba9ta9aš	fourteen
nuṣṣ	half	xamsta9aš	fifteen
θilθ	third	sitta9aš	sixteen
ṣabaaH	morning	sabi9ta9aš	seventeen
'iṣ-ṣabaaH	in the morning	θamaanta9aš	eighteen
gabil	(prep.) before	tisi9ta9aš	nineteen
iẓ̄ - ẓ̄uhr	(at) noontime	čam is-saa9a?	What time is it?

V. GRAMMAR

1. Imperatives

The imperative is used in giving commands, i.e., in telling or asking someone or a group of people to do something, e.g. **ruuH**! 'go (m.s.)! and **tfaḍ̄ḍ̄al stariiH**! 'Please sit down (m.s.)!' There are four imperative forms in GA: masculine singular, masculine plural, feminine singular, and feminine plural. Nearly all the imperative forms are formed from the imperfect stems of verbs. The masculine singular form of the imperative is the base of all other forms. The following rules pertain to the formation of the masculine singular imperative from the imperfect stems of the verbs we have had so far :

a. **'i–** is prefixed to the imperfect stem if it is of the pattern –CCV– in which CC is not permissible in GA.

Examples : **–šrab–** → **'išrab**! 'Drink (m.s.)!'

–dfa9– → **'idfa9**! 'Pay (m.s.)!'

–dris– → **'idris**! 'Study (m.s.)!'

–ktib– → **'iktib**! 'Write (m.s.)!'

b. If the stem is of the pattern –CCV– and CC is permissible in GA, **'i–** is prefixed optionally.

Examples : –štaġil– → ('i)štaġil! 'Work (m.s.)!'

–tkallam– → ('i)tkallam! 'Talk (m.s.)!'

–t9allam– → ('i)t9allam! 'Learn (m.s.)!'

–tfaḍ̄ḍ̄al– → ('i)tfaḍ̄ḍ̄al! 'Please (m.s.)!'

–stariiH– → ('i)stariiH! 'Rest (m.s.)!'

c. In all other cases (except for some irregular forms, which will be pointed out later) the masculine singular form of the imperative is the same as the imperfect stem.

Example : –ruuH– → ruuH! 'Go (m.s.)!'

The masculine plural form (said to two or more people) takes the suffix **–u**:

'išrab! 'Drink (m.s.)!' → 'išrabu! 'Drink (m.p.)!'

The feminine singular and plural forms take the suffixes **–i** and **–in**, respectively:

'išrab! 'Drink (m.s.)!' → 'išrabi! 'Drink (f.s.)!'
→ 'išrabin! 'Drink (f.p.)!'

(Drills 7, 8, 11)

2. Telling Time

The word **saa9a** 'hour; clock; watch' should be used in asking and stating the time:

kam is-saa9a?	'What time is it?'
'is-saa9a xams.	'It's five o'clock.'

Up to and including the half hour, minutes are added to the hour by using the proper numeral after **u** 'and'; between the half hour and the next hour they are subtracted from the next hour by using **'illa** 'except'. If the time is 'thirty-five minutes past...' or 'thirty-five minutes to...', it is usually expressed by **u nuṣṣ u xams** or **u nuṣṣ illa xams**. The fractions

rub9, **θilθ**, and **nuṣṣ** are usually used for a quarter of an hour, a third of an hour, and a half hour, respectively. The word for minutes is seldom used.

'is-saa9a xams.	'It is five o'clock.'
'is-saa9a xams u 9ašir.	'It is 5:10.'
'is-saa9a xams illa 9ašir.	'It is 4:50.'

'iṣ-ṣabaaH 'in the morning' is usually up to but not including noon. Noon is literally **'iđ̣-đ̣uhr. 9ugb iđ̣-đ̣uhr** is usually any time after twelve-noon up to 4:00 or 5:00 p.m. After 5:00 p.m. it is **'il-masa** 'in the evening' or simply 'p.m.'

'aji s-saa9a tisi9 iṣ-ṣabaaH.	'I come at 9:00 a.m.'
'aji s-saa9a θna9aš iđ̣-đ̣uhr.	'I come at 12:00 noon.'
'aji s-saa9a waHda 9ugb iđ̣-đ̣uhur.	'I come at 1:00 p.m.'
'aji s-saa9a xams il-masa.	'I come at 5:00 p.m.'

(Drills 9, 10)

3. Cardinal Numerals

The independent forms of the cardinal numerals 11 – 19 end in **–a9aš** (11 – 12) or **–ta9aš** (13 – 19). The first part of each of these cardinals is derived from the ordinals 'one' through 'nine':

Hda9aš	'eleven'	xamsta9aš	'fifteen'
θna9aš	'twelve'	sitta9aš	'sixteen'
θalatta9aš	'thirteen'	sabi9ta9aš	'seventeen'
'arba9ta9aš	'fourteen'	θamaanta9aš	'eighteen'
		tisi9ta9aš	'nineteen'

If they are followed by nouns, they end in –a9šar (11 – 12) or –**ta9šar** (13 – 19). The noun following any number between 'eleven' and 'nineteen' is singular, not plural as in English:

xamsta9ašar yoom	'fifteen days'
tisi9ta9ašar saa9a	'nineteen hours'

(Drills 13, 14)

VI. DRILLS

Drill 1 *Chain*

S_1: ṣabbaHk aḷḷa bi l-xeer ya (saalim).' 'Good morning, Salim!'

S_2: 'ahlan wa sahlan. 'Welcome.'

Drill 2 *Substitution*

tišrab **gahwa**? 'Would you like to drink coffee? '

1. čaay
2. Haliib
3. biira
4. wiski
5. mayy
6. šayy
7. gahwa
8. baarid
9. čaay u Haliib
10. gahwa wiyya šakar
11. šayy baarid
12. šayy Haarr
13. biira
14. Haliib baarid
15. Haliib Haarr
16. čaay wiyya Haliib
17. mayy baarid
18. gahwa

Drill 3 *Repetition*

1. huwa yriid yišrab čaay.
2. hum yriiduun yišrabuun čaay.
3. hiya triid tišrab čaay.
4. hin yriidin yišrabin čaay.
5. ʹinta triid tišrab čaay.
6. ʹintum triiduun tišrabuun čaay.
7. ʹinti triidiin tišrabiin čaay.
8. ʹintin triidin tišrabin čaay.
9. ʹaana ʹariid ʹašrab čaay.
10. niHin nriid nišrab čaay.

Drill 4 *Variable Substitution*

Base Sentence: ʹabi ʹǎsrab gahwa. ʹI want to drink coffee.ʹ

1. huwa	8. ʹinti	15. ʹintum
2. hiya	9. Haliib	16. ʹintin
3. čaay	10. hum	17. ʹaana
4. čaay u Haliib	11. niHin	18. gahwa
5. triid	12. nabi	19. šayy baarid
6. biira	13. baarid	20. šayy Haarr
7. ʹinta	14. wiski	21. ʹinta

Drill 5 *Substitution*

ween **il-mudiir** min faḏ̣lak? 'Where is the director, please?'

1. wazaarat it-tarbiya
2. wazaarat il-batrool
3. wazaarat iṣ-ṣiHHa
4. il-mustašfa
5. mustašfa l-Hukuuma
6. 'uteel il-waaHa
7. id-daxtar
8. il-baagi
9. il-mu9allim
10. il-kaatib
11. il-jaami9a
12. mudiir iš-šarika
13. il-mumarriḏ̣a
14. ič-čaay
15. il-gahwa

Drill 6 *Substitution*

'aana **mariiḏ̣** il-yoom. 'I am sick today.'

1. mṣaxxan
2. mariiḏ̣
3. mašġuul
4. mistaanis
5. 9indi šuġul
6. killiš mariiḏ̣
7. mašġuul waajid
8. 'adris 9aṛabi
9. 'aktib 9aṛabi
10. 'aštaġil waajid
11. mṣaxxan
12. mašġuul
13. mistaanis
14. 'ariid 'ašrab gahwa
15. 'ariid 'aruuH

Drill 7 *Repetition*

a.	ruuH	tfaϑ̣ϑ̣al	stariiH	'išrab	štaġil
	'idfa9	tkallam	'idris	t9allam	'iktib
b.	ruuHi	tfaϑ̣ϑ̣ali	stariiHi	'išrabi	štaġli
	'idfa9i	tkallami	'idrisi	t9allami	'iktibi

Drill 8 *Variable Substitution*

Base Sentence : 'inta ruuH stariiH! 'You go rest!'

1. 'inti
2. 'intum
3. 'intin
4. drink coffee
5. 'inti
6. 'inta
7. learn Arabic
8. 'inti
9. 'intum
10. 'intin
11. work
12. 'inta
13. 'inti
14. 'intin
15. 'intum
16. drink tea
17. 'inta
18. 'inti
19. 'intum
20. 'intin

Drill 9 *Repetition*

1. halHiin is-saa9a tisi9. 'Now it's nine o'clock.'
2. halHiin is-saa9a tisi9 u xams.
3. halHiin is-saa9a tisi9 u 9ašir.
4. halHiin is-saa9a tisi9 u rub9.

5. halHiin is-saa9a tisi9 u θilθ.
6. halHiin is-saa9a tisi9 u nuṣṣ.
7. halHiin is-saa9a 9ašir illa xams.
8. halHiin is-saa9a 9ašir illa 9ašir.
9. halHiin is-saa9a 9ašir illa rub9.
10. halHiin is-saa9a 9ašir illa θilθ.

Drill 10 *Repetition*

1. 'is-saa9a tisi9 iṣ-ṣabaaH. 'It's 9:00 a.m.'
2. 'is-saa9a tisi9 il-masa.
3. 'is-saa9a θna9aš iđ̣-đ̣uhr.
4. 'is-saa9a θna9aš u nuṣṣ 9ugb iđ̣-đ̣uhr.
5. 'is-saa9a Hda9aš u nuṣṣ gabl iđ̣-đ̣uhr.
6. 'is-saa9a θna9aš illa rub9.
7. 'is-saa9a θna9aš illa θilθ.
8. 'is-saa9a θna9aš illa rub9.
9. 'is-saa9a θna9aš u rub9.
10. 'is-saa9a θna9aš u θilθ.

Drill 11 *Transformation:* indicative → imperative

Example: 'inta tišrab gahwa. → 'išrab gahwa!
'You (m.s.) drink coffee.' → 'Drink (m.s.) coffee!'

1. 'inta tištaġil hini.
2. 'inti tištaġliin hini.
3. 'intum tišrabuun gahwa.
4. 'intin tidrisin 9aṛabi.

5. ʼinta titkallam 9aṛabi.	10. ʼinta tišrab Haliib.
6. ʼintum tišrabuun čaay.	11. ʼintum titkallamuun zeen.
7. ʼinta tidfa9 dirhim.	12. ʼinti tidrisiin ingiliizi.
8. ʼinti tistariiHiin hini.	13. ʼintum tidfa9uun diinaareen.
9. ʼinta tištaġil wiyya 9ali.	14. ʼinta tit9allam 9aṛabi.

Drill 12 *Question – Answer*

1. šu tabi tišrab?
2. keef Haalak? nšaaḷḷa zeen?
3. kam is-saa9a halHiin?
4. čam iṭ-ṭamaaṭ il-yoom?
5. 9indak šuġul il-masa?
6. ween tabi truuH?
7. kam ṣaarlak hini?
8. nšaaḷḷa a9jabatk il-baHreen?
9. haaðʼi ʼawwal marra taji hini?
10. čam tabi ʼila ʼuteel il-hilton?
11. kam tabi tidfa9?
12. keef iṭ-ṭaqs il-yoom?
13. ʼinta mitzawwij? 9indak 9aayla?
14. čam walad 9indak?

Drill 13 *Chain*

a. T. asks individual students to say the **ordinals, one** through **ten**.

b. T. asks individual students to say the numerals 11 – 19.

Drill 14 *Translation*

1. 11 hospitals	6. 16 girls	11. 14 times
2. 12 doctors (m.)	7. 17 women	12. 11 taxis
3. 15 days	8. 18 dinars	13. 17 hotels
4. 19 teachers (f.)	9. 14 years	14. 12 clerks
5. 13 boys	10. DH 12.50	15. 15 hours

UNIT 16

I. TEXT

maryam: čam iṭ-ṭamaaṭ il-yoom?

seef : θalaaθimyat fils ir-rub9a.

maryam: ġaali kaθiir !

seef : laa muub ġaali. ʼil-yoom maa fii ṭamaaṭ waajid fi s-suug.

maryam: ʼadfa9 miteen fils bas.

seef : laa. haađa galiil.

maryam: zeen. fi maan illaa.

seef : ta9aali. miteen u xamsiin fils?

maryam: laa. miteen bas. ʼariid aštiri beeḏ u burtaqaal ba9ad.

seef : zeen. čam tabiin?

maryam: 9aṭni θalaaθa keelu ṭamaaṭ u darzan beeḏ u darzaneen burtaqaal.

II. TRANSLATION

Mary : How much are tomatoes today?

Seif : 300 fils per rub'a.

Mary : Very expensive.

Seif : No, (it's) not expensive. There aren't many tomatoes in the market today.

Mary : I (will) pay 200 fils only.

Seif : No, this is little.

Mary :	O.K. Bye!
Seif :	Come back! 250 fils?
Mary :	No, 200 only. I want to buy eggs and oranges, too.
Seif :	Fine. How much do you want?
Mary :	Give me three kilos of tomatoes, a dozen eggs, and two dozen oranges.

III. VOCABULARY

ṭamaaṭ	(coll.) tomatoes
rub9a	rub'a
ġaali	expensive
kaθiir	very; much; many
fii	there is; there are
suug	market
galiil	little; few
ta9aali	(imp.) come (back, here)
xamsiin	fifty
'aštiri	I buy
beeđ̣	(coll.) eggs
burtaqaal	(coll.) oranges
ba9ad	too, also
9aṭni	(imp.) give me
keelu	kilogram
darzan	dozen

IV. ADDITIONAL VOCABULARY

jiHH	(coll.) watermelons
baṭṭiix	(coll.) cantaloupes, muskmelons
mooz	(coll.) bananas
tiffaaH	(coll.) apples
laHam	(coll.) meat
simač	(coll.) fish
dihin	(coll.) butter; shortening
jibin	(coll.) cheese
9eeš	(coll.) rice
xubiz	(coll.) bread
raxiiṣ	cheap

V. GRAMMAR

1. Cardinal Numerals

The tens, 30 – 90, are formed by dropping the **–a** (or **–ya**) ending from the corresponding units 3 – 9 and adding **–iin**:

θalaaθa	'three'	θalaaθiin	'thirty'
xamsa	'five'	xamsiin	'fifty'
θamaanya	'eight'	θamaaniin	'eighty'

The noun following the tens is also singular, not plural: **xamsiin yoom** 'fifty days'.

GA has a special system for saying the cardinals. Any number between 21 and 99 is expressed by a phrase consisting of the units numeral followed by the conjunction **w** (or **u**) 'and', and then followed by the tens numeral :

xamsa w xamsiin	'fifty-five'
waaHid u sittiin	'sixty-one'

Numbers between 101 and 999 are expressed by saying the hundreds numeral first followed by the conjunction **w** (or **u**), then the units numeral or the numeral phrase:

miya w xamsa	'105'
θallaaθimya w xamsa w 9išriin	'325'
miteen u sitta w tis9iin	'296'

If a number has **'alf** 'one thousand' as its biggest numeral, you say the thousand first, followed by **w** (or **u**), and then followed by the appropriate phrase as described above:

'alf u tisi9imya w 'arba9a w sab9iin '1974'

(Drills 2, 3, 10)

2. Collective Nouns

ṭamaaṭ 'tomatoes', **beeđ̣** 'eggs', **burtaqaal** 'oranges', **jiHH** 'watermelons', **baṭṭiix** 'cantaloupes, sweet melons', **jibin** 'cheese', **xubiz** 'bread', and **dihin** 'butter, shortening' are examples of collective nouns. Almost all kinds of vegetables, fruits, grains, flowers, fruit trees, grasses, etc., are collective nouns. The singular item or unit associated with a collective noun is known as a "unit noun". Thus, **beeđ̣** is '(some) eggs' and **beeḍ̄a** is 'an egg'. All unit nouns are formed by adding **–a** to the collective noun, sometimes with appropriate stem changes, which will be explained as we go along. Unit nouns are all feminine singular and they have a dual form (e.g., **beeḍ̄ateen** 'two eggs'), and a plural form, as we will see later.

It should be pointed out that almost all collectives are masculine singular, though the English translation may be plural, e.g. **beeḍ̄** 'eggs'. If collectives are used in a general sense, they should take the article prefix, like any other noun:

'iṭ-ṭamaaṭ ġaali l-yoom.	'Tomatoes are expensive today.'
fii ṭamaaṭ fi s-suug.	'There are (some) tomatoes in the market.'

(Drills 1, 3, 6,7, 9)

3. Imperatives

The imperfect stem of a verb with a final vowel, e.g., **–štiri–** 'to buy' is also the form of the masculine or feminine singular imperative. The final vowel drops when the imperative suffixes **–u** or **–in** (See UNIT 13, GRAMMAR 1) are added:

štiri ṭamaaṭ !	'Buy (m.s. or f.s.) some tomatoes!'
štiru ṭamaaṭ !	'Buy (m.p.) some tomatoes !'
štirin ṭamaaṭ !	'Buy (f.p.) some tomatoes !'

The imperative forms of –ji– 'to come' are: **ta9aal, ta9aalu, ta9aali,** and **ta9aalin** 'Come (back, here)!'

(Drill 8)

4. The Negative Particle **ma**

Note that **fii** (with a longer vowel than **fi** 'in') means 'there is; there are'. The negative is **ma fii** 'there isn't; there aren't':

fii ṭamaaṭ fi s-suug.	'There are tomatoes in the market.'
ma fii ṭamaaṭ fi s-ssug.	'There aren't (any) tomatoes in the market.'

ma negates verbs, as apposed to **muub** (or **muu**) that negates nouns, phrases, and adjectives. (**fii** is a verb-like word, like **9ind–** 'to have, possess'):

huwa ma yidris halHiin.	'He is not studying now.'

(Drill 6)

VI. DRILLS

Drill 1 *Substitution*

čam iṭ-ṭamaaṭ il-yoom? 'How much are tomatoes today?'

1. šakar
2. Haliib
3. beeđ̣
4. burtaqaal
5. jiHH
6. baṭṭiix
7. mooz
8. tiffaaH
9. laHam
10. simač
11. jibin
12. 9eeš
13. xubiz
14. si9r il-beeđ̣

15. si9r il-gahwa
16. si9r ič-čaay
17. darzan il-mooz
18. darzan il-beeḏ̣
19. darzan il-burtaqaal
20. darzan it-tiffaaH

Drill 2 *Double Substitution*

θalaaθ**imyat** fils **ir-rub9a** '300 fils a rub'a'

1. 750 – dozen
2. 200 – dozen
3. 125 – dozen
4. 900 – kilogram
5. 605 – kilogram
6. 875 – kilogram
7. 615 – rub9a
8. 580 – rub9a
9. 470 – rub9a
10. 320 – dozen
11. 245 – dozen
12. 950 – kilogram
13. 300 – rub9a
14. 105 – dozen
15. 400 – kilogram

Drill 3 *Chain*

T :	ṭamaaṭ	'tomatoes'
S_1 :	čam iṭ-ṭamaaṭ il-yoom?	'How much are tomatoes today?'
T :	600 fils/kilogram	'600 fils – kilogram'
S_2 :	sittimyat fils il-keelu.	'600 fils per kilo.'

1. šakar – 600 fils/kilogram
2. beeḏ̣ – 500 fils/dozen
3. burtaqaal – $\frac{1}{2}$ dinar/dozen

4. jiHH – 200 fils/rub'a
5. baṭṭiix – 100 fils/kilogram
6. mooz – 400 fils/dozen
7. tiffaaH – 800 fils/dozen
8. laHam – 2 dinars/rub'a
9. simač – 200 fils/kilogram
10. jibin – $\frac{1}{2}$ dinar/kilogram
11. 9eeš – 100 fils/kilogram
12. xubiz – 2 dirhams/dozen
13. gahwa – 1 $\frac{1}{2}$ dinars/rub'a
14. čaay – 2 dinars/kilogram

Drill 4 *Transformation:* masculine → feminine

haaða ġaali. → haaði ġaalya. 'This is expensive.'

1. haaða raxiiṣ.
2. haaða galiil.
3. haaða kaθiir.
4. ṣabbaHk aḷḷa bi l-xeer!
5. maškuur ya ṣaaliH.
6. š tabi?
7. tišrab šayy?
8. čaay min faḍlak!
9. keef Haalak ya mbaarak?
10. waḷḷa muub zeen il-yoom.
11. mariiḍ u mṣaxxan waajid.
12. tfaḍḍal išrab gahwa!
13. haaða 'awwal daxtar hini.
14. 'inta tidris 9aṛabi?
15. huwa yitkallam 9aṛabi zeen.
16. 'il-mu9allim mitzawwij.

Drill 5 *Variable Substitution*

Base Sentence : 'adfa9 miteen fils bas. 'I pay 200 fils only.'

1. hiya
2. hum
3. niHin
4. 2 dinars
5. 2 dirhams
6. DH 1.50
7. huwa
8. 'inta
9. hiya
10. 'aana
11. one dinar
12. one rupee
13. one riyal
14. two riyals
15. hin
16. 'inti
17. 'intin
18. 900 fils
19. 100 fils
20. niHin

Drill 6 *Transformation:* positive → negative

fii ṭamaaṭ fi s-suug. → ma fii ṭamaaṭ fi s-suug.

'There are tomatoes in the market. → There are no (there aren't any) tomatoes in the market.'

1. fii čaay fi s-suug.
2. fii Haliib fi s-suug.
3. fii biira fi s-suug.
4. fii burtaqaal fi s-suug.
5. huwa yišrab gahwa.

6. hiya tišrab biira.
7. 'aana 9indi šuġul il-yoom.
8. fii šuġul il-yoom.
9. 'il-yoom il-xamiis. fii šuġul.
10. 'aana štiri simač kill yoom.
11. hiya tit9allam fi l-jaami9a.
12. hum yabuun yruuHuun wiyyaaha.
13. 'a9jabatni l-baHreen waajid.
14. huwa yištaġil hini.

Drill 7 *Double Substitution*

kam keelu ṭ-ṭamaat? 'How much is a kilogram of tomatoes?'

1. keelu – šakar
2. keelu – gahwa
3. keelu – čaay
4. keelu – jibin
5. darzan – xubiz
6. darzan – burtaqaal
7. darzan – mooz
8. darzan – tiffaaH
9. darzan – beeđ̣
10. rub9a – jiHH
11. rub9a – 9eeš
12. rub9a – simač
13. rub9a – baṭṭiix
14. keelu – dihin

Drill 8 *Transformation:* indicative → imperative

Example : T : 'inta tišrab gahwa. 'You (m.s.) drink coffee.'

S : 'išrab gahwa. 'Drink (m.s.) coffee.'

1. 'inta taji wiyyaay.	7. 'inti truuHiin il-madrasa.
2. 'inti tajiin wiyyaana.	8. 'inta truuH id-daxtar.
3. 'intum tajuun wiyyaana.	9. 'intum tišrabuun biira.
4. 'intin tajin wiyyaa.	10. 'inta tidris 9aṛabi.
5. 'inta tištiri ṭamaaṭ.	11. 'inti tištaġliin fi l-bank.
6. 'intum tištiruun beeđ̣.	12. 'inta tišrab čaay wiyyaahum.

Drill 9 *Variable Substitution*

Base Sentence : 'ariid 'aštiri beeđ̣.

'I want to buy (some) eggs.'

1. huwa	11. burtaqaal
2. hiya	12. hum
3. laHam	13. mooz
4. ṭamaaṭ	14. question
5. negative	15. 'inta
6. simač	16. 'inti
7. tiffaaH	17. 'intin
8. 'inta	18. answer
9. 'inti	19. negative
10. statement	20. 'intum

Drill 10 *Identification*

Individual students are asked to say the following numbers:

35	72	106	1000	1001
20	24	1116	1914	672
1937	1967	1066	111	312
1975	1111	1831	1579	1248

Drill 11 *Chain*

T :	'is-sabt	'Saturday.'
S_1 :	'is-sabt gabl il-'aHad.	'Saturday is before Sunday.'
S_2 :	'il-'aHad 9ugb is-sabt.	'Sunday is after Saturday.'

Carry on with all the days of the week.

UNIT 17

I. TEXT

maryam tabi truuH is-suug li'anha triid tištiri ṭamaṭ u baamya w beeđinjaan 'aswad u filfil 'axđ̣ar. baačir 9indhum xuṭṭaar fi l-beet is-saa9a tisi9 fi l-leel. maryam tabi tiṭbax 'akil 9aṛabi. ba9ad triid tištiri laHam u tiffaaH libnaani Hamar. yamkin ma tHaṣṣil laHam zeen il-yoom. hiya tigdar tištiri l-laHam baačir. šeexa, sadiigaṭ maryam, triid taji beet maryam u taakil wiyyaahum.

II. TRANSLATION

Mary wants to go shopping because she wants to buy tomatoes, okra, black eggplant, and green peppers. Tomorrow they have guests at home at nine in the evening. Mary wants to cook Arabic food. She also wants to buy meat and red Lebanese apples. She might not find good meat today. She can buy meat tomorrow. Shaikha, Mary's friend, wants to come to Mary's home and eat with them.

III. VOCABULARY

li'an	because	tiṭbax	she, you (m.s.) cook
baamya	(coll.) okra	'akil	food
beeđinjaan	(coll.) eggplant	Hamar	red
'aswad	black	yamkin	perhaps, maybe
filfil	(coll.) pepper	tHaṣṣil	she, you (m.s.) find, get
'axđ̣ar	green	tigdar	she, you (m.s.) can

xuṭṭaar	guests (s.**xaaṭir**)	taakil	she, you (m.s.) eat
leel	night, evening	beet	house; home

IV. ADDITIONAL VOCABULARY

xass	(coll.) lettuce	bunni	brown
xyaar	(coll.) cucumbers	rumaadi	grey
loon	color	ðahabi	gold, golden
'abyaḏ̣	white	'azrag	blue
'aṣfar	yellow	burtaqaali	orange
		Habba	piece of, grain of

V. GRAMMAR

1. Collective Nouns

It was pointed out in UNIT 16 (GRAMMAR 2) that unit nouns are formed by adding –**a** to the collective noun, sometimes with appropriate stem changes. Note the following stem changes:

simač ----- simča	'a fish'
xubiz ----- xubza	'a piece (loaf) of bread'
laHam ----- laHma	'a piece of meat'
jibin ----- jibna	'a piece of cheese'

dihin 'butter' does not usually have a unit noun. The unit noun of a collective noun that ends with –**a**, e.g., **baamya** 'okra', is indicated by using the word **Habba** 'piece': **Habbat baayma** or the word **waHda** 'one (f.)': **baamya waHda.** The unit noun for **leel** 'night' is **leela** 'a night'.

(Drills 1, 5, 10, 13)

2. Colors

Colors, commonly known as color adjectives, behave syntactically like adjectives: they modify nouns and agree with them in gender, number (only singular and plural) and definiteness. In this section we are concerned with the singular form only. Most masculine singular color adjectives fit the pattern 'aC_1 C_2 aC_3. The feminine singular pattern is C_1 aC_2 C_3a. The last two examples in the following are irregular:

'axḍ̱ar	→	xaḍ̱ra	'green (f.)'
Hamar	→	Hamra	'red (f.)'
'aṣfar	→	ṣafra	'yellow (f.)'
'azrag	→	zarga	'blue (f.)'
'aswad	→	sooda	'black (f.)'
'abyaḍ̱	→	beeḍ̱a	'white (f.)'

Those that end with –i form their singular feminine forms by adding –iyya (like nisba adjectives):

bunni	→	bunniyya	'brown (f.)'
rumaadi	→	rumaadiyya	'grey (f.)'

(Drills 10, 11, 12)

3. The Conjunction li'ann

Like prepositions, the conjunction **li'ann** 'because' takes suffixed pronouns:

li'anna	'because he'
li'anhum	'because they (m.)'
li'anha	'because she'

li'anhin	'because they (f.)'
li'annak	'because you (m.s.)'
li'ankum	'because you (m.p.)'
li'annič	'because you (f.s.)'
li'ankin	'because you (f.p.)'
li'annaa	'because we'
li'anni	'because I'

(Drills 2,3)

Note that the form is **li'an–** before consonants and **li'ann** before vowels.

4. The Verb –gdar–

–gdar– is the imperfect stem of the verb which means 'to be able to, can'. It can be used by itself or in a string with other verbs:

'ii na9am 'agdar.	'Yes, I can.
yigdar yruuH.	'He can go.'
yigdar yruuH yišrab.	'He can go to (have a) drink.'

The negative is expressed by placing **ma** before **–gdar–**:

ma nigdar nruuH.	'We cannot go.'

(Drills 7, 8, 9)

5. Imperatives

The imperative forms of the verbs –**akil**– ʹto eatʹ and –**ṭbax**– ʹto cookʹ are: ʹ**ikil**! ʹEat (m.s.)!ʹ and ʹ**iṭbax**! ʹCook (m.s.)!ʹ

VI. DRILLS

Drill 1 *Substitution*

a. ʹariid ʹaakil **baamya.** ʹI want to eat (some) okra.ʹ

1. beeđ̣	6. jiHH	11. mooz
2. beeđinjaan	7. simač	12. baamya
3. xass	8. xubiz	13. filfil
4. xyaar	9. laHam	14. ṭamaaṭ
5. burtaqaal	10. jibin	15. baṭṭiix

b. Replace the collective nouns in a, above, with unit nouns.

Drill 2 *Repetition*

ʹaana :	liʹanni	hum :	liʹanhum
huwa :	liʹanna	hin :	liʹanhin
hiya :	liʹanha	ʹintum :	liʹankum
ʹinta :	liʹannak	ʹintin :	liʹankin
ʹinti :	liʹannič	ʹniHin :	liʹannaa

Drill 3 *Combination*

ʹaana ʹabi ʹaruuH is-suug. ʹariid ʹaštiri ṭamaaṭ. → ʹaana ʹabi ʹaruuH is-suug liʹanni ʹariid ʹaštiri ṭamaaṭ.

'I want to go to market. I want to buy (some) tomatoes.' → 'I want to go to market because I want to buy (some) tomatoes.'

1. hiya tabi taruuH id-daxtar. hiya mariiđ̣a.
2. 'inta ma tigdar taji. 'inta mariiđ̣.
3. ma nigdar naji baačir. 9indana šuġul.
4. tigdariin tištiriin ṭamaaṭ waajid. 'iṭ-ṭamaaṭ raxiiṣ il-yoom.
5. ma 'agdar 'ašrab haađi l-biira. 'il-biira Haarra.
6. yabi yruuH il-beet. yriid yaakil.
7. 'abi 'aruuH il-madrasa. 'ariid 'at9allam.
8. yabuun yruuHuun dbayy.yriiduun yšuufuun halhum.

Drill 4 *Substitution*

maryam tabi tiṭbax 'akil 9aṛabi.	'Maryam wants to cook Arabic food.'

1. American
2. Lebanese
3. Bahraini
4. English
5. Canadian
6. French
7. Egyptian
8. Tunisian
9. Kuwaiti
10. Qatari
11. Syrian
12. Jordanian
13. Iraqi
14. Persian
15. Indian
16. Libyan

Drill 5 *Variable Substitution*

yamkin tHaṣṣil simač fi s-suug.

'You (m.s.) may find fish in the market.'

1. beeđ̣	11. 'intum
2. baamya	12. hum
3. beeđinjaan	13. baamya
4. xass	14. mooz
5. xyaar	15. 'aana
6. 'inti	16. mooz 'axđ̣ar
7. 'aana	17. tiffaaH Hamar
8. huwa	18. filfil 'aswad
9. tiffaaH	19. baamya xađ̣ra
10. filfil	20. beeđinjaan

Drill 6 *Chain*

S_1 : kam is-saa9a? 'What time is it?'

T : 10:15

S_2 : 'is-saa9a 9ašir u rub9.

1. 10:30	5. 12:55	9. 2:15	13. 5:40
2. 10:45	6. 12:05	10. 2:25	14. 7:50
3. 11:00	7. 11:45	11. 2:55	15. 1:03
4. 12:15	8. 1:30	12. 3:20	16. 12:54

Drill 7 *Completion*

a. 'aana 'agdar ..... 'I can .....'

T : speak Arabic

S : 'aana 'agdar 'atkallam 9aṛabi. 'I can speak Arabic.'

1. speak English
2. speak French
3. buy red apples
4. get green okra
5. get green cheese
6. come at 5:30 a.m.
7. come at night
8. go to market
9. eat Arabic food
10. go home now
11. drink beer
12. pay 800 fils
13. write Arabic
14. study at school
15. work now

b. 'inta tigdar ..... 'You (m.s.) can .....'

c. huwa yigdar ..... 'He can .....'

Use substitutions from **Drill 7 a**, above.

Drill 8 *Transformation:* positive → negative

Change the sentences in **Drill 7**, above, into the negative.

Example : 'aana 'agdar 'atkallam 9aṛabi. → 'aana ma gdar atkallam 9aṛabi.

'I can speak Arabic. → I can't speak Arabic.'

Drill 9 *Addition*

T : huwa yigdar yHaṣṣil simač. 'He can get (find) fish.'

S : 'aana 'agdar 'aHaṣṣil simač ba9ad. 'I can get (find) fish, too.'

1. hiya tigdar taji.
2. huwa yigdar yaakil filfil.
3. 'inta tigdar truuH halHiin.
4. 'aana 'agdar 'ašrab wiski.
5. huwa yigdar yruuH.
6. huwa yigdar yaji wiyyaay.
7. hiya tigdar tidris.
8. 'inta tigdar taakil hini.
9. 'inta tigdar tištiri baamya.
10. 'inta tigdar truuH il-beet.
11. huwa yigdar yidfa9.
12. huwa yigdar yaji halHiin.
13. 'aana 'agdar 'aštaġil hini.
14. 'aana 'agdar 'aruuH.

Drill 10 *Repetition*

1. 'il-mooz 'aṣfar.
2. 'il-mooza ṣafra.
3. 'it-taksi 'axđ̣ar.
4. 'il-baamya xađ̣ra.
5. 'il-beeđinjaan 'aswad.
6. 'il-beeđinjaana sooda.
7. it-tiffaaH Hamar.
8. 'it-tiffaaHa Hamra.
9. 'il-Haliib 'abyađ̣.
10. 'il-beeđ̣a beeđ̣a.
11. 'it-taksi bunni.
12. 'il-gahwa bunniyya.
13. 'il-beet rumaadi.
14. 'il-burtaqaal burtaqaali.
15. 'il-jiHHa burtaqaaliyya.
16. 'il-loon đahabi.
17. 'ič-čaay Hamar.
18. haađa 'azrag.
19. haađi zarga.
20. haađi il-baṭṭiixa ṣafra.

Drill 11 *Chain*

a. S_1: šu loon haaðа? 'What color is this?'

T : 'aswad 'black'

S_2: loona 'aswad. 'It's (lit: 'it's color') black.'

1. 'abyaḏ̣	11. white
2. 'axḏ̣ar	12. black
3. Hamar	13. brown
4. 'aṣfar	14. orange
5. bunni	15. green
6. rumaadi	16. red
7. 'azrag	17. grey
8. burtaqaali	18. blue
9. ðahabi	19. green
10. yellow	20. black

Drill 12 *Transformation:* masculine → feminine

1. haaða 'aswad.	9. huwa burtaqaali.
2. haaða 'aṣfar.	10. huwa ðahabi.
3. 'il-walad 'abyaḏ̣	11. huwa 'aswad.
4. haaða 'axḏ̣ar.	12. 'il-mudiir 'abyaḏ̣.
5. haaða 'aswad.	13. 'il-mu9allim 'aswad.
6. 'il-walad bunni.	14. huwa 'aṣfar.
7. haaða Hamar.	15. haaða 'axḏ̣ar.
8. haaða rumaadi.	16. huwa Hamar.

Drill 13 *Variable Substitution*

huwa yaakil laHam kill yoom. 'He eats meat every day.'

1. hiya	13. niHin
2. beeḏ̣	14. nHaṣṣil
3. 9eeš	15. Haliib
4. 'aana	16. simač
5. simač	17. 'intum
6. 'aštiri	18. laHam
7. xubiz	19. tiṭbaxuun
8. ṭamaaṭ	20. hiya
9. huwa	21. simač
10. 'inta	22. baamya
11. mooz	23. hum
12. tiffaaH	24. 'intum

UNIT 18

I. TEXT

9ali   : Hajji jaasim! maHHad yšuufak. xeer nšaaḷḷa!

Hajji jaasim: waḷḷa 9indi šuġul waajid. 'aruuH iš-šuġul iṣ-ṣabaaH
is-saa9a sitt u 'abannid is-saa9a θalaaθ kill yoom.

9ali   : čeef il-9aayla w li-9yaal?

Hajji jaasim: la baas. zeeniin. baačir tiftaH il-madrasa, w halHiin
'aruuH il-bank li'anni 'ariid 'asHab fluus. 'il-'awlaad
yriiduun kutub u dafaatir u gḷaama, ...

9ali   : 'il-madrasa ba9iida?

Hajji jaasim: la gariiba. hum yimšuun. marraat 'aaxiðhum bi
s-sayyaara w marraat yruuHuun bi l-paaṣ.

II. TRANSLATION

Ali   : Hajji Jasim! No one sees you'. Everything is well,
I hope.

Hajji Jasim: Really, I have a lot of work. I go to work in the
morning at six and finish at three every day.

Ali   : How are the famiḷy and the children?

Hajji Jasim: Not bad. (They are) well. Tomorrow school
opens, and now I want to go to the bank because
I want to withdraw some money. The children
want books, notebooks (copy books), pencils, etc.

Ali   : Is the school far?

Hajji Jasim: No, (it's) close. They walk. Sometimes I take
them by car and sometimes they go by bus.

III. VOCABULARY

'aHad	somebody, someone
—šuuf—	to see
—bannid—	to finish (work), to close, shut
9yaal	(s. **9ayyil**) children
la baas	not bad; fine
zeeniin	(s. **zeen**) fine, good
—ftaH—	to open
—sHab—	to withdraw (e.g., money); to pull (e.g., door)
fluus	money (f.)
kutub	(s. **ktaab**) books
dafaatir	(s. **daftar**) notebooks; copy books
gḷaama	(s. **gaḷam**) pens; pencils
ba9iida	far
gariiba	close, nearby
—mši—	to walk
marraat	(s. **marra**) sometimes
—aaxiđ—	to take
sayyaara	car
paaṣ	bus

IV. ADDITIONAL VOCABULARY

hađeel	(s. **haađa**) these (m., f.)
bi l-9aṛabi	in Arabic
kill il-yoom	all day long, the whole day

V. GRAMMAR

1. Verbs – Imperfect Tense

The imperfect prefixes of the verbs –**ftaH**– 'open', –**sHab**– 'withdraw (money); pull', and –**mši**– 'walk' usually take the vowel –i:

'il-madrasa tiftaH baačir. 'The school opens tomorrow.'

The imperative form of these verbs takes the prefix –i:

'isHab fluus! 'Withdraw (m.s.) (some) money!'

The imperfect stems –**šuuf**– 'see', –**bannid**– 'close, shut; finish (work)', –**aaxið**– 'take' and –**aakil**– 'eat' do not have initial consonant clusters; therefore, they do not normally need a vowel with their imperfect prefixes:

huwa yaaxið taksi.	'He takes a taxi.'
hiya taakil halHiin.	'She is eating now.'

The imperative forms of –**šuuf**– and –**bannid**– do not take the prefix –i; –**aaxið**– and –**aakil**– either drop –aa– or drop –aa– and take the prefix –i:

xiði taksi! 'Take (f.s.) a taxi!'

or :

'ixði taksi! (Drill 5)

2. Plurals of Nouns

There are two kinds of plurals of nouns in GA: masculine sound or feminine sound plurals and broken plurals.

a. Most masculine sound plural nouns refer to male human beings or to a group in which there is only one male. They are formed by adding –**iin** to the masculine singular noun, sometimes with stem changes. If the masculine singular noun ends with a –VC, the –V– is usually dropped, e.g., **muhandis** --- **muhandsiin** 'engineers'; **muhandisiin** is also heard. If it ends with –i, the stem adds –**yy** before –**iin**: **giṭari** --- **giṭariyyiin** 'Qataris', **maṣri** --- **maṣriyyiin** 'Egyptians'.

b. The feminine sound plural is formed by adding –**aat** to the singular. It is used for four general classes of nouns:

(1) Those referring to females, e.g.

daxtoora → daxtooraat   maṣriyya → maṣriyyaat
bint → banaat (irreg.)   'uxut → 'axawaat (irreg.)

(2) Most feminine singular nouns ending in –**a**:

saa9a → saa9aat   Hukuuma → Hukuumaat
marra → marraat   wazaara → wazaaraat
sana → sanawaat (irreg.)

Included here are unit nouns formed from collectives:

baṭṭiixa → baṭṭiixaat   tiffaaHa → tiffaaHaat

The feminine nouns **madrasa** 'school', **leela** 'night', and **madiina** 'city, town' take a broken plural form. (See c, below.)

(3) Some masculine nouns of foreign origin:

'uteel → 'uteelaat   paaṣ → paaṣaat
keelu → keeluwaat (**u** + **aa** → **uwaa**)

(4) Certain masculine nouns ending in –**a**, such as:

mustašfa → mustašfayaat

c. Broken plurals are formed from the singular not by adding suffixes but by changing the internal structure of the word. There are a number of different such patterns which will be learned separately. It will be sufficient here to illustrate two types that have already shown up:

fils 'a fils' → fluus '(some) fils'

Here the singular pattern CiCC changes to the plural pattern CCuuC. Other examples of the plural pattern CCuuC are: **bank** 'bank' → **bnuuk, beet** 'house' → **byuut,** and **hindi** 'Indian' → **hnuud.** Another example of the other pattern is **šuġul** 'work, job' → **'ašġaal,** where the singular pattern CuCul changes into 'aCCaal. Other examples are: **suug** 'market' → **'aswaag, si9ir** 'price, tariff' → **'as9aar,** and **loon** 'color' → **'alwaan.** These two patterns, CCuuC and 'aCCaaC, are probably the two most common broken plural patterns.

(Drill 3 a.)

Note : All plurals of nouns in VOCABULARY and ADDITIONAL VOCABULARY will be parenthesized as of UNIT 19.

3. Noun – Adjective Concord

Adjectives in GA should agree with the nouns they modify in gender and definiteness. As for number, they have two numbers: singular and plural only. If a noun is singular, the adjective should be singular; if it is dual or plural, the adjective should be plural:

haaðа mudiir zeen.	'This is a good director (m.).'
haðeel mudiireen zeeniin.	'These are two good directors (m.).'
haðeel mudiiriin zeeniin.	'These are good directors (m.).'
haaði mudiira zeena.	'This is a good director (f.).'
haðeel mudiirteen zeenaat.	'These are two good directors (f.).'
haðeel mudiiraat zeenaat.	'These are good directors (f.).'

4. maHHad 'no one, nobody'

maHHad is a combination of **ma 'aHad** (lit. 'not anyone, no one'). **'aHad** 'someone, anyone' should be used in a question or a negative statement: **fii 'aHad?** 'Is there anyone?' **la. ma fii 'aHad.** 'No, there isn't anybody.' **waaHid** 'someone' can be used in a positive statement:

fii waaHid yištaġil hini. 'There is someone working here.'

waaHid yidris u waaHid yiktib.
'Someone is studying and another (the other) is writing.'

wa la waaHid means 'no one; not even a single one.' The phrase **waaHid min** (m.) (f. **waHda min**) means 'one of':

waaHid min 'aṣdiqaa'i	'one of my friends'
waHda min il-banaat	'one of the girls'

5. Object Pronouns

When a pronoun suffix is added to a verb, it always functions as the object of that verb, e.g., **'aaxiðhum** 'I take them.' Other examples are:

'aaxiðha	'I take her.'	**'aaxða**	'I take him, it.'
'aaxðak	'I take you (m.s.).'		
'aaxðič	'I take you (f.s.).'		
yaaxiðni	'He takes me.'		
naaxða	'We take him, it.'		

These suffixed pronouns are the same as those that are suffixed to nouns, except the one that corresponds to the first person singular, **–ni**, as in the example above.

(Drill 1)

VI. DRILLS

Drill 1 *Substitution*

'inta : maHHad yšuufak. 'You: no one sees you (m.s.).'

Example : T : huwa 'he'

S : huwa: maHHad yišuufa. 'He:no one sees him.'

1. hiya	11. huwa
2. hum	12. 'inta
3. 'inti	13. hum
4. 'intum	14. 'inti
5. 'inta	15. 'intum
6. huwa	16. 'intin
7. niHin	17. hin
8. hin	18. niHin
9. 'intin	19. huwa
10. hiya	20. hiya

Drill 2 *Transformation :* conjugation

ʼaana : ʼaruuH iš-šuġul iṣ-ṣabaaH u ʼabannid is-saa9a xams.
ʼI : I go to work in the morning and finish at five.ʼ

1. hiya	11. hiya
2. huwa	12. huwa
3. ʼinta	13. niHin
4. ʼinti	14. hin
5. ʼintum	15. ʼintin
6. ʼintin	16. ʼintum
7. ʼaana	17. ʼinta
8. niHin	18. ʼinti
9. hum	19. ʼintin
10. hin	20. hum

Drill 3 *Repetition* (singular → plural)

a.	ʼasim	---	ʼasaami	ṭaalib	---	ṭullaab
	daftar	---	dafaatir	kaatib	---	kuttaab
	taksi	---	takaasi	xaaṭir	---	xuṭṭaar
	fundug	---	fanaadig	--------		----------
	darzan	---	daraazin	ʼamrikaani	---	ʼamrikaan
	daxtar	---	daxaatir	galam	---	gḷaama
	madrasa	---	madaaris	ryaal	---	ʼaryil
	9aayla	---	9awaayil	diinar	---	danaaniir

------------------------ ---------------------------

ktaab	---	kutub	šuġul	----	'ašġaal
'axḏ̣ar	---	xuḏ̣ur	suug	---	'aswaag
'aṣfar	---	ṣufur	si9ir	---	'as9aar
Hamar	---	Humur	yoom	---	'ayyaam
'azrag	---	zurg	walad	---	'awlaad
bank	---	bnuuk	loon	---	'alwaan
fils	---	fluus	sadiig	---	'asdiga
beet	---	byuut	'abyaḏ̣	---	biiḏ̣
hindi	---	hnuud	'aswad	---	suud

---

b.

wazaara	---	wazaaraat
šarika	---	šarikaat
keelu	---	keeluwaat
'uteel	---	'uteelaat
ryaal	---	ryaalaat
paaṣ	---	paaṣaat
mustašfa	---	mustašfayaat

---

c.

muhandis	---	muhandisiin
mudiir	---	mudiiriin
mumarriḏ̣	---	mumarriḏ̣iin
maṣri	---	maṣriyyiin

giṭari --- giṭariyyiin

kweeti --- kweetiyyiin

baHreeni --- baHreeniyyiin

(b) bint --- banaat

'uxut --- 'axawaat

sana --- sanawaat

(c) zeen --- zeeniin

maškuur --- maškuuriin

mašġuul --- mašġuuliin

mṣaxxan --- mṣaxxniin

mistaanis --- mistaansiin

mariið̣ --- mariið̣iin

mitzawwij --- mitzawwjiin

galiil --- galiiliin

kaθiir --- kaθiiriin

ba9iid --- ba9iidiin

gariib --- gariibiin

bunni --- bunniyyiin

Drill 4 *Transformation:* singular → plural

1. haaðа walad.
2. huwa fi l-madrasa.
3. 'il-paaṣ gariib.
4. haaða daxtar 'abyaḍ̣.
5. haaða ktaab Hamar.
6. huwa kaatib maṣri.

7. haađi 'amrikaaniyya.
8. 'aana 'aštağil kill šayy.
9. fii šuğul waajid hini.
10. 'il-walad zeen.
11. čeef Haalak? nšaaḷḷa mistaanis.
12. fi 'abu ḓabi 9ašar (bank)
13. ma 9indi (fils) waajid.
14. 'il-bint tabi ktaab u daftar u gaḷam.

Drill 5 *Repetition* (imperative → negative statement)

1. šuuf il-mudiir! → ma 'agdar 'ašuuf il-mudiir.
2. ruuH id-daxtar! → ma 'agdar 'aruuH id-daxtar.
3. 'ixiđ taksi! → ma 'agdar 'aaxiđ taksi.
4. 'iftaH li-ktaab! → ma 'agdar 'aftaH li-ktaab.
5. 'isHab fluus min il-bank! → ma 'agdar 'asHab fluus min il-bank.
6. 'iktib 'asmak bi l-9aṛabi! → ma 'agdar 'aktib 'asmi bi l-9aṛabi.
7. ruuH bi s-sayyaara! → ma 'agdar 'aruuH bi s-sayyaara.
8. ta9aal bi l-paaṣ! → ma 'agdar 'aji bi l-paaṣ.
9. 'imši 'ila s-suug! → ma 'agdar 'amši 'ila s-suug.
10. štiri dafaatir u gḷaama! → ma 'agdar 'aštiri dafaatir u gḷaama.
11. Haṣṣil sayyaara! → ma 'agdar 'aHaṣṣil sayyaara.
12. 'ikil 9eeš u laHam! → ma 'agdar 'aakil 9eeš u laHam.
13. 9aṭni 'alf diinaar! → ma 'agdar 'a9ṭiik 'alf diinaar.
14. 'išrab wiski w gahwa! → ma 'agdar 'ašrab wiski w gahwa.
15. 'ištağil fi šarikat ADMA! → ma 'agdar 'aštağil fi šarikat ADMA.

16. 'idfa9 fluus 'ila l-bank! → ma 'agdar 'adfa9 fluus 'ila l-bank.

17. tkallam wiyya l-muhandis! → ma 'agdar 'atkallam wiyya l-muhandis.

18. 'idris 9aṛabi kill yoom! → ma 'agdar 'adris 9aṛabi kill yoom.

Drill 6 *Variable Substitution*

'ariid 'ašuuf il-mudiir. 'I want to see the director.'

1. huwa
2. his friend (m.)
3. the clerk (m.)
4. hiya
5. today
6. 'inta
7. the minister (m.)
8. 'inti
9. tomorrow
10. at 10:30 a.m.
11. at 12:55 p.m.
12. niHin
13. today
14. after tomorrow
15. hin
16. 'intin
17. the doctor (f.)
18. at home

Drill 7 *Variable Substitution*

'il-madrasa tiftaH il-yoom. '(The) school opens today.'

1. tomorrow
2. in the morning
3. at 8:30
4. 'il-bank
5. today
6. at noon
7. at night
8. tomorrow

9. after tomorrow
10. the ministry
11. closes
12. tomorrow
13. the school
14. at 3:45
15. all day (long)
16. on Friday
17. on Thursday
18. opens

Drill 8 *Substitution*

'is-sayyaara **ġaalya.** 'The car is expensive.'

1. blue
2. far away
3. close by
4. expensive
5. cheap
6. black
7. white
8. red
9. green
10. yellow
11. grey
12. brown
13. gold
14. cold
15. hot
16. American

Drill 9 *Substitution*

hiya tabi tištiri **ṭamaat.** 'She wants to buy (some) tomatoes.'

1. car
2. books
3. notebooks
4. bananas
5. everything
6. something
7. milk
8. cheese

9. sugar
10. tea
11. coffee
12. oranges
13. eggs
14. tomatoes
15. watermelons
16. bread
17. rice
18. cucumbers
19. fish
20. apples

Drill 10 *Translation*

1. Eggs are white and yellow.
2. This eggplant is black.
3. The car is blue.
4. The pepper is black.
5. These apples are green.
6. This apple is red.
7. These apples are yellow.
8. The book is brown.
9. The car is grey.
10. The pen is gold.
11. The notebook is orange.
12. Okra is green.
13. The color is white.
14. The color is blue.

Drill 11 *Question – Answer*

1. ween tištaġil?
2. nšaaḷḷa šuġlak zeen?
3. čam ṣaarlak hini?
4. nšaaḷḷa a9jabatk bu ḏ̣abi?
5. ʹinta mitzawwij?
6. čam walad 9indak?
7. čeef il-9aayla w il-ʹawlaad?
8. ʹil-ʹawlaad yruuHuun il-madrasa?

9. čeef yruuHuun il-madrasa?
10. bi l-paaṣ, bi s-sayyaara ... ?
11. ʼil-madrasa ba9iida min hini?
12. dbayy ba9iida min 9umaan?
13. čam saa9a bi s-sayyaara?
14. š tabi tišrab?
15. bas gahwa?
16. ma tišrab biira marraat?

Drill 12 *Translation*

1. I am not working today because today is Friday.
2. How are you, Ali? Not bad, thank you.
3. I want to go to the bank because I want to withdraw some money.
4. The American bank opens at 9:00 today. You can't go tomorrow because tomorrow is Friday.
5. He goes to work at 6:30 a.m. and comes home at 3:30 p.m.
6. I would like to get some good tomatoes.
7. I hope I will be able to write my name in Arabic.
8. Go take (m.p.) a taxi. The school is far away from here.
9. You (m.s.) can go to Qatar by plane and by car.
10. She can't go by car because she is an old woman. Besides, Dubai is far away from here.
11. No one is working today because it is Friday.
12. No one sees him. He is always busy.
13. One of my friends is an engineer.

UNIT 19

I. TEXT

šiišt il-batrool

Attendant : 9aadi walla mumtaaz?

mHammad: 9aadi min faḍ̄lak.

Attendant : čam galan tabi?

mHammad: ʼitris it-taanki!

Attendant : nšaaḷḷa.

mHammad: naḍ̄ḍ̄if il-jaam min faḍ̄lak! killiš waṣix. čayyik it-taayraat!

Attendant : nšaaḷḷa. ʼit-taayraat killiš zeeniin.

mHammad: čayyik ir-radeetar w il-ʼaayil!

Attendant : nšaaḷḷa. ʼir-radeetar yiHtaaj šwayy mayy. ʼil-ʼaayil galiil. tiHtaaj guuṭi ʼaayil.

mHammad: čam yiṣiir?

Attendant : diinaar u θalaaθimyat fils.

mHammad: haaḏ̄a diinaar u nuṣṣ. ʼil-baagi ʼilak baxšiiš.

Attendant : maškuur.

II. TRANSLATION

The Gas Station

Attendant : Regular or Super?

Muhammad: Regular please.

Attendant : How many gallons do you want?

Muhammad: Fill the tank!

Attendant : Yes, sir.

Muhammad: Clean the glass, please. (It's) very dirty. Check the tires!

Attendant : Yes, sir. The tires are very good.

Muhammad: Check the radiator and the oil!

Attendant : O.K. The radiator needs a little water. The oil is low. It needs a can of oil.

Muhammad: How much is it?

Attendant : One dinar and 300 fils.

Muhammad: This is one dinar and a half. The remainder is a tip for you.

Attendant : Thank you.

III. VOCABULARY

šiiša	('išyaš) gasoline station
9aadi	(–yyiin) regular, ordinary
walla	(conj.) or
mumtaaz	(–iin) super, excellent
galan	(–aat) gallon
–tris–	to fill (up)
taanki	(tawaanki) tank
nšaaḷḷa	yes (sir); certainly
–naḏ̣ḏ̣if–	to clean
jaam	(–aat) glass

waṣix	(–iin) dirty
–čayyik–	to check
taayir	(–aat) tire
radeetar	(–aat) radiator
'aayil	oil, motor oil
–Htaaj–	to need, lack
guuṭi	(gawaaṭi) can (e.g., oil); package (e.g., cigarettes)
–ṣiir–	to be; to become
baxšiiš	tip, something free

IV. ADDITIONAL VOCABULARY

naọ̌iif	(–iin) clean
ṭawiil	(ṭwaal) tall; long
gaṣiir	(gṣaar) short
jigaara	(jigaayir) cigarette
jadiid	(jiddad) new
9atiij	(–iin) old, ancient
jamiil	(–iin) beautiful; handsome
ọ̌aruuri	(–yyiin) necessary
guuṭi jigaayir	(gawaaṭi) package of cigarettes

V. GRAMMAR

1. **'ila** 'to; for' may take a suffixed pronoun like any other preposition:

'ila	'to (for) him'	'ilkum	'to (for) you (m.p.)'
'ilhum	'to (for) them (m.)'	'ilič	'to (for) you (f.s.)'
'ilha	'to (for) her'	'ilkin	'to (for) you (f.p.)'
'ilhin	'to (for) them (f.)'	'ili	'to (for) me'
'ilak	'to (for) you (m.s.)'	'ilna	'to (for) us'

The preposition la– also expresses possession, but it can only take suffixed pronouns; it cannot occur independently: **la, lahum, laha, lahin, lak, lakum, lič, lakin, li, lana.**

(Drill 7)

2. Cardinal Numerals

We have had all the cardinal numerals except for thousands and millions. **'alf** is one thousand and its dual form is **'alfeen** '2,000'. The plural is **'aalaaf,** which, unlike English is used in case of three or more thousands. Thus 3,563 is **θalaaθ aalaaf u xamsimya w θalaaθa w sittiin.** Remember to use the conjunction **w/u** with every word in the number.

The word for 'million' is **malyoon,** with a dual **malyooneen** 'two million' and a broken plural **malaayiin** 'millions', which should be used with three million onwards.

The noun counted after any number is always singular except after 3 – 10. Thus:

xams kutub	'five books'
'alf u xamsimya w sitt kutub	'1,506 books'
'alf u xamsimya w 9išriin ktaab	'1,520 books'
sitt 'aalaaf ktaab	'6,000 books'

If the units digit in a number over 100 is two, then the dual is used:

'arba9 'aalaaf u miya w ktabeen '4,102 books'

(Drill 12)

3. Note the following two constructions:

haaðī s-sayyaara ġaalya.	'This car is expensive.'
haaðī sayyaara ġaalya.	'This is an expensive car.'

In the first sentence, the definite noun **s-sayyaara** is part of the subject of the sentence: **haaðī s-sayyaara** 'this car'. In the second sentence **haaðī** 'this (f.)' is the entire subject of the sentence. Due to interference from English, English speakers have a tendency to equate **haaðī sayyaara** with 'this car', which is wrong. Remember that if the noun after the demonstrative is definite, you have a phrase and not a sentence, e.g., **haaða l-walad** 'this boy...'; if it is indefinite, you have a sentence, e.g., **haaða walad** 'this is a boy.'

(Drill 9)

NOTES ON TEXT

1. **nšaaḷḷa** as a response to an imperative has the meaning of 'yes, certainly, sure... etc.', and it implies respect.

'itris it-taanki!	'Fill the tank (m.s.)!'
nšaaḷḷa.	'Certainly.'

2. **čam yiṣiir?** The imperfect stem –ṣiir– means 'to become; to happen, take place'. The phrase **čam yiṣiir?** is used to mean 'How much will it be?' or 'How much does it add up to?' If you want to inquire about the price of something, e.g., apples, you say **čam it-tiffaaH?**, but you say **čam yiṣiir?** to a grocer, for instance, after you have asked for, e.g., tomatoes, apples, eggplant, and now you want to know how much the whole lot costs.

VI. DRILLS

Drill 1 *Substitution*

haaða 9aadi. 'This is regular.'

1. handsome
2. good
3. feverish
4. happy
5. busy
6. necessary
7. far away
8. close by
9. super
10. cheap
11. expensive
12. regular
13. a lot
14. a little
15. short
16. tall
17. clean
18. dirty
19. old
20. new

Drill 2 *Substitution*

9aadi walla mumtaaz? 'regular or super?'

1. cheap – expensive
2. a lot – a little
3. short – long
4. clean – dirty

5. new – old
6. far – near
7. black – white
8. sick – fine
9. hot – cold
10. dry – humid
11. American – Arab
12. nurse – doctor
13. clerk – director
14. boy – girl
15. necessary–not necessary

Drill 3 *Chain – Cued*

T : car

S_1: haaδi sayyaara. 'This is a car.'

T : beautiful

S_2: haaδi sayyaara jamiila. 'This is a beautiful car.'

1. oil – regular
2. oil – super
3. boy – tall
4. girl – beautiful
5. pen – yellow
6. bus – big
7. car – red
8. book – red
9. bananas – cheap
10. okra – green
11. pepper – hot
12. eggplant – black
13. an apple – green
14. meat – good
15. bread – Arabic
16. cheese – Canadian
17. fish – fresh
18. an orange – green
19. pen – gold
20. notebook – small
21. car – big
22. house – dirty
23. tire – old
24. glass – clean

Drill 4 *Combination*

haaðī sayyaara + 'is-sayyaara jamiila → haaðī s-sayyaara jamiila.
'This is a car + The car is beautiful → This car is beautiful.'

1. This is gas. The gas is regular.
2. This is a car. The car is excellent.
3. These are apples. The apples are expensive.
4. This is a girl. The girl is tall and beautiful.
5. This is a boy. The boy is sick and feverish.
6. This is water. The water is clean and cold.
7. This is a manager. The manager is busy.
8. This is a car. The car is black and white.
9. This is a doctor (f.). The doctor is new but good.
10. This is a book. The book is old but necessary.
11. This is a tire. The tire is excellent.
12. This is a cigarette. The cigarette is long.
13. This is a house. The house is new also.
14. This is a can of tomatoes. The can of tomatoes is cheap.
15. This is a house. The house is cheap but far away.

Drill 5 *Variable Substitution*

huwa yiHtaaj guuṭi jigaayir. 'He needs a pack of cigarettes.'

1. 'aana w 'inta
2. 'intum
3. guuṭi ṭamaaṭ
4. hiya w huwa
5. niHin
6. 'inta

7. guuṭi ʼaayil
8. Haliib
9. ʼaana
10. li-9yaal
11. hiya
12. fresh meat
13. ʼintin
14. apples
15. fresh eggs
16. new car
17. ʼaana
18. ʼil-9aayla

Drill 6 *Variable Substitution*

hiya tnaððif is-sayyaara. 'She is cleaning the car.'

1. il-beet
2. is-simač
3. hin
4. il-jaam
5. ʼaana
6. ʼinta
7. ʼinti
8. ʼintum
9. niHin
10. ir-radeetar
11. huwa
12. hum
13. ʼit-taanki
14. ʼaana
15. ʼinta
16. ʼintum
17. hum
18. ʼil-paaṣ
19. ʼil-xass
20. li-xyaar
21. ʼaana
22. hiya
23. hin
24. ʼinti

Drill 7 *Substitution*

a. ʼil-baagi ʼimyat fils lak baxšiiš.

'The remainder, 100 fils, is a tip for you.'

1. miteen fils	10. nuṣṣ rubbiyya
2. θalaaθimyat fils	11. nuṣṣ dirhim
3. rub9 diinaar	12. diinaar
4. nuṣṣ diinaar	13. 'arba9imyat fils
5. dirhim	14. xamsimyat fils
6. ryaal	15. sittimyat fils
7. ryaaleen	16. ryaal u nuṣṣ
8. dirhimeen	17. diinaar u nuṣṣ
9. xamsimyat fils	18. dirhim u nuṣṣ

b. haaðа d-daftar 'ilak. 'This notebook is yours (m.).'

'inti : haaða d-daftar 'ilič. 'This notebook is yours (f.).'

1. huwa	11. 'inti
2. 'aana	12. 'inta
3. 'inta	13. huwa
4. 'inti	14. 'aana
5. 'intum	15. niHin
6. 'intin	16. 'intin
7. hum	17. 'intum
8. hin	18. hum
9. niHin	19. hin
10. hiya	20. hiya

c. Use the above forms with the preposition la–.

Drill 8 *Chain – Cued*

T : ġaali 'expensive'

S_1 : haað̄a ġaali? 'Is this expensive?'

S_2 : la muub ġaali. raxiiṣ. 'No, not expensive. (It is) cheap.'

1. 9aadi
2. galiil
3. ṭawiil
4. nað̣̄iif
5. jadiid
6. ba9iid
7. 'abyað̣̄
8. raxiiṣ
9. mariið̣̄
10. baarid
11. Haaff
12. waajid
13. ð̣̄aruuri
14. zeen
15. jamiil
16. mašġuul
17. mistaanis
18. 9aadi
19. gaṣiir
20. waṣix

Drill 9 *Chain – Cued*

T : haað̄i s-sayyaara ġaalya? 'Is this car expensive?'

S : la. muub ġaalya. raxiiṣa waajid.
'No, not expensive. (It is) very cheap.'

1. haað̄a l-'aayil 9aadi?
2. haað̄a l-beet raxiiṣ?
3. haað̄a l-mayy nað̣̄iif?
4. haað̄i l-bint ṭawiila?
5. haað̄i s-sayyaara jadiida?
6. haað̄i l-madrasa ba9iida?
7. haað̄a l-walad mṣaxxan?
8. haað̄a l-mayy Haarr?

9. haađa l-muhandis mašġuul?
10. haađa li-ktaab đ̣aruuri?
11. haađi j-jigaayir zeena?
12. haađi s-sayyaara ġaalya?
13. haađa l-beet 9atiij?
14. haađi l-jaami9a jadiida?
15. haađa t-taanki nađ̣iif?
16. haađa s-simač zeen?

Drill 10 *Transformation.* imperative → negative statement

Example : 'itris it-taanki! → ma 'agdar 'atris it-taanki.

'Fill (m.s.) the tank'. → I can't fill the tank.'

1. nađ̣đ̣if il-jaam!
2. čayyik it-taayir!
3. šuuf il-waziir!
4. bannid il-mayy!
5. 'iftaH il-guuṭi!
6. 'isHab li-fluus!
7. 'imši wiyyaay!
8. 'ixiđ il-'awlaad bi s-sayyaara!
9. 'ikil tiffaaH 'axđ̣ar!
10. 'iṭbax 9eeš u laHam!
11. štiri beet jadiid!
12. 9aṭni 'alf diinaar!
13. 'išrab wiski w mayy!
14. ta9aal is-saa9a xams!
15. štaġil fi l-leel!
16. ruuH beruut fi l-geeđ̣!

Drill 11 *Transformation:* imperative → negative statement

Example : 'itrisu t-taanki → ma nigdar nitris it-taanki.

'Fill (m.p.) the tank! → We cannot fill the tank!'

Use imperatives from **Drill 10**, above.

Drill 12 *Identification*

Individual students give the GA words for the following numbers:

80	10	50	93	71
100	200	600	900	513
918	730	818	209	1,000
1,217	2,914	3,976	4,492	1,666,317
2,000,014		120,134,270	5,568,900	

UNIT 20

I. TEXT

fi garaaj iš-šarg

sabt : ṣabbaHk aḷḷa bi l-xeer, ya seef!

seef : ṣbaaH il-xeer. weeš fi sayyaaratak il-yoom?

sabt : waḷḷa il-leet Haggha muub zeen. ð̣a9iif muub gawi.

seef : yamkin il-batri muub zeen.

sabt : ʼaḷḷa ysallimk! il-leet ṣaarla subuu9 u huwa muub zeen. ma dri šu l-miškila.

seef : zeen xaḷḷn ašuufa.

sabt : zeen xaḷḷha 9indak. baddil il-ʼaayil min fað̣lak!

seef : nšaaḷḷa.

sabt : tabriz baačir?

seef : ʼaḷḷa ysallimk baačir il-jum9a 9uṭla. ta9aal 9ugub baačir.

II. TRANSLATION

At the East Garage

Sabt : Good morning, Seif!

Seif : Good morning. What's wrong with your car today?

Sabt: Its light is not good. (It's) weak, not strong.

Seif : Probably the battery is not good.

Sabt : God protect you! It's light hasn't been good for a week. I don't know what the problem is.

Seif : O.K. Let me see it.

Sabt : Fine. Keep it at your place. Change the oil, please.

Seif : Surely.

Sabt : Will it be ready tomorrow?

Seif : God protect you! Tomorrow is Friday, a holiday. Come after tomorrow.

III. VOCABULARY

garaaj	(–aat) garage
šarg	east
weeš?	(inter.) what?
weeš fi?	what's the matter?
leet	(–aat) light
Hagg	belonging to
ḓ̣a9iif	(–iin) weak
gawi	(–yyiin) strong
batri	(bataari) battery
–sallim–	to protect, keep safe
subuu9	('asaabii9) week
–dri–	to know, realize
miškila	(mašaakil) problem
–xal̤l̤–	to leave, leave alone
–baddil–	to change
–briz–	to be ready
9uṭla	(9uṭal) holiday, vacation

IV. ADDITIONAL VOCABULARY

fagiir	(–iin) poor
ġani	(–yyiin) rich
mitiin	(–iin) fat
mxabbaḷ	(–iin) crazy, mad
9aagil	(iin) rational, wise
ṣaaHi	(–yiin) conscious; sober
šahar	('aš̌hir) month

V. GRAMMAR

1. Negative Commands

A negative command (or request) is used to tell someone not to do something. In GA, a negative command consists of the negative particle la followed by the imperfect tense of the verb:

Commands

baddil!	'Change (m.s.)!'
baddli!	'Change (f.s.)!'
baddlu!	'Change (m.p.)!'
baddlin!	'Change (f.p.)!'

Negative Commands

la tbaddil!	'Do not change (m.s.)!'
la tbaddliin!	'Do not change (f.s.)!'

la tbaddluun!	'Do not change (m.p.)!'
la tbaddlin!	'Do not change (f.p.)!'

(Drill 14)

2. The Particle **Hagg**

There are two ways of expressing possession in GA:

(a) Noun Construct: N + N or N + Pronoun:

sayyaarat il-waziir	'the minister's car'
sayyaarta	'his car'

(b) N + Hagg + N or N + Hagg + Pronoun:

'is-sayyaara Hagg il-waziir	'the minister's car'
'is-sayyaara Hagga	'his car'

Hagg, like any other particle or noun, takes suffixed pronouns:

'il-guuṭi Haggi	'my can'	
'il-beet Haggna	'our house'	(Drills 4,5)

3. xaḷḷ– (+ imperfect)

The imperative construction **xaḷḷn ašuufa** is made up of –**xaḷḷ**– 'to let someone do something' + a suffixed pronoun + the imperfect of –**šuuf**– 'to see' and the suffixed pronoun –**a** (obj. of 'to see'). It means 'let me see it (him)!' The –**i** in **xaḷḷni** 'let me' is omitted because of the initial 'a– in '**ašuufa** 'I see it.' Below are sentences with **xaḷḷ**– and suffixed pronouns:

xaḷḷa yšuufa	'Let him see it (him).'
xaḷḷhum yšuufuunhum	'Let them (m.) see them (m.).'
xaḷḷha tšuufha	'Let her see her.'
xaḷḷhin yšuufinhin	'Let them (f.) see them (f.).'
xaḷḷn ašuufa	'Let me see it (him).'
xaḷḷna nšuufa	'Let us see it (him).'

(Drill 7)

NOTES ON TEXT

1. **ṣbaaH il-xeer**! and **ṣabaaH il-xeer**! 'Good morning!' are used interchangeably. The former is more commonly used.

2. You learned that **'aḷḷa ysallimk**! as a response to **ma9 is-salaama**! 'Good-bye! (lit.: 'with safety') means 'God keep you safe:' Here it is used at the beginning of a sentence, with the same meaning, as a courtesy expression.

3. **šu** and **weeš** 'what' are used interchangeably. They are sometimes reduced to š, especially in rapid speech:

š tabi	'What do you (m.s.) want?
š fii sayyaaratk?	'What's wrong with your (m.s.) car? '

VI. DRILLS

Drill 1 *Substitution*

a. š fi s-**sayyaara**? 'What's wrong with the car? '

1. batri
2. taanki
3. jaam
4. taayir

5. radeetar
6. 'aayil
7. guuṭi
8. walad
9. 'awlaad
10. paaṣ
11. 9yaal
12. gḷaama
13. Haliib
14. gahwa
15. sikirteer
16. mu9allim
17. kaatib
18. kuuli
19. leet
20. ṭaalib

Drill 2 *Substitution*

ma dri **ween is-sayyaara.** 'I don't know where the car is.'

1. where the East Garage is
2. where the Battery is
3. where the gas station is
4. where the boys are
5. how he studies at night
6. how to go to the market
7. how to change the tire
8. how she works all day long
9. what her name is
10. what the problem is
11. what to buy in the market
12. what he wants to drink
13. where he comes from
14. what he makes (gets) per month

Drill 3 *Variable Substitution*

'aana ma dri keef aji. 'I do not know how to come.'

1. huwa
2. yruuH is-suug
3. ybannid il-leet
4. hiya

5. niHin	12. hum
6. 'inta	13. hiya
7. tbaddil il-'aayil	14. tičayyik il-batri
8. 'inti	15. 'aana
9. 'aana	16. 'inta
10. 'atris it-taanki	17. 'it-taayraat
11. huwa	18. tbaddil it-taayir

Drill 4   *Substitution*

haaða Haggi.   'This is mine.'

hiya : haaða Haggha.   'This is hers.'

1. 'inta	11. hum
2. 'inti	12. huwa
3. 'intum	13. hiya
4. 'intin	14. 'intum
5. hum	15. 'intin
6. 'aana	16. 'inta
7. huwa	17. hin
8. hiya	18. huwa
9. hin	19. 'aana
10. niHin	20. niHin

Drill 5 *Double Substitution*

ʼis-sayyaara Hagg iš-šarika. ʼThe car belongs to the company.ʼ

1. garage – Ali
2. battery – car
3. light – house
4. books – school
5. pens – clerk
6. tank – ministry
7. tire – car
8. cigarettes – Salim
9. pencils – student
10. house – family
11. bus – boys
12. food – coolie
13. notebook – manager
14. car – secretary
15. taxi – hotel
16. money – bank
17. watch – doctor
18. bread – girl

Drill 6 *Transformation:* indicative → imperative

ʼariid ašuufa. → xaḷḷn ašuufa.

ʼI want to see it (him). → Let me see it (him).ʼ

1. ʼariid ʼaaxđa.
2. yriid yišraba.
3. triid tšuufa.
4. yriiduun yaaxđuuna
5. nriid nbannda.
6. yriid ybaddla.
7. yriiduun yidrusuuna.
8. ʼariid ʼaktiba.
9. nriid ništiri sayyaara.
10. triid taakil hini.
11. ʼariid ʼasHab fluus.
12. yriid yaaxiđ taksi.
13. yriiduun yimšuun wiyyaay.
14. triid tnađđif il-beet.
15. nriid nit9allam 9aṛabi.
16. ʼariid ʼašrab gahwa.

Drill 7 *Substitution*

	xaḷḷn ašuufa.	'Let me see it (him).'
hiya :	xaḷḷha tšuufa.	'Let her see it (him).'

1. hum
2. hin
3. niHin
4. 'aana
5. hiya
6. maryam
7. 9ali w xamiis
8. layla w šeexa
9. 'il-'awlaad
10. 'il-bint
11. 'aana w hiya
12. hiya
13. huwa
14. 'il-kaatib
15. 'is-sikirteer
16. 'il-banaat
17. saalim
18. jum9a
19. 'aamna
20. 'il-muhandis

Drill 8 *Variable Substitution*

baddil il-'aayil min faḏ̣lak! 'Change (m.s.) the oil, please!'

1. 'il-batri
2. halHiin
3. čayyik
4. 'intum
5. baačir
6. 'is-saa9a xams
7. 'inti
8. 'inta
9. naḏ̣ḏ̣if
10. 'il-yoom
11. 'ir-radeetar
12. baačir

13. baddil	17. 'intum
14. 'il-yoom	18. 'inti
15. 'it-taanki	19. 'intin
16. 'itris	20. naḍ̄ḍ̄fin

Drill 9 *Chain –Cued*

T : Change (m.s.) the oil, please!

S_1: baddil il-'aayil min faḍ̄lak!

S_2: nšaaḷḷa.

1. Go to the gas station, please!
2. Fill the tank, please!
3. Clean the house, please!
4. Check the oil, please!
5. Change the tires, please!
6. See the manager, please!
7. Talk to the minister, please!
8. Open the can, please!
9. Come with me, please!
10. Clean the car, please!
11. Pay sixty dinars, please!
12. Buy some tomatoes, please!
13. Drink this milk, please!
14. Go withdraw some money, please!
15. Come take this, please!
16. Go fill this tank, please!

Drill 10 *Substitution*

'is-sayyaara tabriz baačir. 'The car will be ready tomorrow.'

1. 9ugub baačir
2. 9ugub yoomeen
3. 9ugub subuu9
4. yoom il-jum9a
5. yoom is-sabt
6. yoom il-xamiis
7. halHiin nšaaḷḷa
8. 9ugub šwayy
9. 9ugub saa9a
10. 'il-yoom
11. 9ugub šahar
12. 9ugub šahreen
13. yoom il-'arba9a
14. baačir nšaaḷḷa
15. yoom il-'aHad
16. yoom il-'aθneen
17. 9ugb iđ̣ - đ̣uhr
18. 'il-yoom il-masa
19. baačir iṣ-ṣabaaH
20. baačir il-masa
21. 9ugub subuu9

Drill 11 *Repetition*

→

9ašara	9išriin	θalaaθiin	'arba9iin
xamsiin	sittiin	sab9iin	θamaaniin
tis9iin	'imya	'imya w 9išriin	
xamsimya w sab9iin		'alf u tisi9imya w 'arba9a w sab9iin	

Drill 12 *Identification*

Individual students give the GA words for the following numbers:

90	70	60	40	30	20
100	200	300	900	800	700
130	240	350	670	920	560
1,000	1,360	1,420	1,510	1,901	1,974

Drill 13 *Combination*

haað̄a kuuli. 'il-kuuli fagiir. → haað̄a l-kuuli fagiir.

'This is a coolie. The coolie is poor. → This coolie is poor.'

1. haað̄a muhandis. 'il-muhandis ġani.
2. haað̄a mudiir. 'il-mudiir mitiin.
3. haað̄a kaatib. 'il-kaatib mxabbaḷ.
4. haað̄a mu9allim. 'il-mu9allim 9aagil.
5. haað̄a mariiḏ̣̄. 'il-mariiḏ̣̄ muub ṣaaHi.
6. haað̄a daxtar. 'id-daxtar mumtaaz.
7. hað̄eel muhandisiin. 'il-muhandisiin mumtaaziin.
8. hað̄eel sayyaaraat. 'is-sayyaaraat biiḏ̣̄.
9. hað̄eel 'amrikaan. 'il-'amrikaan ġaniyyiin.
10. hað̄eel madaaris. 'il-madaaris jadiida.
11. haað̄i bint. 'il-bint mitiina.
12. haað̄i mumarriḏ̣̄a. 'il-mumarriḏ̣̄a 9aagla.
13. haað̄i daxtoora. 'id-daxtoora ġaniyya.
14. hað̄eel banaat. 'il-banaat jamiilaat.
15. hað̄eel muwaḏ̣̄ḏ̣̄afiin. 'il-muwaḏ̣̄ḏ̣̄afiin fagiiriin.

Drill 14 *Transformation:* Imperative → negative command

Example : ruuH! 'Go (m.s.)!' → la truuH! 'Do not go!'

1. baddil il-'aayil.
2. tkallami 9aṛabi.
3. 'ixðu taksi.
4. ruuHi l-madrasa.
5. 'išrab gahwa.
6. ruuH ištiri ṭamaaṭ.
7. čayyik it-taayir.
8. naẓẓfu l-jaam.
9. ta9aal wiyyaay.
10. ta9aalu l-yoom.
11. 'iṭbaxi baamya.
12. ruuH garaaj iš-šarg.
13. 'imši 'ila s-suug.
14. 'itris it-taanki.
15. 'a9ṭiiha fluus.
16. 'išrabi haaða.
17. 'iktibi bi l-'ingiliizi.
18. štaġlu hini.
19. 'idfa9 li-fluus.
20. 'isHab fluus min il-bank.

UNIT 21

REVIEW

Drill 1 *Question – Answer*

Example : T : fii šuġul il-yoom?
'Is there work today?'

S_1 : la. ma fii šuġul il-yoom.
'No, there is no work today.'

T : baačir? 'tomorrow?'

S_2 : fii šuġul baačir. 'There is work tomorrow.'

1.	fii daxtar fi l-madrasa?	fi l-mustašfa
2.	fii mayy hini?	fi l-madrasa
3.	fii burtaqaal il-yoom?	baačir iṣ-ṣabaaH?
4.	fii madrasa yoom il-jum9a?	yoom is-sabt
5.	fii jaami9a fi 9ajmaan?	fi li-kweet
6.	fii gahwa 'amrikaaniyya fi l-wazaara?	fii gahwa 9aṛabiyya
7.	fii kutub hini?	fi s-suug
8.	fii banaat fi l-madrasa?	fii 'awlaad
9.	fii Haliib fi č-čaay?	fii šakar
10.	fii jibin fi l-beet?	fi s-suug
11.	fii mooz fi s-suug?	fii tiffaaH
12.	fii 9eeš fi l-beet?	fii xubiz
13.	fii jigaayir 'amrikaaniyya hini?	fii jigaayir ingiliiziyya
14.	fii gḷaama ṣufur 9indak?	fii gḷaama Humur
15.	fii tiffaaH 'axḏ̣ar fi s-suug?	fii tiffaaH 'aṣfar
16.	fii paaṣ 'ila l-fundug?	fii taksi

Drill 2 *Transformation:* positive ––– negative

1. ʹaana min ʹingiltara.
2. haað̄a walad 9aagil.
3. haað̄i bint mitiina.
4. hað̄eel ʹawlaad zeeniin.
5. hað̄eel muhandisiin libnaaniyyiin.
6. huwa yidris 9aṛabi kill yoom.
7. ʹinta tigdar tištiri sayyaara?
8. bannid il-leet!
9. ruuHi s-suug bi s-sayyaara!
10. ta9aal is-saa9a xams.
11. šiili l-janṭa!
12. fii šuġul il-yoom.
13. Huṭṭ li-fluus fi l-bank!
14. 9indi maw9id il-yoom.
15. ʹil-hawa Haarr waajid il-yoom.
16. hin yidrisin faṛansi.
17. ʹil-yoom il-xamiis.
18. baddil il-leet!
19. ʹisHab fluus min il-bank!
20. ʹiklu simač u 9eeš kill yoom!

Drill 3 *Transformation:* statement ––– question

Ask questions to which the words in heavy type are the short answers.

1. 'abi 'aštiri **laHam.**
2. **ṭayyib maškuur.**
3. **la. 'atkallam 9aṛabi šwayy.**
4. 'il-hawa **baarid** il-yoom.
5. tabi tidris **9aṛabi.**
6. yidfa9uun **dinaareen** bas.
7. 'is-saa9a θinteen halHiin.
8. **'ii na9am. 'il-yoom is-sabt.**
9. **la baas.** maškuur.
10. **na9am.** 'a9jabatni giṭar waajid.
11. la. **'il-xamiis** 9ugb il-'arba9a.
12. **mariið̣ u mṣaxxan.**
13. hum min **beruut** fi libnaan.
14. 'id-daxtar yaji is-saa9a **tisi9.**
15. hum yištağluun **fi wazaarat il-ma9aarif.**
16. ma yigdar yimši fi s-suug **li'an il-hawa Haarr.**
17. **'ii.** 'il-burtaqaal raxiiṣ killiš il-yoom.
18. ṣaarli hini, aḷḷa ysallimk, **xams siniin.**

Drill 4 *Transformation:* singular ––– plural

1. haaða muwað̣ð̣af fagiir.
2. haaða 'uteel naðiif.
3. haaði bint jamiila.
4. haaði madrasa jadiida.
5. yriid yištiri daftar u gaḷam.
6. fii šuğul waajid fi bu ð̣abi.
7. tigdar taji baačir?
8. mudiir iš-šarika yamm il-waziir.

9. haaᵭa s-sadiig mumtaaz.
10. ʹiṭ-ṭaalib fi l-madrasa.
11. ʹil-mu9allim mašġuul halHiin.
12. čeef Haalak? nšaaḷḷa mistaanis.
13. ʹil-mustašfa 9atiij u waṣix.
14. huwa yištaġil kill šayy.
15. haaᵭa kweeti ġani.
16. huwa kaatib zeen.

Drill 5 *Variable Substitution*

9indi maw9id il-yoom. ʹI have an appointment today.ʹ

1. at 1:00 p.m.
2. in the morning
3. you (m.s.)
4. you (f.s.)
5. you (m.p.)
6. you (f.p.)
7. tomorrow morning
8. after tomorrow
9. negative
10. huwa
11. hiya
12. at 9:45
13. at 2:30
14. at 1:55
15. today
16. hum
17. positive
18. question
19. ʹintin
20. hin
21. tomorrow evening
22. on Friday
23. answer
24. on Thursday
25. on Sunday
26. with the doctor
27. on Monday
28. at 12:30
29. on Wednesday
30. on Saturday

Drill 6 *Completion*

'aana 'abi ..... 'I want to ..... '

1. go to the market
2. work at the garage
3. buy a gas station
4. know what the problem is
5. take a holiday tomorrow
6. change the tires
7. check the lights
8. see the company manager
9. withdraw 100 dinars
10. get an increase
11. eat Arabic food
12. come to Bahrain
13. go pay (some) money
14. speak Arabic very well
15. write to my family
16. give you (m.s.) a book

Drill 7 *Combination*

haađa walad + 'il-walad mitiin. → haađa l-walad mitiin.

'This is a boy. + The boy is fat.' → 'This boy is fat.'

1. This is gasoline. The gasoline is regular, not super.
2. This is a book. The book is new, not old.
3. These are tomatoes. The tomatoes are expensive, not cheap.
4. These are boys. The boys are fat, not thin.
5. This is a garage. The garage is far away, not close.
6. This is a patient (m.). The patient is running a temperature.
7. This is cheese. The cheese is green, not white.
8. These are teachers (f.). The teachers are poor, not rich.

9. This is a battery. The battery is weak, not strong.
10. This is a girl. The girl is sane, not crazy.
11. This is a secretary (f.). The secretary is beautiful but fat.
12. This is water. The water is hot, not cold.
13. This is a house. The house is new but dirty.
14. This is a car. The car is expensive but necessary.
15. This is a holiday. The holiday is long, not short.
16. This is money. The money is little, not much.
17. This is a nurse (f.). The nurse is English.
18. This is a problem. The problem is old, not new.

Drill 8 *Chain*

S_1: haaði 'awwal marra taji bu ð̣abi?

'Is this the first time you come to Abu Dhabi? '

S_2: la. haaði muub 'awwal marra 'aji bu ð̣abi. haaðiθaani marra.

'No, this is not the first time I come to Abu Dhabi. This is the second time.' ..... etc.

Drill 9 *Question ——— Answer*

1. šloon it-tiffaaH?
2. šloon il-mooz?
3. šloon il-baamya?
4. šloon il-xass?
5. šloon il-jiHH?
6. šloon il-baṭṭiix?
7. šloon il-beeðinjaan?
8. šloon il-filfil?
9. šloon il-9eeš?
10. šloon il-xubiz?

11. šloon is-simač?
12. šloon id-dihin?
13. šloon il-mayy?
14. šloon il-burtaqaal?
15. šloon li-xyaar?
16. šloonak?

Drill 10 *Chain*

S_1:	'is-saa9a waHda.	'It's one o'clock.'
S_2:	'is-saa9a waHda w waHda.	'It's 1:01.'
S_3:	'is-saa9a waHda w θinteen.	'It's 1:02.'
		(etc.)

Drill 11 *Identification*

Individual students read the following numerals:

20	15	18	19	13	17
100	130	170	190	200	210
201	317	325	940	1,000	1,005
1,492	1,914	1,930	1,948	1,973	2,730
21	215	1,967	7,002		

UNIT 22

I. TEXT

fi l-maṭaar (i)

Airline Clerk: 'it-taðkara wi l-jawaaz min faḍ̣lak!

Passenger : tfaḍ̣ḍ̣al.

Airline Clerk: 9indak wiiza Hagg libnaan?

Passenger : la ma 9indi. baaxiðha fi maṭaar beruut.

Airline Clerk: čam janṭa 9indak?

Passenger : janṭateen.

Airline Clerk (to Porter): Huṭṭ haðeel il-jinaṭ 9ala l-miizaan ya byaat! 9indak jinaṭ θaanya?

Passenger : la. ma fii.

Airline Clerk: 9indak ziyaada xamsa keelu. 9aṭni 9ašara diinaar Hagg iz-ziyaada w diinar waaHid ḍ̣ariiba Hagg il-maṭaar. kill msaafir laazim yidfa9 diinaar.

Passenger : tfaḍ̣ḍ̣al haaða Hda9aš diinaar.

Airline Clerk: 'itris haaði l-biṭaaqa w ba9deen laazim truuH il-jawaazaat.

Airline Clerk (to Porter). šiil il-jinaṭ ya byaat!

II. TRANSLATION

At the Airport (i)

Airline Clerk: The ticket and the passport please!

Passenger : Here.

Airline Clerk: Do you have a visa for Lebanon?

Passenger : No, I don't. I'll get it in Beirut Airport.

Airline Clerk: How many bags do you have?

Passenger : Two

Airline Clerk (to Porter): Put these bags on the scales, Byat:

Airline Clerk: Do you have (any) other bags?

Passenger : No, I don't.

Airline Clerk: You have five kilograms of excess baggage. Give me ten dinars for excess baggage and one dinar airport tax. Every passenger must pay one dinar.

Passenger : Here. Here is eleven dinars.

Airline Clerk: Fill this card and then you should go to the passports (department).

Airline Clerk (to Porter): Lift the bags, Byat!

III. VOCABULARY

maṭaar	(–aat) airport
taðkara	(taðaakir) ticket
jawaaz	(–aat) passport
wiiza	(wiyaz) visa
janṭa	(jinaṭ) suitcase, bag
Huṭṭ	(imp.) put
miizaan	(mawaaziin) scales, balance
–šiil–	to lift, carry

ziyaada	excess, surplus
ḏ̣ariiba	(ḏ̣araayib) tax, duty
msaafir	(–iin) passenger
biṭaaqa	(baṭaayiq) card; ticket
laazim	(with foll. imperfect; must, should, have to, ought to
ʼil-jawaazaat	the passports (department)

IV. ADDITIONAL VOCABULARY

pooliis	police
širṭi	(širṭa) policeman, officer
jindi	(jnuud) soldier
jeeš	army
jimrig	(jamaarig) customs, duty
(ha)ḏaak	(f. **haḏiič**) that; that one
Hammaal	(Hamaamiil) porter, carrier

V. GRAMMAR

1. laazim

laazim 'must; have to; ought to; (it is) necessary that' is always followed by the imperfect form of the verb. It is invariable, i.e., it has only one form, but the verb form varies according to the subject:

laazim ʼaruuH halHiin.	'I have to (must) go now.'
laazim tiṭbax.	'She ought to cook.'
laazim yaji l-yoom.	'He should come today.'

The negative of such constructions is made by using the negative particle **ma** before laazim:

ma laazim 'aruuH halHiin. 'I do not have to go now.'
'I must not go now.'

2. The Particle b–

The particle b– is sometimes prefixed to the indicative form of the verb when it has habitual, progressive or future meaning.

1. hiya btišrab biira.
   1. 'She drinks beer (usually).'
2. hiya btišrab gahwa l-Hiin.
   2. 'She is drinking coffee now.'
3. hiya btišrab biira hnaak.
   3. 'She will have beer there.'

It does not affect the meaning of the verb, and it is not commonly used; it is less commonly used in GA than in other dialects of Arabic, such as Palestinian, Syrian, or Egyptian.

3. Elative Adjectives

Elative adjectives correspond in meaning to comparative and superlative adjectives in English, e.g., the comparative adjective **'aṭwal** (from **ṭawiil** 'long; tall') can be used to mean 'longer; taller' or 'longest; tallest', depending upon the construction in which it is used. In this lesson, we will deal with the comparative meaning, i.e., those constructions in which the elative adjective is used when comparing two people or things.

The elative adjective is formed on the pattern 'aC_1 C_2 aC_3 from the corresponding simple form of the adjective. Examples:

Simple		Elative	
jadiid	'new' ———	'ajdad	'newer; newest'
mitiin	'fat' ———	'amtan	'fatter; fattest'
waṣix	'dirty'———	'awṣax	'dirtier; dirtiest'

Other adjectives that are governed by this rule are: **ṭawiil** 'tall; long', **raxiiṣ** 'cheap', **9atiij** 'old; ancient' **naḍ̄iif** 'clean', **ḍ̄a9iif** 'weak; thin', **baarid** 'cold', **raṭib** 'wet, humid', **mariiḍ̄** 'sick', **kaθiir** 'many; much', **gaṣiir** 'short', **fagiir** 'poor', and **9aagil** 'sensible, rational'.

Note the following variations:

(a) Most adjectives ending with –i form their elative forms on the pattern 'aC_1 C_2a:

Simple		Elative	
ġaali	'expensive'	'aġla	'more (most) expensive'
gawi	'strong'	'agwa	'stronger, strongest'
ġani	'rich'	'aġna	'richer; richest'
ṣaaHi	'conscious'	'aṣHa	'more (most) conscious'

(b) Adjectives in which the second and third consonants are identical form their elatives on the pattern 'aC_1 aC_2 C_3 (except for **jadiid** 'new'): **Haarr** 'hot' → **'aHarr** 'hotter; hottest' and **galiil** 'little; few' → **'agall** 'less; least'.

(c) Other adjectives (including color adjectives) form their elatives by postposing the elative **'akθar** 'more' to the adjective :

ḍ̄aruuri	'necessary'	→	ḍ̄aruuri 'akθar	'more necessary'
bunni	'brown'	→	bunni 'akθar	'browner'

Other examples are: **mumtaaz 'akθar** 'more excellent', **9aadi 'akθar** 'more regular, usual', **'aṣfar 'akθar** 'yellower', etc.

Note that the elative of **čibiir** 'big; old' is usually **'akbar,** though **'ačbar** is also heard. The elative of **zeen** is **'azyan,** according to the pattern, but **'aHsan** 'better; best' (UNIT 32) is more commonly used.

Elatives in GA are, unlike adjectives, not inflected for gender or number :

saalim 'akbar.	'Salim is older.'
'il-bint 'akbar.	'The girl is older.'
'il-banaat 'ajmal.	'The girls are more beautiful.'
'il-'awlaad 'aṭwal.	'The boys are taller.'
haađa bunni 'akθar	'This (m.) is browner.'
haađi bunniyya 'akθar.	'This (f.) is browner.'

Like adjectives, elatives can function as predicates of equational sentences or modifiers of indefinite nouns:

haađa 'azyan.	'This (m.) is better.'
haađi sayyaara 'aġla.	'This is a more expensive car.'

The preposition **min** is used after the elative to express the meaning of 'than' in English:

haaða 'awṣax min ðaak. 'This (m.) is dirtier than that (m.).'

beeta 'akbar min beeti. 'His home is bigger than mine.'

(Drills 11, 12)

VI. DRILLS

Drill 1 *Transformation:* singular ––– plural

1. haaða maṭaar jadiid
2. haaði taðkara ġaalya.
3. haaða jawaaz 9atiij.
4. haaði wiiza ḏaruuriyya.
5. haaði janṭa sooda.
6. haaða miizaan zeen.
7. haaði ḏariiba ḏaruuriyya.
8. haaða msaafir.
9. haaði biṭaaqa Hamra.
10. haaða walad ṭawiil.
11. haaða beet naḏiif.
12. haaða Hammaal mitiin.
13. haaða leet gawi.
14. ḥaaði bint ḏa9iifa.

Drill 2 *Variable Substitution*

'aana 'aHuṭṭ fluus fi l-bank. 'I put money in the bank.'

1. hiya
2. 'ibraahiim
3. niHin
4. 'intum
5. 'inti
6. 'inta
7. 'intin
8. hum
9. hin
10. 'aana
11. 'asHab (min)
12. kalθuum

13. Hiṣṣa
14. 9abdaḷḷa
15. baačir
16. 9ugub baačir
17. yaaxiđ
18. saalim
19. hum
20. niHin

Drill 3 *Repetition*

1. huwa yšiil il-jinaṭ.
2. hum yšiiluun il-jinaṭ.
3. hiya tšiil il-jinaṭ.
4. ʼinta tšiil il-jinaṭ.
5. ʼintum tšiiluun il-jinaṭ.
6. ʼinti tšiiliin il-jinaṭ.
7. ʼintin tšiilin il-jinaṭ.
8. hiya tšiil il-jinaṭ.
9. ʼaana ʼašiil il-jinaṭ.
10. niHin nšiil il-jinaṭ.

Drill 4 *Repetition*

1. šiil il-jinaṭ!
2. Huṭṭ il-janṭa hini!
3. xall is-sayyaara fi l-garaaj!
4. baddil il-ʼaayil!
5. šuuf il-mudiir!
6. ʼitris it-taanki!
7. nađđif il-batri!
8. čayyik it-taayir!
9. bannid il-leet!
10. ʼiftaH id-dariiša!
11. ʼisHab fluus!
12. ʼimši wiyyaay!
13. ʼixiđ taksi!
14. 9aṭni fluus!
15. štiri biṭaaqa!
16. ʼišrab čaay!
17. štaġil hini!
18. ruuH is-suug!
19. tkallam 9aṛabi!
20. ʼidfa9 li-fluus!

Drill 5 *Transformation:* imperative → negative command

šiil il-janṭa! → laa tšiil il-janṭa.

'Carry (m.s.) the suitcase!' → Don't carry the suitcase.'

Use the commands in **Drill 4**, above.

Drill 6 *Completion*

'aana laazim..... 'I have to, must, should, ... '

1. study Arabic every day
2. put money in the bank
3. lift the tomatoes
4. pay airport tax
5. change the tires
6. let him work every day
7. fill the card
8. clean the car
9. check the oil
10. open the tomato can
11. give her a tip
12. see the minister
13. withdraw money from the bank
14. take a taxi to the hotel
15. buy a new battery
16. turn off the light

Drill 7 *Transformation:*
imperative ––– **maa laazim** + imperfect

'idris 9aṛabi kill yoom: ––– ma laazim 'adris 9aṛabi kill yoom.

'Study (m.s.) Arabic every day. ––– I don't have to study Arabic every day.'

'I must not study Arabic every day.'

Use the commands in **Drill 4**, above.

Drill 8 *Repetition*

1. 'aana laazim 'aštağil halHiin li'an is-saa9a θamaan.
2. 'aana laazim 'asHab fluus li'an ma 9indi fluus.
3. 'aana laazim 'aštiri tiffaaH li'an it-tiffaaH raxiiṣ il-yoom
4. 'aana laazim 'amši 'ila s-suug li'an ma 9indi sayyaara.
5. 'aana laazim 'aruuH il-mustašfa li'anni mariiđ̣.
6. 'aana laazim 'ašuuf il-mudiir li'anni muub ṣaaHi.
7. 'aana laazim 'aaxiđ taksi li'anni ma gdar 'amši.
8. 'aana laazim 'adris 9aṛabi li'anni ma 'atkallam 9aṛabi zeen.
9. 'aana laazim 'a9ṭiihum fluus li'anhum fagiiriin.
10. 'aana laazim 'ašrab gahwa li'an is-saa9a 9ašir.

Drill 9 *Substitution*

a. Substitute **huwa** 'he' for '**aana** 'I' in **Drill 8,** above.

b. Substitute **hiya** 'she' for '**aana** 'I' in **Drill 8,** above.

c. Substitute '**inta** 'you' for '**aana** 'I' in **Drill 8,** above.

d. Substitute '**inti** 'you' for '**aana** 'I' in **Drill 8,** above.

e. Substitute **niHin** 'we' for '**aana** 'I' in **Drill 8,** above.

Drill 10 *Question ––– Answer*

Example : T : leeš laazim tištağil halHiin?
'Why do you have to work now?'

S : laazim 'aštağil halHiin li'an is-saa9a θamaan.
'I have to work now because it's 8 o'clock.'

Teacher forms questions from the verbs in **Drill 8**, above, with **leeš laazim** and students answer according to the example in this drill.

Drill 11 *Transformation:* positive → elative

Example : T : haađa ktaab jadiid. 'This is a new book.'

S : đaak ktaab 'ajdad. 'That is a newer book.'

1. haađa beet čibiir.
2. 9inda fluus kaθiira.
3. haađi tađkara ġaalya.
4. haađa Hammaal mitiin.
5. haađa jawaaz jadiid.
6. haađi bint ṣaġiira.
7. haađa jindi ṭawiil.
8. haađi bint đ̣a9iifa.
9. haađi janṭa sooda.
10. haađa čaay Haarr.
11. haađa ṭaqs baarid.
12. haađa šeex ġani.
13. haađi mariiđ̣a mṣaxxna.
14. haađi madiina zeena.
15. haađa maṭaar nađ̣iif.
16. haađi bint gaṣiira.

Drill 12 *Comparison –– Cued*

Example : T : maktab –– ṣaff –– nađ̣iif
'office –– class –– clean'

S : 'il-maktab 'anđ̣af min iṣ-ṣaff.
'The office is cleaner than the class (room).'

1. bint – walad – čibiir
2. tiffaaH – burtaqaal – kaθiir
3. beeđinjaan – jiHH – ṣaġiir
4. beruut – 'il-qaahira – jamiil

5. sayyaarati – sayyaaratk – jadiid
6. 'abu ḍ̄abi – dbayy – čibiir
7. giṭar – 'is-su9uudiyya –ṣaġiir
8. 'uxtha – 'uxtič – ṭawiil
9. gahwa – čaay – ḍ̄aruuri
10. laHam – simač – ġaali
11. mudiira – mu9allima – ġani
12. 'il-baHreen – libnaan – Haarr
13. bint – walad – ḍ̄a9iif
14. Hammaal – kuuli – mitiin
15. 9ajmaan – giṭar – baarid
16. sayyaara – ṭayyaara – 9atiij

UNIT 23

I. TEXT

fi l-maṭaar (ii)

Hasan : ween msaafir ya Hamad?

Hamad : landan nšaaḷḷa.

Hasan : 9ala ʼay ṭayyaara?

Hamad : ʼil-xaliij. ṭayaraan il-xaliij w inta?

Hasan : ʼaana raayiH il-qaahira.

Hamad : wiyya ʼay šarika?

Hasan : ʼiš-šarg il-ʼawṣaṭ.

Hamad : ʼinta raayiH siida ʼila landan?

Hasan : la. 9an ṭariig il-baHreen. banaam leela fi ʼuteel ʼil-xaliij 9ala čiis iš-šarika. t9arif ʼaHad fi landan?

Hamad : ʼii na9am. 9indi ʼaṣdiga waajid ihnaak.

Hasan : ʼaana ma ʼa9rif ʼaHad fi l-qaahira. haaði ʼawwal marra ʼaruuH il-qaahira.

Hamad : ʼaguul! ʼinta leen tooṣal ihnaak guul Hagg raa9i t-taksi yaaxðak ʼila ʼuteel il-hilton u hum yrawwuunak il-balad.

II. TRANSLATION

At the Airport (ii)

Hasan : Where are you traveling, Hamad?

Hamad : London, I hope.

Hasan : On which plane?

Hamad : Gulf. Gulf Aviation. And you?

Hasan : I ' m going to Cairo.

Hamad : With which company?

Hasan : Middle East Airlines.

Hamad : Are you going straight (nonstop) to London?

Hasan : No, by way of Bahrain. I will stay overnight at the Gulf Hotel at the company expense. Do you know anybody in London?

Hamad : Yes, I have a lot of friends there.

Hasan : I do not know anybody in Cairo. This is the first time I go to Cairo.

Hamad : By the way! When you get there, ask a cab driver to take you to the Hilton Hotel, and they will show you the city.

III. VOCABULARY

landan	London (f.)
ṭayyaara	(–aat) airplane
xaliij	(xiljaan) gulf
ṭayaraan	aviation, flight
ṭayaraan il-xaliij	Gulf Air (Aviation)
raayiH	(–iin) going to
'awṣaṭ	middle
'iš-šarg il-'awṣaṭ	Middle East
siida	(adv.) straight, direct, nonstop

ṭariig	(ṭurug) road, way
—naam—	to sleep
leela	(layaali) one night
čiis	expense
—9arif—/—9rif—	to know
'ihnaak	there, over there
'aguul!	by the way!
leen	(conj.) when; whenever
—ooṣal—	to reach, arrive
raa9i	owner, proprietor
—rawwi—	to show

IV. ADDITIONAL VOCABULARY

—saafir—	to travel
—rja9—	to return, go back
'il-xaliij il-9aṛabi	Arabian Gulf

V. GRAMMAR

1. Elative Adjectives

huwa 'akbar walad.	'He is the biggest boy.'
hiya 'akbar bint.	'She is the biggest girl.'
huwa 'akbar 'il-'awlaad.	'He is the biggest of (the) boys.'
hiya 'akbar il-banaat.	'She is the biggest of (the) girls.'

There are two major constructions in which the superlative meaning of the GA elatives is expressed. In the first two sentences the elative **'akbar** is followed by a singular indefinite noun, which corresponds to English 'The biggest boy (girl)'. In the third and the fourth sentences the elative construction contains a plural definite noun, and corresponds to English 'The biggest of (the) boys (girls)'. Note that the elative is invariable; it is not inflected for gender or number.

If the elative is used predicatively, i.e., if it is the predicate of an equational sentence, it should take the article prefix for expressing the superlative meaning:

huwa l-'amtan.	'He is the fattest.'
hiya l-'azyan.	'She is the most beautiful.'

The superlative meaning of adjectives that do not have associated elative forms (see UNIT 22, GRAMMAR, 1.) is expressed by the adjective followed by the elative 'akθar 'more; most' followed by **šayy** 'thing' or **waaHid** 'one':

huwa mašġuul 'akθar šayy.	'He is the busiest.'
huwa mašġuul 'akθar waaHid.	'He is the busiest (one).

(Drills 8,9)

2. The Conjunction leen

leen is a conjunction in GA and has the following range of English equivalents: 'when', 'whenever', 'as soon as', 'any time that', etc.:

leen tooṣal ruuH il-'uteel.	'When you (m.s.) arrive, go to the hotel.'

leen yooṣal laazim yiji yammi.	'As soon as he arrives, he should come to me.'
leen yištaġil yištaġil zeen.	'Whenever he works, he works hard.'

(Drill 10)

3. Verbs – Imperfect Tense

The imperfect stem of the verb 'to arrive' is **–ooṣal–**. It takes the inflectional prefixes **y–**, **t–**, **'–**, **n–** and drops the stem vowel **–a–** when the inflectional suffixes **–iin** and **–uun** are added. (See the verb **–aaxiđ–** 'to take' in UNIT 18.) Following are the imperfect forms of this verb:

huwa yooṣal	hum yooṣluuun
hiya tooṣal	hin yooṣlin
'inta tooṣal	'intum tooṣluun
'inti tooṣliin	'intin tooṣlin
'aana 'ooṣal	niHin nooṣal

The imperative forms are: **'ooṣal**! 'Arrive (m.s.)!'; **'ooṣli**! 'Arrive (f.s.)!'; **'ooṣlu** 'Arrive (m.p.)!'; and **'ooṣlin** 'Arrive (f.p.)!'

(Drill 10)

The imperfect tense of the verb 'to know' has two stems: one for the first person singular, **–9rif** (**'aana 'a9rif** 'I know') and **–9arif–** for the other persons. Examples:

'inta t9arif.	'You (m.s.) know'
'intum t9arfuun.	'You (m.p.) know.'

hum y9arfuun. 'They (m.) know.'

niHin n9arif. 'We know.'

(Drills 4, 5)

4. raayiH

raayiH 'going, going to' is a participle, that is, an adjective derived from a verb. As an adjective, it is inflected for gender, number, and definiteness, and is usually negated by **muu(b)**. As a participle derived from a verb of motion (i.e., a verb of coming or going, etc.), it may also have future meaning:

huwa raayiH dbayy halHiin, walaakin 'aana raayiH baačir.
'He is going to Dubai now, but I am going tomorrow.'

Another participle from a verb of motion is **msaafir**: niHin msaafriin 9ugub yoomeen. 'We are leaving in two days.'

raayiH, however, has a unique role among participles: it may be used with a following imperfect verb to give that verb future meaning:

huwa raayiH yooṣal wiyya š-šarg il-'awṣaṭ.
'He's going to arrive via Middle East Airlines.'

mata raayHiin taaxðuun taksi?
'When are you going to take a taxi?'

(Drills 2, 3)

VI. DRILLS

Drill 1 *Transformation:* singular → plural

1. haaðˉi ṭayyaara jadiida.
2. haaðˉa maṭaar ba9iid.
3. haaðˉa ṭariig ṭawiil.
4. haaðˉi leela zeena.
5. huwa y9arif il-miškila.
6. leen tooṣal ruuH il-'uteel.
7. rawwiini il-'uteel!
8. ruuH siida!
9. haaðˉi ṭayyaarat il-xaliij.
10. haaðˉa 9ala čiisi.
11. hiya tidfa9 min čiisha.
12. haaðˉi šarikat ṭayaraan il-xaliij.
13. ween msaafir?
14. t9arif 'aHad fi landan?

Drill 2 *Repetition*

a. 1. 'aana raayiH baačir.
2. huwa raayiH baačir.
3. 'inta raayiH baačir.
4. 'inti raayHa baačir.
5. hiya raayHa baačir.
6. hum raayHiin baačir.
7. niHin raayHiin baačir.
8. 'intum raayHiin baačir.
9. 'intin raayHaat baačir.
10. hin raayHaat baačir.

b. 1. 'aana msaafir il-yoom.
2. huwa msaafir il-yoom.
3. 'inta msaafir il-yoom.
4. 'inti msaafra il-yoom.
5. hiya msaafra il-yoom.
6. hum msaafriin il-yoom.
7. niHin msaafriin il-yoom.
8. 'intum msaafriin il-yoom.
9. 'intin msaafraat il-yoom.
10. hin msaafraat il-yoom.

Drill 3 *Variable Substitution*

'aana raayiH il-qaahira. 'I am going to Cairo.'

1. hiya
2. huwa
3. hum
4. 'intum
5. 'intin
6. niHin
7. 'inta
8. 'inti
9. 'aana
10. hin
11. baġdaad
12. landan
13. dimašq
14. beruut
15. maṣir
16. 'amriika
17. 9ali
18. šeexa
19. 'iṭ-ṭayyaara
20. 'ingiltara

Drill 4 *Repetition*

'aana ma 'a9rif 'aHad ihnaak. 'I do not know anybody there.'

huwa ma y9arif 'aHad ihnaak. 'He doesn't know anybody there.'

1. hiya ma t9arif 'aHad ihnaak.
2. 'inta ma t9arif 'aHad ihnaak.
3. 'inti ma t9arfiin 'aHad ihnaak.
4. hum ma y9arfuun 'aHad ihnaak.
5. hin ma y9arfin 'aHad ihnaak.
6. 'intum ma t9arfuun 'aHad ihnaak.
7. 'intin ma t9arfin 'aHad ihnaak.
8. niHin ma n9arif 'aHad ihnaak.

Drill 5 *Completion*

'aana ma 'a9rif... 'I do not know...'

1. what his name is
2. what the time is
3. what these are
4. what to say
5. what to buy
6. what to take
7. what I should say
8. what she should clean
9. what the problem is
10. where he is going
11. where she is traveling
12. how to go home
13. how much tomatoes are today
14. how many children he has
15. how the weather will be tomorrow
16. how much he wants for the car

Drill 6 *Substitution*

haaðа raa9i **t-taksi.** 'This is the taxi owner (driver).'

1. hotel
2. car
3. tickets
4. customs
5. suitcase
6. tax
7. card
8. garage
9. gas station
10. cigarettes
11. books
12. bus
13. tea
14. oranges
15. milk
16. tires

Drill 7 *Double Substitution*

'aana raayiH siida 9an ṭariig **il-baHreen.**

'I am going straight by way of Bahrain.'

1. he - London
2. they (m.) - France
3. we - Kuwait
4. you (m.s.) - Egypt
5. you (f.s.) - Qatar
6. we - Abu Dhabi
7. they (f.) - Dubai
8. you (m.p.) Libya
9. you (f.p.) - Bahrain
10. I - Iraq
11. he - Lebanon
12. we - Iran
13. they (m.) - Canada
14. you (m.s.) - Lebanon
15. you (f.s.) - Jordan
16. she - Syria
17. you (f.p.) - Damascus
18. you (m.p.) - Pakistan
19. I - Saudi Arabia
20. we - Beirut
21. he - Paris

Drill 8 *Transformation:* positive → elative

Example : ṭawiil → 'aṭwal 'tall → taller'

jadiid	mitiin	waṣix	ġaali	đ̣aruuri
raxiiṣ	9aadi	bunni	ġani	fagiir
Haarr	galiil	kaθiir	Hamar	9atiij
'aṣfar	raṭib	mariiđ̣	ṣaġiir	mṣaxxan
ṣaaHi	gaṣiir	raṭib	đ̣a9iif	gawi
čibiir	baarid	9aagil	jamiil	mumtaaz

Drill 9 *Transformation:* positive → elative

Example :

T : haaða l-walad ṭawiil. 'This boy is tall.'

S_1 : haaða l-walad 'aṭwal min haðaak il-walad. 'This boy is taller than that boy.

S_2 : haaða 'aṭwal walad. 'This is the tallest boy.'

1. haaða l-maktab naḍ̄iif.
2. haaða l-maṭaar čibiir.
3. haaði l-janṭa ṣaġiira.
4. haaða l-hawa zeen.
5. haaði ṭ-ṭayyaara jadiida.
6. haaða ṭ-ṭariig ṭawiil.
7. haaði š-šarika čibiira.
8. haaði t-taðkara ġaalya.
9. haaða l-maṭaar naḍ̄iif.
10. haaða l-jindi gawi.
11. haaði l-bint mitiina.
12. haaða l-beet waṣix.
13. haaða l-hawa Haaff.
14. haaði l-mudiira gaṣiira.
15. haaða l-walad 9aagil.
16. haaða l-batrool 9aadi.

Drill 10 *Substitution*

Teacher: see the director

S : leen tooṣal ihnaak **šuuf il-mudiir.**

'When you get there, see the director.'

1. go to the hotel
2. go to the hospital
3. buy some apples
4. take a taxi
5. pay the money
6. change the oil

7. sleep in the hotel
8. fill the tank
9. clean the car
10. withdraw your money
11. put the money in the bank
12. walk to the office
13. eat Arabic food
14. come see me
15. get some fish
16. see Shaikh Zayid

UNIT 24

I. TEXT

ʹaskin fi beet čibiir. ʹil-beet fi šaari9 iš-šeex Hamdaan fi bu ᵭabi. fii xams Hijar: θalaaθ Hijar Hagg noom u maylis u Hijrat ʹakil. Hijra min Hijar in-noom Haggi w Hagg Hurmiti liʹanni mitzawwij u 9indi waladeen u bint. ʹil-Hijra θ-θaanya Hagg il-ʹawlaad w iθ-θaalθa Hagg ʹummi w ʹubuuy liʹanhum yiskinuun wiyyaana. ʹubuuy rayyaall čibiir 9umra sittiin sana w ʹummi mara čibiira ba9ad; 9umurha xamsa w xamsiin sana.

Hijrat il-ʹakil fiiha meez maal ṭa9aam u sitt karaasi. ʹil-maṭbax fii θallaaja w ġassaala w firn. ʹil-maylis fii kanabateen u ʹarba9 karaasi. Hijar in-noom fiihum xams kirfaayaat. fii Hammaameen fi l-beet: waaHid čibiir Haggna w iθ-θaani ṣaġiir Hagg li-9yaal.

II. TRANSLATION

I live in a large house. The house is on Shaikh Hamdan Street. There are five rooms in it: three bedrooms, a living room, and a dining room. One of the bedrooms is for me and for my wife because I am married, and I have two boys and a girl. The second bedroom is for the children, and the third bedroom is for my father and my mother because they live with us. My father is an old man; he is sixty years old. And my mother is an old woman; she is fifty-five years old.

There are a dining table and six chairs in the dining room. There are a refrigerator, a washing machine, and a stove in the kitchen. There are two sofas and four chairs in the living room. There are five beds in the bedrooms. There are two bathrooms in the house: a large one for us, and the other one is small; it is for the children.

III. VOCABULARY

–skin–	to live, dwell
šaari9	(šawaari9) street
šeex	(šyuuk) Shaikh
Hijra	(Hijar) room
noom	sleep, sleeping
maylis	(mayaalis) living room
ʼumm	(ʼummahaat) mother
ʼubu	(ʼaabaaʼ) father
ʼubuuy	my father
9umur	(9maar) age
rayyaal	(rayaayiil) man
mara	(Hariim) woman
meez	(myuuz) table
maal	belonging to
ṭa9aam	food
kirsi	(karaasi) chair
maṭbax	(maṭaabix) kitchen
θallaaja	(–aat) refrigerator
ġassaala	(–aat) washing machine
firn	(fraan) stove

kanaba	(–aat) sofa
kirfaaya	(–aat) bed
Hammaam	(--aat) bath; bathroom

IV. ADDITIONAL VOCABULARY

'uxu	('ixwaan) brother
baab	(biibaan) door
dariiša	(daraayiš) window
teebil	(tawaabil) table (f.), desk

V. GRAMMAR

1. Telling Ages

When you are asked how old you are in English, you say, "I am... years old." In French, e.g., you say the equivalent of English "I have... years." Other languages have other ways of telling age. In GA, as in most other dialects of Arabic, you say the equivalent of English "My age is... years." The word for 'age' is **9umur**. You add suffixed pronouns to **9umur**–to get 'my, your, his, ... age : '

9umri 9išriin sana.	'I am twenty years old.'
9umrak xamsiin sana?	'Are you (m.s.) fifty years old? '
9umurha xamsiin sana.	'She is fifty years old.'

(Drill 8)

2. **maal**

maal may be translated as 'property of' or 'belonging to'. It is similar to **Hagg** (UNIT 20) in meaning and use. **Hagg**, however, is more commonly used. Examples:

haaða l-kirsi maali.	'This chair is mine.'
haaði t-teebil maalič.	'This table is yours (f.s.).'

maal is often used instead of a noun construct, especially if the first noun is one borrowed from another language:

meez maal ṭa9aam	'dining room table'
kanaba maal maylis	'living room sofa'

(Drill 6)

3. In GA words that end with –**CCa** the final vowel –**a** changes into –**i** when a suffixed pronoun is added:

Hurma	'wife, woman'	———	Hurmiti	'my wife'
Hijra	'room'	———	Hijritha	'her room'

4. Note that the preposition **fii** (cf. **fi** 'in') in the construction **Hijrat il-'akil fiiha**——— 'The dining room has...' should have a suffixed pronoun referring to the noun head **Hijra** 'room'. Other examples are:

'il-maṭbax fii θallaaja.	'The kitchen has a refrigerator.' 'There is a refrigerator in the kitchen.'

li-9yaal ma9hum gḷaama. 'The children have pens (pencils).' 'There are pens (pencils) with the children.'

'is-suug fii simač. 'There is fish in the market.'

(Drills 2, 3)

5. Suffixed Pronouns

When a suffixed pronoun is added to a noun or a particle ending with a vowel, that vowel is lengthened. Below is the full paradigm of pronouns suffixed to 'ubu 'father':

'ubuu	'his father'
'ubuuha	'her father'
'ubuuk	'your (m.s.) father'
'ubuuč	'your (f.s.) father'
'ubuuy	'my father'
'ubuuhum	'their (m.) father'
'ubuuhin	'their (f.) father'
'ubuukum	'your (m.p.) father'
'ubuukin	'your (f.p.) father'
'ubuuna	'our father'

Other examples are: fi → fii, fiiha, fiik, fiič, fiina, ... etc.; wiyya → wiyyaa, wiyyaaha, wiyyaak, wiyyaač, ... etc.

VI. DRILLS

Drill 1 *Chain – Cued*

T : beet 'house'

S : haað̄a beet 'This is a house.'

1. šaari9
2. šeex
3. šyuux
4. θallaaja
5. ġassaala
6. firn
7. maylis
8. 'ubuuy
9. 'ummi
10. rayyaal
11. rayaayiil
12. mara
13. Hariim
14. Hammaam
15. myuuz
16. kirfaaya
17. kanaba
18. kanabaat
19. maṭbax
20. kirsi

Drill 2 *Substitution*

haað̄a beet. 'il-beet fii **maylis.**

'This is a house. The house has a living room.'

1. table
2. dining table
3. kitchen
4. four rooms
5. two rooms
6. dining room
7. six chairs
8. refrigerator
9. washing machine
10. stove

11. four beds
12. big sofa
13. three sofas
14. bathroom
15. two bathrooms
16. two doors
17. four windows
18. four bedrooms
19. large kitchen
20. small bathroom

Drill 3 *Combination*

haaða beet. il-beet fii maylis čibiir. → haaða l-beet fii maylis čibiir.

'This is a house. The house has a large living room. → This house has a large living room.'

1. haaða beet. 'il-beet fii xams Hijar.
2. haaða beet. 'il-beet fii maylis.
3. haaða beet. 'il-beet fii 'ummi w 'ubuuy.
4. haaða beet. 'il-beet fii two tables.
5. haaða beet. 'il-beet fii dining table.
6. haaða beet. 'il-beet fii dining room.
7. haaða beet. 'il-beet fii large kitchen.
8. haaða beet. 'il-beet fii θallaaja čibiira.
9. haaða beet. 'il-beet fii washing machine.
10. haaða beet. 'il-beet fii two bathrooms.
11. haaða beet. 'il-beet fii 3 sofas.
12. haaða beet. 'il-beet fii 5 beds.
13. haaða beet. 'il-beet fii nice stove.
14. haaða jawaaz. 'il-jawaaz fii wiiza Hagg landan.
15. haaða maṭaar. 'il-maṭaar fii ṭayyaaraat waajid.

Drill 4 *Substitution*

'il-beet fi šaari9 iš-šeex Hamdaan.

'This house is in Shaikh Hamdan Street.'

1. jaasim
2. zaayid
3. xaadim
4. 9iisa
5. xaliifa
6. Hamad
7. Hamdaan
8. raašid
9. 'aHmad
10. Haamid
11. mHammad
12. ṣagir
13. sulṭaan
14. saalim
15. xaalid
16. jum9a
17. mbaarak
18. seef
19. yuusif
20. 'ibraahiim

Drill 5 *Variable Substitution*

'askin fi beet čibiir. 'I live (am living) in a large house.'

1. 'ubuuy
2. 'ummi
3. ṣaġiir
4. 'aana
5. 'ahli
6. jadiid
7. 'intum
8. 'inti
9. 'inta
10. čibiir
11. niHin
12. hiya

13. hin
14. jadiid
15. 9atiij
16. 'intin
17. 'uxti
18. zeen
19. 'aana
20. hiya

Drill 6 *Repetition*

1. meez maal 'akil
2. kanaba maal maylis
3. tiffaaH maal libnaan
4. jiHH maal li-9raag.
5. laHam maal kanada
6. jibin maal hoḷanda
7. batri maal sayyaara
8. Hijra maal noom
9. batrool maal giṭar
10. Hijar maal noom
11. kirfaaya maal mustašfa
12. batrool maal is-su9uudiyya

Drill 7 *Double Substitution*

waaHid minhum čibiir w iθ-θaani ṣaġiir.

'One of them is large (old) and the other is small (young).'

1. expensive - cheap
2. tall - short
3. clean - dirty
4. new - old
5. long - short
6. rich - poor
7. far - near
8. white - black
9. sick - fine
10. sane - crazy
11. American - Arab
12. nurse - doctor
13. clerk - director
14. fat - thin
15. strong - weak
16. expensive - cheap
17. feverish - well
18. busy - not here

Drill 8 *Substitution*

9umra sittiin sana. 'He is 60 years old.'

1. 50 years
2. 30 years
3. 55 years
4. 100 years
5. 73 years
6. 10 years
7. 6 years
8. 2 years
9. $1\frac{1}{2}$ years
10. 8 months
11. 11 months
12. 9 months
13. 15 days
14. 12 days
15. 20 days
16. 1 week
17. 2 weeks
18. 3 weeks
19. 20 years
20. 17 years

Drill 9 *Translation*

1. This is expensive and that is expensive, too.
2. This airport is big and that house is big, too.
3. This room is small and that one is small, too.
4. My passport is new and your passport is new, too.
5. My son is young, and your (m.) son is young, too.
6. This suitcase is black, and that one is black, too.
7. This traveler (m.) is sick, and that one is sick, too.
8. This porter is strong and that one is strong, too.
9. This policeman is tall, and that one is tall, too.

10. This army is strong and that one is strong, too.
11. My father is an old man, and my mother is an old woman, too.
12. One of the two bathrooms is for the children.

Drill 10 *Repetition*

čibiir – kbaar	mara – Hariim
šaari9 – šawaari9	meez – myuuz
šeex – šyuux	kirsi – karaasi
Hijra – Hijar	maṭbax – maṭaabix
maylis – mayaalis	θallaaja – θallaajaat
rayyaal – rayaayiil	ġassaala – ġassaalaat
firn – fraan	Hammaam – Hammaamaat
kanaba – kanabaat	baab – biibaan
dariiša – daraayiš	teebil – tawaabil

Drill 11 *Transformation:* singular → plural

1. haaða kirsi čibiir.
2. haaða šeex zeen.
3. haaða šaari9 naðiif.
4. haaða rayyaal zeen.
5. haaði mara jamiila.
6. haaða meez maal 'akil.
7. haaði Hijra maal noom.
8. haaða kirsi ṣaġiir.
9. haaða maṭbax 9atiij.
10. haaði θallaaja ġaalya.
11. haaði ġassaala čibiira.
12. haaða firn naðiif.
13. haaði kanaba jadiida.
14. haaða baab il-beet.
15. haaði dariiša ṣaġiira.
16. haaði teebil ṭawiila.

Drill 12 *Questions* (based on TEXT)

1. beeti ṣaġiir walla čibiir?
2. ween il-beet?
3. ween haað̵a š-šaari9?
4. čam Hijra fii fi l-beet?
5. čam Hijra Hagg noom?
6. kam maylis?
7. kam Hijrat ʼakil?
8. ʼaana mitzawwij?
9. kam walad 9indi?
10. ween ʼummi w ʼubuuy?
11. čam 9umur ʼubuuy?
12. ʼummi mara ṣaġiira?
13. čam 9umurha?
14. weeš fii fi l-maṭbax?
15. čam kirsi fii fi l-maylis?
16. kam Hammaam fii fi l-beet?

UNIT 25

I. TEXT

fi maṭ9am beruut

Waiter : 'ahlan wa sahlan! tfað̣ð̣alu!

saalim : š tabi taakil ya mbaarak?

mbaarak : (to Waiter): weeš fi 9indakum?

Waiter : 9indana kill šayy: dijaaj u laHam ġanam u kabaab u kubba w simač mašwi .....

mbaarak : (to Waiter): 9aṭni 9eeš u simač!

Waiter : Haað̣ir. nšaaḷḷa.

saalim : 'aana 'abi kabaab. jiib ṣaHin Hummoṣ u ṣaHin zalaaṭa min fað̣lak!

Waiter : nšaaḷḷa. šu triiduun tišrabuun?

mbaarak : 'aana 'ariid 'ašrab baarid: bebsi zeen.

saalim : 9aṭni gahwa 9ugb il-'akil!

---

saalim : ta9aal ya walad: čam li-Hsaab?

Waiter : θalaaθiin dirhim.

mbaarak : la waḷḷa 'inta ma tidfa9. 9alayy 'aana.

II. TRANSLATION

At Beirut Restaurant

Waiter : Welcome! Please!

Salim : What do you want to eat, Mbarak?

Mbarak	:	(to Waiter): What do you have?
Waiter	:	We have everything: chicken, lamb, kabob, kubba, baked fish, ...
Mbarak	:	Give me rice and fish!
Waiter	:	Yes, sir.
Salim	:	I want kabob. Bring a dish of hummos and salad, please.
Waiter	:	Yes. What would you like to drink?
Mbarak	:	I would like to have a soft drink.. Pepsi Cola is fine.
Salim	:	Give me coffee after the food.

Salim	:	Waiter! How much is the bill?
Waiter	:	Thirty dirhams.
Mbarak	:	No, no! You won't pay. It's on me.

III. VOCABULARY

dijaaj	(coll.) chicken; hens
ġanam	(coll.) lambs, goats
laHam ġanam	lamb, mutton
kabaab	kabob
kubba	a dish made of ground meat, cracked wheat, and onions
mašwi	(–yyiin) baked, grilled
Haaḏ̣ir	Yes, sir; (lit.: 'I ' m ready').
–jiib–	to bring, fetch

ṣaHin	(ṣHuun) plate, dish
Hummoṣ	a dish made of crushed chick peas, sesame seed paste, and lemon juice
zalaaṭa	salad
bebsi	Pepsi Cola

IV. ADDITIONAL VOCABULARY

magḷi	(—yyiin) fried
ṣaaloona	soup
gafša	(gfaaš) spoon; ladle
siččiin	(sičaačiin) knife (f.)
finjaan	(fanaajiin) cup; coffee cup
gḷaaṣ	(—aat) glass of s. th. (f.)
boṭil	(bṭaala) bottle (f.)
kuub	(ʼakwaab) cup (not coffee); drinking cup
čingaaḷ	(činaagiiḷ) fork

V. GRAMMAR

1. Collective Nouns

Three more collective nouns occur in this lesson: **dijaaj** 'chicken; hens', **ġanam** 'sheep (and goats)', and **simač** 'fish'. The unit nouns derived from these collectives are: **dijaaja** 'a chicken', **ġanama** 'a sheep, a goat', and **simča** 'a fish'.

2. Haaḏ̣ir as a response to an imperative literally means 'I am ready'. It is used in the same way as **nšaaḷḷa** (UNIT 19) 'yes; certainly; surely, etc.' Unlike **nšaaḷḷa, Haaḏ̣ir** functions as an adjective and it is inflected for gender, number, and definiteness:

'aana Haaḏ̣ir.	'I am ready.'
hiya Haaḏ̣ra.	'She is ready.'
hum Haaḏ̣riin.	'They (m.) are ready.'
hin Haaḏ̣raat.	'They (f.) are ready.'

VI. DRILLS

Drill 1 *Repetition*

1. 9aṭni finjaan gahwa!	'Give me a cup of coffee!'
2. 9aṭni finjaan čaay!	'Give me a cup of tea!'
3. 9aṭni finjaan Haliib!	'Give me a cup of milk!'
4. 9aṭni gḷaaṣ Haliib!	'Give me a glass of milk!'
5. 9aṭni gḷaaṣ mayy!	'Give me a glass of water!'
6. 9aṭni gḷaaṣ biira!	'Give me a glass of beer!'
7. 9aṭni boṭil biira!	'Give me a bottle of beer!'
8. 9aṭni kuub čaay!	'Give me a cup of tea!'
9. 9aṭni kuub Haliib!	'Give me a cup of milk!'
10. 9aṭni ṣaHin dijaaj!	'Give me a plate of chicken!'

Drill 2 *Chain – Cued*

S_1: weeš fii 9indkum?	'What do you have?'
9indna **dijaaj**.	'We have chicken.'

1. fish
2. fried fish
3. baked fish
4. chicken
5. fried chicken
6. baked chicken
7. meat
8. mutton
9. kabob
10. kubba
11. hummos
12. salad
13. cold Pepsi
14. coffee, tea,..
15. soup
16. beer, whiskey..
17. dining tables
18. refrigerators
19. plates
20. washing machine

Drill 3 *Substitution*

9aṭni..... min fađlak! 'Give me....., please!'

1. salad plate
2. Lebanese apples
3. regular gasoline
4. fresh eggs
5. fried chicken
6. baked fish
7. glass of beer
8. cup of coffee
9. glass of milk
10. plate of hummos
11. fork and knife
12. fork and spoon
13. soup
14. mutton
15. the bill
16. bottle of beer
17. tea with milk
18. rice and fish

Drill 4 *Substitution*

	9alayy 'aana.	'(It's) on me.'
T :	huwa	'He'
S :	9alee huwa	'(It's) on him.'

1. hiya	11. hum
2. hum	12. hiya
3. hin	13. hin
4. 'inti	14. 'aana
5. 'inta	15. 'inta
6. 'intum	16. 'intum
7. 'aana	17. 'inti
8. niHin	18. 'intin
9. 'intin	19. niHin
10. huwa	20. huwa

Drill 5 *Variable Substitution*

jiib ṣaHin Hummoṣ min faðlak!	'Bring a plate of hummos, please!'

1. ṣaHin dijaaj	6. laHam
2. ṣaHin zalaaṭa	7. 'intum
3. 'inti	8. chicken
4. 9eeš	9. mutton
5. xubiz	10. kabob

11. kubba	16. chair
12. cold Pepsi	17. spoon
13. soup	18. fork
14. bread	19. knife
15. sofa	20. chicken

Drill 6 *Variable Substitution*

huwa yabi yjiib kabaab. 'He wants to bring (some) kabob.'

1. chicken	11. Hummoṣ
2. hiya	12. zalaaṭa
3. simač	13. hum
4. 9eeš	14. bebsi
5. 'aana	15. Haliib
6. laHam	16. gḷaaṣaat
7. biira	17. bṭaala
8. hiya	18. 'akwaab
9. lamb	19. sičaačiin
10. kabob	20. soup

Drill 7 *Chain – Cued*

S_1: čam li-Hsaab? 'How much is the bill?'

T : 3 dinars

S_2: θalaaθa diinaar. 'Three dinars.'

1. 5 dirhams	4. $\frac{1}{2}$ dinar
2. 2 dirhams	5. 3/4 dinar
3. $1\frac{1}{2}$ dinars	6. 750 fils

7. 500 fils
8. 320 fils
9. 1 riyal
10. 2 riyals
11. 7 rupees
12. 12 riyals
13. 10 riyals
14. 16 dirhams
15. 20 riyals
16. 35 dirhams
17. 840 fils
18. 520 fils

Drill 8 *Double Substitution*

'aana 'abi g̣laaṣ mayy. 'I want a glass of water.'

1. huwa – fried fish
2. 'aana – cup of coffee
3. hiya – cup of coffee
4. 'inta – mutton
5. 'inti – baked fish
6. hum – kabob
7. hin – cold Pepsi
8. 'intum – salad
9. niHin – cup of tea
10. huwa – fish and rice
11. 'aana – cold water
12. hiya – fork and spoon
13. hiya – knife
14. 'inta – bread
15. 'inti – fried fish
16. niHin – fried chicken
17. 'aana – baked meat
18. huwa – baked fish

Drill 9 *Variable Substitution*

'abi 'aakil kabaab fi l-maṭ9am.

'I want to eat kabob in the restaurant.'

1. hiya
2. huwa
3. 'inta
4. l-beet

5. simač
6. ʹuteel
7. ʹinti
8. halHiin
9. dijaaj
10. ʹintum
11. hum
12. laazim
13. ʹaana
14. huwa
15. fundug
16. hiya
17. negative
18. niHin
19. hin
20. ʹaana

UNIT 26

I. TEXT

9ala t-talafoon (i)

mHammad: haluw! haluw! ʹil-xaṭṭ muub zeen il-yoom. haluw!

Servant : haluw! man yitkallam?

mHammad: ʹaana mHammad mijrin. haaδa beet 9abdaḷḷa kaddaas?

Servant : ʹii na9am. man triid?

mHammad: ʹariid ʹaHči wiyya 9abdaḷḷa.

Servant : zeen. ṣabir šwayy!

9abdaḷḷa : haluw! marHaba ya mHammad! keef inta?

mHammad: l-Hamdu lillaah. ṣaarli ʹaHaawil attaṣil fiik min muddat saa9ateen w il-xaṭṭ mašǧuul. ʹaguul! baačir il-jum9a. tfaδ̣δ̣alu ṣoobna nsoolif u nil9ab warag u nistaanis.

9abdaḷḷa : zeen. ʹay Hazza?

mHammad: Hawaali s-saa9a tisi9 u nuṣṣ fi l-leel.

9abdaḷḷa : zeen. maškuur ya mHammad. binji nšaaḷḷa.

II. TRANSLATION

On the Telephone (i)

Muhammad: Hello! Hello! The line is not good today. Hello!

Servant : Hello! Who is speaking?

Muhammad: I ' m Muhammad Mijrin. Is this Abdalla Kaddas' home?

Servant : Yes. Whom do you want?

Muhammad: I want to speak to Abdalla.

Servant : Fine. Just a minute.

Abdalla : Hello! Hi, Huhammad! How are you?

Muhammad: I ' m fine. I've been trying to contact you for two hours, and the line was busy. By the way: Tomorrow is Friday. Come to our place. We'll talk, play cards, and have a good time.

Abdalla : Fine. What time?

Muhammad: About 9:30 p.m.

Abdalla : O.K. Thank you, Muhammad. We'll be there.

III. VOCABULARY

talafoon	(–aat) telephone
haluw!	Hello!
xaṭṭ	(xṭuuṭ) telephone line
man?	who?
–Hči–	to talk, speak
ṣabir!	(lit: 'patience') wait!
ṣabir šwayy!	Just a minute!
–Haawil–	to try to do s. th.
–ttaṣil–	to contact, reach by telephone

mudda	period (of time), interval
ṣoob	(n.) place, direction; (prep.) at the place of, by, next to
—soolif—	to speak, talk; to chatter
—l9ab—	to play (e.g., cards, games)
warag	(coll.) paper; cards
—staanis—	to have a good time, enjoy oneself
Hazza	period (of time)
'ay Hazza?	What time?
Hawaali	about, approximately

IV. GRAMMAR

1. ṣaarli + Double Imperfect

In an earlier section we had **ṣaarli...** 'I have been... ' followed by an imperfect tense to express an action going on at the present time. In this lesson we have **ṣaarli** followed by a double imperfect verbal construction **ṣaarli 'aHaawil attaṣil...** 'I have been trying to contact...'. Here are some more examples:

ṣaarlana nHaawil naji...	'We have been trying to come...'
ṣaarlaha tHaawil tguul...	'She has been trying to say...'
ṣaarlahin yHaawlin yištaġlin...	'They (f.) have been trying to work...'

(Drills 6, 7)

2. **Hazza** 'time' is limited in use to the following constructions:

'ay Hazza triid taji?	'What time (when) do you (m.s.) want to come?'
hal Hazza zeen.	'This time is fine.'
hal Hazza s-saa9a xams.	'Now it's five o'clock.'

***čam il-Hazza**? is wrong. You should say **čam is-saa9a**? 'What time is it?'

3. **Hawaali** 'nearly, approximately, about' behaves syntactically like a preposition; it should precede the noun or noun phrase it governs.

ṣaarli hini Hawaali sanateen.	'I have been here for about two years.'
min hini 'ila dbayy Hawaali saa9ateen bi s-sayyaara.	'It's about two hours from here to Dubai by car.'

4. The word **ṣoob** can be used as a preposition or as a noun. As a preposition it means 'by, next to; at the place of'. As a noun it means 'direction; place.' Examples:

'il-mustašfa ṣoob iš-šarika.	'The hospital is next to the company.'
'il-mustašfa đaak iṣ-ṣoob.	'The hospital is in that direction.'
ta9aal ṣoobna.	'Come (m.s.) to our place.'

(Drill 12)

V. DRILLS

Drill 1 *Repetition*

9aṭni il-xaṭṭ min faḓlak!	'Give (m.s.) me the line, please!'
jiib il-xaṭṭ min faḓlak!	'Bring (get) (m.s.) the line, please!'
'ixiđ il-xaṭṭ min faḓlak!	'Take (m.s.) the line, please!'
xalli l-xaṭṭ min faḓlak!	'Leave (m.s.) the line, please!'
čayyik il-xaṭṭ min faḓlak!	'Check (m.s.) the line, please!'
bannid il-xaṭṭ min faḓlak!	'Shut (m.s.) the line, please!'
'iftaH il-xaṭṭ min faḓlak!	'Open (m.s.) the line, please!'
Haṣṣil il-xaṭṭ min faḓlak!	'Get (m.s.) the line, please!'

Drill 2 *Variable Substitution*

huwa yriid yiHči ma9 9abdaḷḷa.
'He wants to speak with Abdalla.'

1. 'aana	11. hiya
2. hiya	12. 'aana
3. negative	13. mooza
4. hum	14. 'intin
5. yitkallamuun	15. question
6. niHin	16. 'inti
7. positive	17. tsoolfiin
8. hin	18. 'uxuuč
9. šeexa	19. tittaṣliin
10. yil9abin	20. hiya

Drill 3 *Variable Substitution*

huwa yHaawil yittaṣil ma9 9abdaḷḷa.

'He is trying to contact Abdalla.'

1. hum
2. huwa
3. negative
4. hiya
5. salma
6. hin
7. 'inti
8. 'intin
9. niHin
10. niHči
11. šeexa
12. 'aana
13. positive
14. hiya
15. til9ab
16. til9ab warag
17. question
18. answer
19. niHin
20. 'inti

Drill 4 *Chain –Cued*

T : 9abdaḷḷa

S_1 : 'ariid aHči wiyya 9abdaḷḷa. 'I want to talk to Abdalla.'

S_2 : ṣabir šwayy! 'Just a minute!'

1. saalim
2. jaasim
3. 9ali
4. mHammad
5. xamiis
6. 9eeša
7. salma
8. mooza
9. layla
10. Hiṣṣa

11. li-wlaad	16. 'inta
12. l-banaat	17. 'inti
13. l-waziir	18. 'intum
14. s-sikirteer	19. hum
15. d-daxtar	20. hin

Drill 5 *Double Substitution*

huwa yriid yittaṣil **fiik.**	'He wants to contact you.'
hiya niHin	'She we'
hiya triid tittaṣil fiina.	'She wants to contact us.'

1. 'aana – 'intum	10. hin – 'intin
2. hum – niHin	11. 'intum – niHin
3. 'inti – hin	12. niHin – huwa
4. 'inta – hiya	13. 'aana – 'inti
5. byaat – huwa	14. Hiṣṣa – hiya
6. šamsa – hiya	15. hum – 'inta
7. niHin – 'intum	16. hin – niHin
8. 'intin – hum	17. niHin – 'inta
9. 'inta – 'aana	18. hiya – hin

Drill 6 *Repetition*

'aana : ṣaarli 'aHaawil 'attaṣil fiik min muddat saa9ateen.

I : 'I have been trying to contact you (m.s.) for two hours.'

hiya : ṣaarlaha tHaawil tittaṣil fiik min muddat saa9ateen.

hum : ṣaarlahum yHaawluun yittaṣluun fiik min muddat saa9ateen.

huwa : ṣaarla yHaawil yittaṣil fiik min muddat saa9ateen.

hin : ṣaarlahin yHaawlin yittaṣlin fiik min muddat saa-9ateen.

niHin : ṣaarlana nHaawil nittaṣil fiik min muddat saa9ateen.

'aana : ṣaarli 'aHaawil 'attaṣil fiik min muddat saa9ateen.

Drill 7 *Variable Substitution*

ṣaarli 'aHaawil 'attaṣil fiik min muddat saa9ateen.

'I have been trying to contact you for two hours.'

1. huwa
2. saa9a
3. $\frac{1}{2}$ saa9a
4. hum
5. yoomeen
6. subuu9
7. subuu9een
8. niHin
9. šahar
10. hin
11. šahreen
12. 'aana
13. sana
14. sanateen
15. hiya
16. hum
17. 4 'ayyaam
18. 5 saa9aat
19. 'aana
20. min zamaan

Drill 8 *Repetition*

1. huwa yHaawil ybannid is-saa9a xams.
2. huwa yHaawil yjiib beeṯ̣ jadiid.

3. huwa yHaawil yištiri beet jadiid.
4. huwa yHaawil yHaṣṣil ziyaada.
5. huwa yHaawil yaakil 'akil hindi.
6. huwa yHaawil yitkallam 9aṛabi.
7. huwa yHaawil yiktib bi l-9aṛabi.
8. huwa yHaawil ybaddil is-sayyaara.
9. huwa yHaawil yšuuf il-waziiṛ.
10. huwa yHaawil yimši fi l-leel.
11. huwa yHaawil yaji l-yoom.
12. huwa yHaawil yišrab wiski.
13. huwa yHaawil yruuH baačir.

Drill 9 *Substitution*

'il-xaṭṭ **mašġuul.** 'The line is busy.'

1. good
2. very good
3. not good
4. new
5. busy
6. not busy
7. excellent
8. weak
9. strong
10. very weak
11. old
12. busy

Drill 10 *Translation*

1. I live in a large house.
2. The house has five rooms.
3. My parents are living with us.

4. He is 65 years old.
5. The woman is 30 years old.
6. The kitchen is very small.
7. There isn't a refrigerator.
8. There isn't a stove either.
9. The dining table is new.
10. There is a bathroom for the children.
11. The sofa and the bed are old.
12. I want to eat fried chicken.
13. This restaurant has fish and rice.
14. Bring me a cup of coffee, please!
15. The bill is on me. You won't pay.
16. She wants a glass of milk.

Drill 11 *Transformation: Conjugation*

'aana 'asoolif u 'al9ab warag. 'I (talk) am talking and (play) playing cards.'

1. huwa	6. 'il-'awlaad	11. 'inta
2. 'intum	7. hiya	12. li-9yaal
3. seef	8. 'aana	13. 'inta
4. hum	9. 'il-banaat	14. niHin
5. 'intin	10. hin	15. mooza

Drill 12 *Double Substitution*

tfaḍ̄ḍ̄al ṣoobna! 'Please come to our place!'

T : 'inti – hum 'you (f.s.) –– they (m.)'

S : tfaḍ̄ḍ̄ali ṣoobhum. 'Please come (f.s.) to their (m.) place:'

1. 'inta – niHin
2. 'inti – niHin
3. 'intum – niHin
4. 'intin – niHin
5. 'inta – hum
6. 'inti – hin
7. 'intum – hum
8. 'intin – hin
9. 'intin – hiya
10. 'inti – hiya
11. 'inta – huwa
12. 'intum – huwa

UNIT 27

I. TEXT

9ala t-talafoon (ii)

Operator : wazaarat il-'ašġaal!

sabt : 'abi 'atkallam wiyya s-sayyid jamiil.

Operator : 9inda xaṭṭ θaani. jarrib ir-raqam 9748.

sabt : zeen maškuur.

---

sabt : haluw! 'is-sayyid jamiil mawjuud min faḏlak?

Operator : numra ġalaṭ.

sabt : mit'assif.

---

sabt : 'is-sayyid jamiil mawjuud?

Secretary : la waḷḷa. muub hini. birja9 9ugub saa9a. tabi titrik la risaala?

sabt : 'ii. 'abi 'a9mal maw9id wiyyaa.

Secretary : zeen xalln ašuuf:..... baačir is-saa9a 9ašir zeen?

sabt : zeen maškuur.

II. TRANSLATION

On the Telephone (ii)

Operator : Ministry of Works!

Sabt : I want to talk to Mr. Jamil.

Operator : He has another line. Try the number 9748.

Sabt : O. K. Thanks.

Sabt : Hello! Is Mr. Jamil there, please?

Operator : Wrong number.

Sabt : Sorry.

Sabt : Is Mr. Jamil there?

Secretary : No, he's not here. He will be back in an hour. Would you like to leave him a message?

Sabt : Yes. I'd like to make an appointment with him.

Secretary : Fine. Let me see: ..... Is tomorrow at 10 O.K.?

Sabt : O.K. Thank you

III. VOCABULARY

–jarrib–	to try
wazaarat il-'ašġaal	Ministry of (Public) Works
raqam	('arqaam) number
mawjuud	(–iin) found, available, on hand
numra	(numar) number
ġalaṭ	incorrect, wrong
mit'assif	(–iin) (I'm) sorry
–trik–	to leave (e.g., place, message)
risaala	(rasaayil) message; letter
–9mal–	to do; to make

IV. ADDITIONAL VOCABULARY

jawaab	(–aat) answer, response
santraal	central telephone line/operator
–sma9–	to hear s. th.; to listen
–dugg–	to ring (e.g., bell)
9adil	(lit. 'justice') correct, right
wazaarat il-9adil	Ministry of Justice
ziraa9a	agriculture
wazaarat iz-ziraa9a	Ministry of Agriculture
daayra	(dawaayir) department
wazaarat il-maaliyya	Ministry of Finance
wazaarat il-xaarijiyya	Foreign Ministry
wazaarat id-daaxiliyya	Ministry of the Interior
wazaarat il-muwaaṣalaat	Ministry of Communications

V. GRAMMAR

θaani 'another; other; second'

θaani 'another; other; second' in this lesson follows the noun it modifies and, like any other adjective, can be masculine, feminine, singular, plural, definite, and indefinite, depending upon the noun it modifies. Examples:

walad θaani	'another boy'
bint θaanya	'another girl'

'awlaad θaanyiin	'other boys'
banaat θaanyaat	'other girls'
'il-walad iθ-θaani	'the other boy'

Only the masculine singular form **θaani** can precede the noun it modifies and mean 'another; second'. The noun should be indefinite. In this case **θaani** is also an ordinal:

θaani xaṭṭ	'another line; the second line'
θaani numra	'another number; the second number'

(Drills 2, 3)

VI. DRILLS

Drill 1 *a. Repetition*

1. wazaarat il-maaliyya
2. wazaarat id-daaxiliyya
3. wazaarat il-muwaaṣalaat
4. wazaarat iṣ-ṣiHHa
5. wazaarat il-batrool
6. wazaarat il-xaarijiyya
7. wazaarat il-9adil
8. wazaarat il-'ašġaal
9. wazaarat it-tarbiya
10. wazaarat iz-ziraa9a

b. Substitution

'abi 'attaṣil fi wazaarat **il-'ašġaal.**
'I want to contact the Ministry of Public Works.'

1. petroleum
2. agriculture
3. finance
4. foreign affairs
5. interior
6. justice

7. communications
8. education
9. public works
10. education
11. agriculture
12. justice
13. health
14. finance
15. interior
16. communications
17. justice
18. education
19. petroleum
20. public works

Drill 2 *Transformation: Conjugation*

huwa : 9inda xaṭṭ θaani. 'He has another line.'

1. hiya
2. hum
3. hin
4. 'aana
5. niHin
6. 'inta
7. 'intum
8. 'inti
9. 'intin
10. huwa
11. niHin
12. hiya
13. huwa
14. 'aana
15. hum

Drill 3 *Substitution*

9inda **xaṭṭ** θaani. 'He has another line.'

1. talafoon
2. raqam
3. numra
4. risaala
5. šuġul
6. line
7. jawaab
8. maṭ9am
9. sayyaara
10. kuub

11. gafša
12. siččiin
13. čingaaḷ
14. finjaan
15. gḷaaṣ
16. maw9id
17. walad
18. bint
19. ktaab
20. janṭa

Drill 4 *Transformation:* singular ––– plural

1. 9inda xaṭṭ θaani.
2. 'abi 'atkallam wiyyaa.
3. jaarib haaᵭa r-raqam!
4. zeen maškuur.
5. ma fii jawaab.
6. xalln ašuuf!
7. xallha tšuuf!
8. 'ariid atrik la risaala.
9. haaᵭi daayrat Hukuuma.
10. mata truuH id-daayra?
11. 'il-xaṭṭ muub zeen il-yoom.
12. hiya mawjuuda hini kill yoom.
13. birja9 9ugub saa9a.
14. 'it-talafoon ydigg.

Drill 5 *Chain – Cued*

S_1: 'is-sayyid jamiil mawjuud min faᵭ̣lak?
'Is Mr. Jamil there, please? '

S_2 :	la. numra ġalaṭ!	'No. Wrong number!'
S_1 :	mit'assif.	'(I'm) sorry.'

1. 'is-sayyid 9ali	7. 'il-waziir
2. 'is-sayyida mooza	8. 'iš-šeex jaasim
3. bu saalim	9. 'id-daxtar saami
4. bu 9ali	10. 'il-mudiir jum9a
5. 'ibraahiim	11. 'il-mu9allim byaat
6. šeexa	12. 'is-sayyid Hamad

Drill 6 *Variable Substitution*

'abi 'a9mal gahwa. 'I want to make (some) coffee.'

1. hiya	11. Hafṣa
2. hum	12. 9eeša
3. čaay	13. 'aana
4. niHin	14. maw9id
5. 'aana	15. huwa
6. hin	16. hum
7. sabt	17. raayHiin
8. mHammad	18. gahwa
9. 9abdaḷḷa	19. hiya
10. šeexa	20. 'intum

Drill 7 *Substitution*

xalln'ašuuf! 'Let me (allow me to) see!'

1. go
2. come
3. come back
4. eat
5. leave
6. hear
7. work
8. speak
9. sleep
10. drink
11. make coffee
12. make tea
13. bring food
14. write Arabic
15. go eat
16. go home

Drill 8 *Translation*

1. I am going to London tomorrow by Middle East Airlines.
2. By the way! Are you going direct or by way of Doha?
3. When you get there, contact my friend by phone.
4. Gee, this is very good. I do not know anybody there.
5. He will take you in his car and show you around the city.
6. They live in a large house which has six rooms.
7. We need another stove. This stove is very old.
8. The refrigerator doesn't work well. Go buy a new one.
9. How old is your house? Is it about ten years old?
10. Just a minute! I want to go to the bathroom.

Drill 9 *Question — Answer*

1. čam wazaara fi bu đ̣abi?
2. 9indak talafoon fi l-beet?
3. ʼinta tištaġil fi ʼay wazaara?
4. tabi tišrab biira?
5. ween il-mudiira mawjuuda?
6. ween iš-šaarja mawjuuda?
7. ʼinta mawjuud il-yoom hini?
8. ween wazaarat il-xaarijiyya?
9. man waziir il-maaliyya?
10. man waziir id-daaxiliyya?
11. ʼinta tištaġil fi l-wazaara?
12. ween daayrat iz-ziraa9a?
13. kam raqam talafoonak?
14. ween wazaarat il-muwaaṣalaat?
15. man waziir il-9adil?
16. haađi daayrat iṣ-ṣiHHa?

UNIT 28

I. TEXT

ʹaana min il-manaama fi l-baHreen. dirast fi l-manaama fi l-madrasa l-ʹibtidaaʹiyya w iθ-θaanawiyya. ba9deen tirakt il-baHreen gabil ʹarba9 siniin u jeet id-dooHa. lamma wiṣalt hini sikant fi šigga fiiha θalaaθ Hijar liʹanni mitzawwij u 9indi 9aayla čibiira.

halHiin ʹaana ʹaskin fi beet gariib min il-baHar. kill yoom ʹil-ʹawlaad yruuHuun ṣoob il-baHar yil9abuun u yisbaHuun. baštaġal mu9allim fi markaz it-tadriib Hagg šarikat šal.

II. TRANSLATION

I am from Manama in Bahrain. I studied in Manama at the elementary school and the secondary school. Later I left Bahrain four years ago and came to Doha. When I arrived here, I lived in an apartment which has three rooms because I ' m married and have a big family.

Now I am living in a house close to the sea. The children go to the sea to play and swim every day. I work as a teacher at Shell Training Center.

III. VOCABULARY

diras	(yidris) he studied
ʹibtidaaʹiyya	elementary, primary
θaanawiyya	secondary

tirak	(yitrik) he left, departed
gabil	(prep.) before; ago
ja	(yiji) he came
lamma	(conj.) when; whenever
wiṣal	(yooṣal) he arrived
sikan	(yiskin) he lived, dwelled
šigga	(šigag) apartment
gariib min	(–iin) close to
baHar	(bHaar) sea
li9ab	(yil9ab) he played
sibaH	(yisbaH) he swam, bathed; he took a shower
markaz	(maraakiz) center
tadriib	training
markaz tadriib	training center

IV. ADDITIONAL VOCABULARY

ṣaff	(ṣfuuf) class, grade
gaṣir	(gṣuur) palace, castle
ba9iid 9an	(–iin) far away from
xeema	(xyaam) tent

V. GRAMMAR

Perfect Tense

In previous lessons we have seen most of the forms and uses of the imperfect tense. This UNIT introduces the other verb tense in GA, the perfect tense. The perfect tense in GA corresponds to the following English tenses: simple past, e.g., **he came**; present perfect, e.g., **he has come**; and past perfect, e.g., **he had come**.

We have seen that the inflectional forms of verbs in the imperfect tense are characterized by prefixes and in some cases also by suffixes. The inflectional forms of verbs in the perfect tense are characterized only by suffixes. There are ten inflectional forms of a perfect-tense verb, corresponding to the person-gender-number categories of the imperfect tense. Below is the complete conjugation of the verb **diras** 'to study' and its suffixes, which are the same for all perfect-tense verbs:

Pronoun	Verb	Meaning	Suffix
huwa	diras	'he studied'	—
hum	drisaw	'they (m.) studied'	—aw
hiya	drisat	'she studied'	—at
hin	drisan	'they (f.) studied'	—an
'inta	dirast	'you (m.s.) studied'	—t
'intum	dirastu	'you (m.p.) studied'	—tu
'inti	dirasti	'you (f.s.) studied'	—ti
'intin	dirastin	'you (f.p.) studied'	—tin
'aana	dirast	'I studied'	—t
niHin	dirasna	'we studied'	—na

Note the following comments on the perfect-tense forms:

a. The forms are built on and derived from the 3rd person singular form of the verb, which is referred to as the stem: **diras** 'he studied'. This stem is used to refer to the verb as a whole, in the same way as the infinitive is used in English. Thus, when we say the verb **diras**, which literally means 'he studied', we refer to what corresponds to the English infinitive 'to study'.

b. Note that the stem vowel **–i–** and the second consonant **–r–** are switched before suffixes beginning with a vowel: **drisaw** 'they (m.) studied', **drisat** 'she studied', and **drisan** 'they (f.) studied', although the forms **dirsaw, dirsat,** and **dirsan** are also used.

c. The first syllable of the first four forms is stressed, while the second syllable of the other forms is stressed because of the **CVCC** sequence: díras → dirást 'He studied → I studied.'

The verbs **tirak** 'he left, departed', **wiṣal** 'he arrived', **sikan** 'he lived, dwelled', and **sibaH** 'he swam' are regular, and thus are conjugated like **diras** 'he studied.' The verb **jaa** 'he came' is irregular. It is a so-called "weak" verb because of the final vowel **–aa**:

huwa	ja	'intum	jeetu
hum	jaw	'inti	jeeti
hiya	jat	'intin	jeetin
hin	jan	'aana	jeet
'inta	jeet	niHin	jeena

From now on only the perfect stems of verbs, with the imperfect forms of the 3rd person masculine singular in parentheses, will be listed in the VOCABULARY or ADDITIONAL VOCABULARY of the lessons.

NOTES ON TEXT

SYSTEM OF EDUCATION

The stages of education in the Gulf states and in most other parts of the Arab World are four: elementary, preparatory, secondary, and university. They correspond, respectively, to the American stages of education: elementary —— six years; preparatory (Junior High) —— three years; secondary (Senior High) —— three years; and university —— four years.

VI. DRILLS

Drill 1 *Transformation:* imperfect → perfect

(Use **'ams** 'yesterday' in place of **baačir** 'tomorrow',) **kill yoom** 'every day', **halHiin** 'now' ... etc.)

1. 'adris 9aṛabi kill yoom.
2. 'atrik iš-šuġul baačir.
3. 'ooṣal il-9een 9ugb saa9a.
4. 'askin fi šigga čibiira.
5. 'asbaH kill yoom.
6. 'adris fi markaz it-tadriib.
7. 'atrik il-beet lamma 'asbaH.
8. 'adris kill yoom saa9ateen.

9. ʹatrik giṭar il-yoom.
10. ʹooṣal il-manaama l-yoom.
11. ʹaskin wiyya ʹubuuy.
12. ʹasbaH iṣ-ṣabaaH.
13. ʹasbaH fi l-baHar.
14. ma ʹadris kill yoom.
15. ma ʹaskin fi šigga.
16. ma ʹaskin ṣoob il-baHar.

Drill 2 *Transformation:* imperfect → perfect

Change the sentence in **Drill 1**, above, to: **ʹinta** ʹyou (m.s.), and then to **ʹinti** ʹyou (f.s.)ʹ.

Drill 3 *Transformation:* imperfect → perfect

(Use past time expressions, e.g., **ʹams** ʹyesterdayʹ, **gabil ʹams** ʹthe day before yesterdayʹ, **gabil (sana, šahar, subuu9, yoomeen,** etc.) ʹ(a year, a month, a week, two days) agoʹ, etc.

1. ʹinta tidris fi l-leel.
2. ʹinta titrik šuġlak baačir?
3. ʹinta tooṣal il-yoom
4. ween tiskin?
5. ʹinta tisbaH fi l-baHar baačir?
6. ʹinta tidris fi l-jaami9a?
7. ʹinta titrik bu ḏ̣abi baačir?

8. 'inta tooṣal bi s-sayyaara?
9. 'inta tidris ihnaak halHiin?
10. leeš titrik iš-šuġul?
11. ween tidris halHiin?
12. 'inta tiskin ṣoob il-baHar?
13. 'inta tisbaH kill yoom?
14. 'inta tiskin wiyya 'ahlak?
15. 'inta tidris 'ingiliizi?
16. 'inta tisbaH iṣ-ṣabaaH?

Drill 4 *Transformation:* imperfect → perfect

Change the sentences in **Drill 3**, above, to; **'intin** and then to **niHin**.

Drill 5 *Double Substitution*

'il-walad iṣ-ṣaġiir fi ṣ-ṣaff **il-'awwal** w ič-čibiir fi ṣ-ṣaff **ir-raabi9**.

'The young(er) boy is in the **first** class (grade), and the old(er) one is in the **fourth** class (grade).'

1. second – third
2. third – first
3. first – fourth
4. fourth – fifth
5. fifth – sixth
6. sixth – first
7. first – sixth
8. sixth – second

9. second – third
10. third – fourth
11. fifth – second
12. fourth – fourth
13. fourth – first
14. first – sixth
15. third – fifth

Drill 6 *Chain – Cued*

T : 2 – 3

S_1: ’iṣ-ṣaġiir fi ṣ-ṣaff iθ-θaani fi l-madrasa l-’ibtidaa’iyya.
’The young(er) one is in the second class in the elementary school.

S_2: w ič-čibiir fi ṣ-ṣaff iθ-θaaliθ fi l-madrasa θ-θaanawiyya.
’And the old(er) one is in the third class in the secondary school.

Use cues from **Drill 5**, above.

Drill 7 *Variable Substitution*

sikant fi šigga fiiha θalaaθ Hijar.
’I lived in a three-room apartment.’

1. ’inta
2. xams
3. ’arba9
4. beet
5. ’inti
6. Hijrateen
7. Hijra bas
8. imperfect
9. šigga
10. ’intin
11. perfect
12. sitt

13. beet
14. 'aana
15. Hijra bas
16. šigga
17. negative
18. imperfect
19. niHin
20. 'inta
21. perfect
22. 'inti
23. 'inta
24. 'aana

Drill 8 *Substitution*

yruuHuun ihnaak **yil9abuun u yisbaHuun.**
'They go there to **play and swim.**'

1. play and have a good time
2. play cards
3. talk and drink coffee
4. eat and drink
5. study and learn
6. work and get money
7. pay money and get the car
8. buy rice and meat
9. swim and play
10. talk and play cards
11. take the money and return
12. take the bus and go home

Drill 9 *Substitution*

haađa markaz it-tadriib Hagg **šarikat šal.**
'This is the **Shell Company** Training Center.'

1. ADMA Company	7. ARAMCO Company
2. BP Company	8. Qatar Petroleum Company
3. Phillips Company	9. Kuwait Oil Company
4. the government	10. Iraq Petroleum Co.
5. Ministry of Education	11. Ministry of Public Works
6. Department of Education	12. Ministry of Agriculture

Drill 10 *Transformation:* Conjugation

huwa yabi yisbaH. 'He wants to swim (bathe, take a shower).'

1. hum	9. huwa
2. hin	10. 'intin
3. 'aana	11. hin
4. niHin	12. niHin
5. hiya	13. 'aana
6. 'inta	14. hum
7. 'inti	15. 'inta
8. 'intum	16. 'inti

Drill 11 *Chain – Cued*

T : 'inta sikant fi šigga čibiira?
'Did you live in a big apartment?'

S_1 : 'inta sikant fi šigga čibiira?

S_2 : 'ii na9am. 'aana sikant fi šigga čibiira.
'Yes, I lived in a big apartment.'

1. dirast 9aṛabi l-yoom?
2. dirast faṛansi?
3. tirakt iš-šuġul?
4. tirakt il-jaami9a?
5. wiṣalt il-yoom?
6. wiṣalt ʼams?
7. sikant fi xeema?
8. sikant ṣoob il-baHar?
9. sibaHt fi l-baHar?
10. sibaHt iṣ-ṣabaaH?
11. dirast fi ʼamriika?
12. tirakt iš-šarika?
13. sikant fi gaṣir?
14. wiṣalt min zamaan?

Drill 12 *Transformation:* positive → negative

Change the answers in **Drill 11**, above, into the negative.

Drill 13 *Translation*

1. I can't talk on the telephone because the line is busy.
2. He has been trying to reach me for two hours.
3. They go there to play cards, talk, and have a good time.
4. What time do you (f.s.) go to work? About 8:00 a.m.
5. Who is speaking? Just a minute!
6. Wrong number! Dial the number again!
7. I ' m sorry he isn't here. Would you like to leave him a message?
8. Give me the line, please! He has another line. There's no answer.
9. Let me see. He is busy all day tomorrow. Is (day) after tomorrow O.K.?

10. The Ministry of Education, the Ministry of Agriculture, and the Ministry of Public Works are big ministries. I work in the Ministry of Foreign Affairs.
11. Where did you (m.s.) live two years ago?
12. When I arrived here, I lived in an apartment by the sea.
13. They (m.) played cards, swam, and left at about 6:00 p.m.
14. We did not study in the university; we studied in the secondary school for three years.

UNIT 29

I. TEXT

ʹams fi l-leel ʹaana w sadiigi saalim riHna ʹila maṭ9am ʹiiwaan lajil naakil. kinna juu9aaniin u 9aṭšaaniin waajid. ʹiṭ-ṭaqs kaan Haarr kaθiir. ʹakalna marag u 9eeš u laHam. ʹaana šribt biira w rifiiji saalim širib baarid. 9ugb il-ʹakil ʹakalna baglaawa. ba9deen šribna gahwa bdiwiyya w ba9deen riHna is-siinama. kaan fii filim 9aṛabi zeen ʹasma "9antar u 9abla." ʹaana difa9t Hsaab il-maṭ9am u saalim difa9 θaman it-tađaakir. 9ugb is-siinama sirna l-beet.

II. TRANSLATION

Yesterday in the evening I and my friend, Salim, went to Iwan Restaurant so as to eat. We were very hungry and thirsty. The weather was very hot. We had broth, rice, and meat. I drank beer, and my friend, Salim, drank a soft drink. After the food, we ate baklava. Then we drank Bedouin coffee and later, we went to the movies. There was a good Arabic film called "Antar and Abla." I had paid the restaurant bill, and Salim paid the price of the tickets. After the movies, we went home.

III. VOCABULARY

raaH	(yruuH) he went
lajil	so that, in order that
kaan	(ykuun) he was
kaan fii	there was

juu9aan	(–iin) hungry
9aṭšaan	(–iin) thirsty
širib	(yišrab) he drank
rifiij	(rafaayij) companion, friend
marag	meat broth; gravy
baglaawa	pastry made of puff paste with honey and walnuts or pistachios
bdiwi	(badu) Bedouin; (adj.) Bedouin
siinama	(–aat) cinema, movie, theater
filim	('aflaam) film, movie
difa9	(yidfa9) he paid
θaman	('aθmaan) cost, value
saar	(ysiir) he went; he walked

IV. ADDITIONAL VOCABULARY

gaal	(yguul) he said
maaḏ̣i	(adj.) past; last (e.g., month)
9aam	('a9waam) year (syn. sana)
'is-subuu9 il-maaḏ̣i	last week
'iš-šahar il-maaḏ̣i	last month
'il-9aam il-maaḏ̣i	last year
'is-sabt il-maaḏ̣i	last Saturday

V. GRAMMAR

1. Perfect Tense

In UNIT 28, we discussed the perfect tense of sound verbs such as **diras** 'to study'. In this UNIT we have three more sound verbs: **difa9** 'he paid', **širib** 'he drank', and **'akal** or **kal** 'he ate'. **difa9** is regular and is conjugated like **diras**. The other two are irregular. Below is the conjugation of **širib**:

huwa širib	hin šriban	'inti šribti
hum šribaw	'inta šribt	'intin šribtin
hiya šribat	'intum šribtu	'aana šribt
	niHin šribna	

The verb **kal** 'he ate' has the variant **'akal** which is characteristic of most triradical verbs that have an initial '– (hamzated verbs):

huwa	(kal) 'akal	'intum	(kaleetu) 'akaltu
hum	(kalaw) 'akalaw	'inti	(kaleeti) 'akalti
hiya	(kalat) 'akalat	'intin	(kaleetin) 'akaltin
hin	(kalan) 'akalan	'aana	(kaleet) 'akalt
'inta	(kaleet) 'akalt	niHin	(kaleena) 'akalna

The first form **kal** is more commonly used. The occurrence of the less frequent variant –– **'akal** –– is due to the influence od MSA and the speech of Arab immigrants in the Gulf.

There are four more verbs in this lesson: **raaH** 'he went', **kaan** 'he was', **saar** 'he went; he walked', and **gaal** 'he said'. This class of verbs is known as hollow verbs; they are characterized by the long vowel **–aa–** followed by a final consonant.

These verbs have two stems: **CaaC–**, which is used with the third person endings, and **CiC–**, which is used with the endings of the other persons. Below is the conjugation of **raaH** 'to go':

huwa	raaH	hin	raaHan	'inti	riHti
hum	raaHaw	'inta	riHt	'intin	riHtin
hiya	raaHat	'intum	riHtu	'aana	riHt
		niHin	riHna		

(Drills 1 - 11)

2. The Conjunction **lajil**

lajil as a conjunction introduces a clause; it means 'so that, in order that':

riHna lajil naakil.	'We went so that we might eat.' 'We went to eat.'
yruuH il-madrasa lajil yidris.	'He goes to school so that he might study.
yruuH il-madrasa lajil yidris.	'He goes to school to study.'

lajil can take suffixed pronouns in which case it means 'for the sake of': **lajilna** 'for our sake,' **lajla** 'for his (its) sake, etc.'

3. kaan fii 'there was, there were'

Note that **fii** with the stressed long vowel **ii** means 'there is, there are'. The perfect of **fii** is **kaan fii** 'there was, there were'. **kaan** in this construction is invariable, i.e., not inflected for gender or number:

kaan fii filim.	'There was a movie.'
kaan fii 'aflaam.	'There were movies.'

The negatives of **fii** and **kaan fii** are **ma fii** and **ma kaan fii** :

ma fii filim.	'There's no movie.'
ma kaan fii filim.	'There was no movie.'
ma kaan fii banaat.	'There were no girls.'

VI. DRILLS

Drill 1 *Transformation:* imperfect → perfect

Use past time expressions, e.g., **'is-subuu9, 'iš-šahar, 'il-9aam, 'is-sabt ('il-maaḏ̣i)** '(last) week, month, year, Saturday' in place of the present time expressions.

1. yidfa9 fluus baačir.
2. yruuH il-madrasa kill yoom.
3. yidfa9 θaman it-taḏaakir.
4. yidfa9 li-Hsaab.
5. ysiir il-beet halHiin.
6. yidris 'ingiliizi kill yoom.
7. yitrik landan baačir.
8. yooṣal dbayy il-yoom.
9. yiskin fi gaṣir jadiid.
10. yisbaH fi l-baHar.
11. yaakil fi l-maṭ9am.
12. yišrab gahwa bdiwiyya.
13. yidfa9 θaman is-sayyaara.
14. ysiir il-maṭaar 9ugub saa9a.

15. huwa juu9aan halHiin.
16. huwa 9aṭšaan min zamaan.

Drill 2 *Transformation:* imperfect → perfect

Change the sentences in **Drill 1,** above to **hiya,** then to **hin.**

Drill 3 *Transformation:* imperfect → perfect

1. niHin nidfa9 li-Hsaab.
2. ʼiṭ-ṭamaaṭ raxiiṣ il-yoom.
3. hum juu9aaniin waajid.
4. ma fii filim zeen il-yoom.
5. ʼaana ʼaruuH il-wazaara baačir.
6. hin yišrabin u yaaklin.
7. ʼaana ʼaruuH il-baHar il-yoom.
8. hum 9indahum šuġul baačir.
9. ʼil-hawa zeen il-yoom.
10. hiya tišrab čaay 9ugb il-ʼakil.
11. ʼinta taakil simač kill yoom?
12. huwa yguul 9inda fluus.
13. huwa ma yruuH iš-šuġul il-yoom.
14. ʼinti tišrabiin biira?
15. ʼinta tiskin ihnaak?
16. huwa yiskin fi gaṣir.

Drill 4 *Chain – Cued*

T :	raaH il-madrasa?	'Did he go to school?'
S_1 :	raaH il-madrasa?	'Did he go to school?'
S_2 :	la. ma raaH.	'No, he didn't go.'

1. kaan hini 'ams?
2. šribat biira?
3. difa9t θaman il-kutub?
4. riHti is-siinama?
5. kintum juu9aaniin?
6. sikantin fi šigga?
7. dirsaw 'ingiliizi?
8. sibHan fi l-baHar?
9. kint 9aṭšaan?
10. riHna gabil sana?
11. širib baarid?
12. sibHat wiyyaakum?
13. tirakt iš-šuġul?
14. 'akalti baglaawa?

Drill 5 *Transformation:*

Negative Command → negative statement

T :	la truuH is-siinama!	'Don't go to the movies!'
S :	ma raaH is-siinama.	'He didn't go to the movies.'

1. la tidris kill yoom!
2. la titrik šuġlak!
3. la tiskini hini!
4. la tisbaHuun kill yoom!
5. la truuH il-maṭ9am kill yoom!
6. la taaklin simač kill yoom!
7. la truuH ihnaak!
8. la tišrab wiski kill yoom!
9. la tidfa9 li-Hsaab!
10. la truuHi s-suug!
11. la tiskinuun fi šigga!
12. la tisbaH waajid!
13. la taakil waajid!
14. la tguul ma fii!

Drill 6 *Chain – Cued*

T : ministry

S_1 : man kaan fi l-wazaara? 'Who was in the Ministry?'

T : director

S_2 : 'il-mudiir kaan fi l-wazaara.
'The Director was in the Ministry.'

1. Manama – engineer
2. center – the Shaikh
3. tent – Bedouin
4. class – students
5. palace – Shaikh Jasim
6. sea – boys
7. movies – she
8. work – coolie
9. department - secretary
10. palace – minister
11. street – employees
12. home – my father
13. living room – the shaikhs
14. kitchen – my mother

Drill 7 *Variable Substitution*

huwa kaan ihnaak yoom is-sabt. 'He was there on Saturday.'

1. 'aana
2. 'iš-šyuux
3. on Friday
4. at 1:30 p.m.
5. 'il-banaat
6. on Thursday
7. at 5:15 p.m.
8. 'inta?
9. on Monday
10. at 9:45 a.m.
11. 'inti
12. huwa
13. negative
14. on Tuesday
15. at 12:00 noon
16. positive
17. on Wednesday
18. on Sunday

Drill 8 *Variable Substitution*

ma yidris halHiin. 'He isn't studying now.'

1. 'ams
2. baačir
3. kill yoom
4. 'ams iṣ-ṣabaaH
5. 'ams fi l-leel
6. hum
7. 'intin
8. gabl ams
9. kill yoom
10. niHin
11. 'ams 9ugb iđ̣-đ̣uhr
12. 'inta
13. gabil subuu9
14. baačir il-masa
15. gabil šahar
16. 'iš-šahar il-maađ̣i
17. 'is-subuu9 il-maađ̣i
18. 'il-9aam il-maađ̣i
19. 'il-xamiis il-maađ̣i
20. gabl ams
21. hin

Drill 9 *Questions* (based on TEXT)

1. man saar il-maṭ9am 'ams?
2. 'ay maṭ9am?
3. leeš riHna l-maṭ9am?
4. kinna juu9aaniin?
5. kinna 9aṭšaaniin šwayy?
6. čeef kaan il-hawa?
7. šu kaleena?
8. šu šribt 'aana?

9. sadiigi širib biira ba9ad?
10. šu 'akalna 9ugb il-'akil?
11. šribna gahwa 9aṛabiyya?
12. šu 'asm il-filim?
13. man difa9 li-Hsaab?
14. man difa9 θaman it-taðaakir?

Drill 10 *Transformation:* singular → plural

1. kint juu9aan waajid.
2. huwa diras 9aṛabi.
3. 'inta šribt biira?
4. 'inti wiṣalti l-yoom?
5. 'aana sikant fi šigga.
6. hiya tiskin fi gaṣir.
7. haaða l-filim zeen.
8. huwa difa9 li-fluus.
9. hiya ma kaanat ihni.
10. ma kaan fii filim zeen.
11. ma kaanat juu9aana.
12. li-bdiwi gawi.
13. haaði madrasa zeena.
14. haaða markaz it-tadriib.
15. 'aruuH ṣoob il-baHar 'al9ab u 'asbaH.
16. lamma 'ooṣal 'aštiri beet.

Drill 11 *Translation*

1. When I get a job, I will buy a new car.
2. When he went there, he had a beer.
3. I have to see that film when it comes to Abu Dhabi.
4. We went to the movies and saw "Lawrence of Arabia".
5. Last year I went to Cairo and had a good time there.

6. When he got here, he went to eat because he was very hungry.
7. Give me the line, please! I can't because he has another line.
8. I have been trying to reach you for two hours, and the phone was busy.
9. This is the Ministry of Public Works. You have the wrong number.
10. I am sorry! What's his number? I don't know. Call the operator.

Drill 12 *Translation*

1. We went to see the movie.
2. They went to the restaurant last night in order to eat kabob.
3. She came here in order to see the school.
4. I went to Iwan Restaurant to have a beer because I was very thirsty.
5. Last week we went to Bahrain in order to have a good time.
6. Last year I traveled to Kuwait to see my brother.
7. She goes to the fish market every day to buy fish.
8. He did all of this for the sake of his country.
9. They are studying Arabic so that they might be able to speak Arabic well.
10. He is a very good man. I know that he had done all of this for our sake.

UNIT 30

I. TEXT

mooza : ʹil-Hamdilla 9ala s-salaama ya faaṭma!

faaṭma : ʹaḷḷa ysallimč.

mooza : čeef Haalič?

faaṭma : ṭayyba l-Hamdu lillaah.

mooza : ween činti? min zamaan ma šiftič min gabil sabi9 siniin.

faaṭma : ʹaḷḷa ysallimč xaḷḷaṣt il-madrasa θ-θaanawiyya gabil sitt sanawaat u ba9deen Haṣṣalt bi9θa 9ala Hsaab il-Hukuuma w riHt amriika.

mooza : weeš ta9allamti hnaak?

faaṭma : ta9allamt ingiliizi w tarbiya. ba9dma Haṣṣalt iš-šahaada rija9t il-baHreen u darrast fi daar il-mu9al-limaat muddat sanateen.

mooza : w ba9deen jeeti hni?

faaṭma : ʹii na9am. ṣaarli hni tagriib sanateen.

mooza : ween tištaġliin halHiin?

faaṭma : halHiin baštaġil fi l-ʹiðaa9a fi qism il-ʹingiliizi.

II. TRANSLATION

Moza : Welcome back, Fatima!

Fatima : God protect you.

Moza : How are you?

Fatima : I'm fine. Thank you.

Moza : Where were you? I haven't seen you for seven years.

Fatima : God protect you! I finished the secondary school six years ago and then I got a government scholarship and went to America.

Moza : What did you learn there?

Fatima : I learned English and education. After I had obtained a degree, I returned to Bahrain and taught at the Women's Teacher Training College for two years.

Moza : And you came here later?

Fatima : Yes. I've been here for two years.

Moza : Where are you working now?

Fatima : I am working now in the Broadcasting Station in the English section.

III. VOCABULARY

salaama	safety
sallam	(ysallim) he protected
čaan	(ykuun) he was (var. **kaan**)
xaḷḷaṣ	(yxaḷḷiṣ) he finished
Haṣṣal	(yHaṣṣil) he obtained, got; found
bi9θa	(–aat) scholarship; fellowship
t9allam	(yit9allam) he learned
šahaada	(–aat) degree, certificate
darras	(ydarris) he taught
daar	(duur) home, house

daar il-mu9allimaat	Women's Teacher Training College
tagriib	about, approximately
štaġal	(yištaġil) he worked
'iðaa9a	broadcasting station; broadcasting
qisim	section, part

IV. ADDITIONAL VOCABULARY

čayyak	(yčayyik) he checked
tasallaf	(yitsallaf) he borrowed
bannad	(ybannid) he closed, shut
9arras	(y9arris) he got married
tkallam	(yitkallam) he spoke, talked

V. GRAMMAR

1. Perfect Tense

rija9 'he returned' is conjugated like **diras** 'he studied' (UNIT 28). **čaan** (var. **kaan**) 'he was' and **šaaf** 'he saw' are hollow verbs, and are conjugated like **raaH** 'he went' (UNIT 29).

The verbs **xaḷḷaṣ** 'he finished', **Haṣṣal** 'he got, obtained; found', **darras** 'he taught', etc., are characterized by a double medial consonant. Their conjugation is quite regular:

huwa	xaḷḷaṣ	hin	xaḷḷaṣan	'inti	xaḷḷaṣti
hum	xaḷḷaṣaw	'inta	xaḷḷaṣt	'intin	xaḷḷaṣtin
hiya	xaḷḷaṣat	'intum	xaḷḷaṣtu	'aana	xaḷḷaṣt
		niHin	xaḷḷaṣna		

štaġal 'he worked' is regular. Remember to drop the (second) stem vowel –**a**– when the suffixes –**aw**, –**at**, and –**an** are added: štaġal + **aw** → štaġlaw.

(Drills 8, 9, 10, 12)

Note the use of **min zamaan** 'a long time ago' in a negative sentence to mean '——— for a long time':

ma šiftič min zamaan.	'I have not seen you (f.s.) for a long time.'

min zamaan can precede the negative perfect for emphasis. Examples:

min zamaan ma ja.	'He has not come for a long time.'
min zamaan ma riHt id-dooHa.	'I have not been to Doha for a long time.'
min zamaan ma Haṣṣalt ziyaada.	'I have not had an increase (raise) for a long time.'

With the positive perfect **min zamaan** means 'a long time ago'.

min zamaan jat.	'She came a long time ago.'
9arras min zamaan.	'He got married a long time ago.'

(Drill 4)

2. Perfect Tense with Suffixed Pronouns

When a suffixed pronoun is added to a perfect-tense verb, it functions as the object of that verb. The verb may undergo certain stem changes, as follows:

a. When a suffixed pronoun is added to a form with a final vowel, the final vowel becomes long:

dirasti	'You (f.s.) studied.'
dirastii	'You (f.s.) studied it (m.).'
dirastu	'You (m.p.) studied.'
dirastuu	'You (m.p.) studied it (m.).'
dirasna	'We studied.'
dirasnaa	'We studied it.'

Note the shift in stress : diŕasti → dirastii.

b. The third-person masculine plural form ends with –**aw**, e.g., **drisaw** 'They (m.) studied.' When a suffixed pronoun is added. –**aw** changes to –**oo**, which becomes a vowel stem. The third-person feminine plural form is not used: the masculine form is used instead.

drisaw	'They (m.) studied.
drisoo	'They (m. or f.) studied it (m.).'
šribaw	'They (m.) drank.
šribooha	'They (m. or f.) drank it (f.).'
šaafaw	'They (m.) saw.
šaafoona	'They (m. or f.) saw us.'

Note the shift in stress : dríṡaw → drisóo.

VI. DRILLS

Drill 1 *Chain*

S_1: 'il-Hamdilla 9ala s-salaama ya...'. 'Welcome back, ...:'

S_2: 'aḷḷa ysallimk (ysallimč).'

Drill 2 *Chain*

S_1:	čeef Haalak?	'How are you (m.)?'
S_2:	ṭayyib il-Hamdu lillaah.	'Fine, thanks to God.'

Drill 3 *Chain – Cued*

S_1:	ween čint?	'Where were you (m.)?'
T :	at home	
S_2:	čint fi l-beet.	'I was at home.'

1. at the training center
2. at the ministry
3. at school
4. in class
5. at work
6. at the movies
7. with my friend
8. with šeex xaliifa
9. in the apartment
10. on the telephone
11. in the department
12. in the restaurant
13. at the garage
14. at the gas station
15. in the palace
16. with my family
17. at the market
18. in the Min. of Ag.

Drill 4 *Completion*

ma šiftič min zamaan. 'I haven't seen you (f.) for a long time.'

1. I haven't eaten kabob
2. She hasn't had a beer
3. We haven't gone to Beirut
4. I haven't had an increase
5. They (m.) haven't eaten baklawa
6. You (f.s.) haven't been to the movies
7. You (m.s.) haven't gone swimming
8. You (m.p.) haven't played cards
9. You (f.p.) haven't lived here
10. He hasn't had whiskey
11. They (m.) haven't paid the money
12. They (f.) haven't had a good time
13. We haven't tried this bank
14. I haven't left Bahrain

Drill 5 *Repetition*

xal̤l̤aṣ il-madrasa w Haṣṣal bi9θa. 'He finished school and got a scholarship.'

1. xal̤l̤aṣt – Haṣṣalt
2. xal̤l̤aṣti – Haṣṣalti
3. xal̤l̤aṣtu – Haṣṣaltu
4. xal̤l̤aṣtin – Haṣṣaltin
5. xal̤l̤aṣaw – Haṣṣalaw
6. xal̤l̤aṣan – Haṣṣalan
7. xal̤l̤aṣna – Haṣṣalna
8. xal̤l̤aṣat – Haṣṣalat
9. xal̤l̤aṣ – Haṣṣal
10. xal̤l̤aṣt – Haṣṣalt

Drill 6 *Double Substitution*

t9allam f **amriika** w **darras** fi d-dooHa.
'He learned (studied) in America and taught in Doha.'

1. 'ingiltara – dbayy
2. maṣir – 'il-baHreen
3. libnaan – suuriyya
4. 'amriika – bu ðabi
5. li-9raag – liibya
6. 'il-baHreen – giṭar
7. faṛansa – beruut
8. 'il-hind – 'iš-šaarja
9. li-9raag – tuunis
10. 'is-suudaan – li-kweet
11. 'il-'ardun – 'is-su9uudiyya
12. kanada – 9ajmaan
13. landan – 'id-dooHa
14. beruut – 'il-manaama
15. giṭar – raas il-xeema

Drill 7 *Double Substitution*

a. t9allamt f amriika w darrast fi d-dooHa.

b. t9allamt f amriika w darrasat fi d-dooHa.

Use Substitutions from **Drill** 6,above.

Drill 8 *Transformation:* imperfect → perfect

1. huwa yxaḷḷis iš-šuġul baačir.
2. hiya tHaṣṣil bi9θa 9ugub sana.
3. hum yHaṣṣluun fluus min il-bank.
4. 'aana 'axaḷḷiṣ il-madrasa 9ugub sana.
5. 'inta txaḷḷiṣ iš-šuġul il-yoom?
6. hiya tHaṣṣil šahaada min ihni.

7. huwa ydarris fi daar il-mu9allimiin.
8. hiya tidarris fi daar il-mu9allimaat.
9. hiya tit9allam ihni.
10. niHin nit9allam fi l-madrasa.
11. 'inti tit9allamiin faṛansi.
12. 'aana 'adarris tarbiya.
13. hum yidarrsuun fi li-kweet.
14. 'inta taji hni kill yoom?
15. 'aana 'aji š-šuġul iṣ-ṣabaaH.
16. huwa fi l-'iđ̄aa9a.

Drill 9 *Variable Substitution*

huwa tasallaf fluus u 9arras.
'He borrowed some money and got married.'

1. 'aana
2. 'inta
3. question
4. 'intum
5. hum
6. statement
7. negative
8. huwa
9. Haṣṣal
10. 'aana
11. hum
12. positive
13. trikaw
14. 'intum
15. 'inta
16. niHin
17. huwa
18. 'aana
19. t9allamt
20. dirast

Drill 10 *Variable Substitution*

Faaṭma darrasat fi daar il-mu9allimaat.
'Fatima taught at the Women's Training College.'

1. šeexa
2. saalim
3. Hasan
4. negative
5. 'aana
6. niHin
7. positive
8. 'inti
9. question
10. tarbiya
11. 'ingiliizi
12. 9aṛabi
13. statement
14. hum
15. 'il-mu9allimiin
16. tarbiya
17. 'il-jaami9a
18. 'ingiliizi
19. 'il-madrasa
20. 'iθ-θaanawiyya

Drill 11 *Completion*

huwa ja lajil .... 'He came in order to ...'

1. take money from the bank
2. finish his work
3. work and get (some) money
4. obtain a degree in English
5. obtain a degree in Education
6. borrow money and get married
7. speak with šeex zaayid
8. check the tires and the battery

9. close the window
10. close the door
11. work in the Qatar Broadcasting Station
12. eat kabob and kubba
13. see this film
14. drink Bedouin coffee

Drill 12 *Transformation:* imperfect → perfect

1. ʼinta tiskin fi šigga?
2. huwa fi š-šuġul il-yoom.
3. ʼinta juu9aan halHiin?
4. hiya 9aṭšaana halHiin?
5. ʼaana ʼadris ʼingiliizi.
6. hum yisbaHuun fi l-baHar.
7. niHin nišrab gahwa bdiwiyya.
8. huwa yidfa9 Hsaab il-maṭ9am?
9. hin yitrikin baačir.
10. huwa mawjuud ihni l-yoom.
11. ma fii jawaab.
12. ma fii šuġul il-yoom.
13. lamma yooṣal yHaṣṣil šuġul.
14. ʼaana ʼadris fi markaz it-tadriib.
15. hiya fi l-madrasa l-ʼibtidaaʼiyya.
16. hum yruuHuun beruut kill sana.

UNIT 31

REVIEW

DRILLS

Drill 1 *Aural Comprehension*

Listen twice to the following passage on tape and then give complete answers to the questions below.

9indi sadiig 'asma ṣaaliH min il-9een fi bu ḏ̣abi. sadiigi ṣaaliH mitzawwij u 9inda θalaaθ 9yaal: walad waaHid u binteen. ṣaaliH 9umra 'aθneen u θalaaθiin sana walaakin zawjata šeexa 9umraha 9išriin sana bas. šeexa ma 9indaha šuġul. hiya fi l-beet. ṣaaliH yištaġil kuuli wiyya šarika 'ingiliiziyya. yHaṣṣil xamsimyat dirhim fi š-šahar bas.

'ubu ṣaaliH u 'umma yiskinuun wiyya ṣaaliH u zawjitah w 9yaala. 'il-beet muub kabiir waajid; fii θalaaθ Hijar noom bas: Hijra Hagg ṣaaliH u Hurmita, w iθ-θaanya Hagg li-9yaal w iθ-θaalθa Hagg 'ubu ṣaaliH u 'umma. ma fii maylis wala ġassaala fi l-beet. fii θallaaja w fii Hammaam waaHid bas.

1. šu 'asim sadiigi?
2. min ween ṣaaliH?
3. čam walad 9inda?
4. čam 9umur ṣaaliH?
5. šu 'asim Hurmita?
6. 9umraha θalaaθiin sana?

7. weeš tištaġil šeexa?
8. weeš yištaġil ṣaaliH?
9. yaaxiđ̣ fluus waajid?
10. 'inta čam taaxiđ̣ fi š-šahar?
11. man yiskin wiyya ṣaaliH u 9aayilta?
12. beet ṣaaliH čibiir?
13. čam Hijra fii?
14. čam Hijra fii Hagg li-9yaal.
15. fii θallaaja w ġassaala?
16. čam Hammaam fii?

Drill 2 *Reproduction*

Reproduce the aural comprehension passage in **Drill 1** with the following key words:

ṣaaliH ———	bu đ̣abi ———	9yaal ———	θalaaθiin
9išriin ———	šeexa ———	beet ———	kuuli
dirham ———	beet ———	Hijar ———	θallaaja

Drill 3 *Aural Comprehension*

Listen twice to the following passage on tape and then indicate whether the statements below are true or false. If the statement is false, correct it.

'aana baHreeni min il-manaama. dirast ingiliizi fi daar il-mu9allimiin sanateen. Haṣṣalt iš-šahaada l-9aam il-maađ̣i. 'aana mitzawwij il-Hamdu lillaah. Haṣṣalt šuġul mu9allim fi bu ḏ̣abi. 'aana ma riHt bu ḏ̣abi min zamaan. riHna 'aana w Hurmiti l-maṭaar. difa9t θaman it-taḏaakir bas čaan 9indana jinaṭ waajid. difa9t tagriib 9išriin diinaar baHreeni Hagg iz-ziyaada w diinaareen ḏ̣ariiba Hagg il-maṭaar. tirakna l-maṭaar u wiṣalna bu ḏ̣abi 9ugub nuṣṣ saa9a. bu ḏ̣abi 'aḷḷa ysallimk gariiba min il-baHreen. 9indi rifiij fi bu ḏ̣abi. činna xuṭṭaar 9inda. sikanna wiyyaa w wiyya 9aayilta šahar waaHid u ba9deen Haṣṣalna beet min il-Hukuuma. 'il-beet fii kill šayy: θallaaja w ġassaala w kanabaat u karaasi w kirfaayaat. 'il-beet ṣaġiir walaakin niHin ma nibġa beet čibiir li'an ma 9indana 9yaal u halna ma yiskinuun wiyyaana.

'il-jum9a l-maaḏ̣i riHna 'aana w Hurmiti w rifiiji w 9aayilta ṣoob il-baHar. li9abna w sibaHna w ba9deen riHna n-naadi lajil naakil u nistaanis. 'akalna simač u šribna biira. rifiiji difa9 li-fluus. 9ugb il-'akil riHna s-siinama 9ala Hsaabi 'aana. čaan fii filim 9aṛabi. 'aana min zamaan ma šift filim 9aṛabi. yamkin inta šift aflaam 9aṛabi. 'il-filim čaan zeen. li-9yaal staanasaw waajid min il-filim. 9ugb is-siinama činna ta9baaniin waajid. sirna l-beet u nimna li'an činna ta9baaniin waajid. li-9yaal naamaw killiš zeen haḏiič il-leela.

1. dirast ingiliizi fi l-jaami9a fi l-manaama.
2. Haṣṣalt iš-šahaada gabil sana.
3. 'aana mitzawwij u 9indi 9aayla čibiira.
4. ṣaarli 'aštaġil fi bu ḏ̣abi sanateen.
5. 'aana w Hurmiti riHna bu ḏ̣abi bi s-sayyaara.
6. min il-manaama 'ila bu ḏ̣abi tagriib nuṣṣ saa9a bi s-sayyaara.
7. difa9t 9išriin diinaar Hagg iz-ziyaada w diinaareen ḏ̣ariiba.

8. sikanna wiyya rifiiji w 9aayilta sana waHda.
9. Haṣṣalt beet min il-Hukuuma 9ugub šahar waaHid bas.
10. hali w 'ahil Hurmiti yiskinuun wiyyaana fi l-beet.
11. riHna wiyya rifiiji w 9aayilta l-baHar gabil subuu9.
12. li9abna w sibaHna w riHna s-siinama.
13. 'akalna 9eeš u laHam u šribna čaay fi n-naadi.
14. rifiiji difa9 θaman it-tađaakir w il-'akil kaan 9ala Hsaabi.
15. šifna filim 9aṛabi w čaan il-filim zeen.
16. 9ugub il-filim riHna beet rifiiji w li9abna warag.

Drill 4 *Reproduction*

Reproduce the aural comprehension passage in **Drill 3**, above, with the help of the following key words:

baHreeni ———	'ingiliizi ———	šahaada ———	mu9allim
mitzawwij ———	raaH ———	ṭayyaara ———	jinaṭ
đ̣ariiba ———	tađaakir ———	nuṣṣ saa9a ———	rifiij
Haṣṣal ———	ṣaġiir ———	θallaaja ———	baHar
naadi ———	simač ———	siinama ———	Hsaab
θaman ———	siinama ———	9yaal ———	naam

Note to Teacher :

Ask individual students to tell short stories or describe events of daily occurrence. Members of the class are encouraged to ask questions or comment on the stories told or the events described.

UNIT 32

I. TEXT

muršid : weeš fiik ya ṣaaliH? mariiḏ̣?

ṣaaliH : la muub mariiḏ̣. ta9baan waajid.

muršid : 'ixiḏ ruxṣa! saafir 'ila beruut 'aw il-qaahira walla landan. ruuH twannas!

ṣaaliH : 9adil! 'aḷḷa ysallimk 'aana gaddamt ṭalab Hagg 'ijaaza. il-mudiir laazim ywaafig.

muršid : 'aguul! 'il-mudiir xooš rayyaal. yHibb ysaa9id kill waaHid. huwa saa9adni l-9aam il-maaḏ̣i. Haṣṣalt ziyaada. 'aana mit'akkid 'inna raayiH ywaafig.

ṣaaliH : huwa gaal li ma 9inda maani9.

muršid : ween raayiH tsaafir?

ṣaaliH : 'il-qaahira nšaaḷḷa.

muršid : wiyya jamaa9a?

ṣaaliH : la bruuHi. čiḏi 'aHsan. 'aana saafart il-qaahira ṣ-ṣeef il-maaḏ̣i ba9ad.

II. TRANSLATION

Murshid: What's wrong with you, Salih? Sick?

Salih : No, not sick. I am very tired.

Murshid: Take leave! Travel to Beirut, or Cairo, or London. Go have a good time!

Salih : True. (God protect you.) I submitted a request for leave. The director has to approve (it).

Murshid: By the way! The director is a good man. He likes to help everyone. He helped me last year. I got an increase (raise). I 'm sure he will approve (it).

Salih : He told me that he had no objection.

Murshid: Where are you going to travel?

Salih : To Cairo, God willing.

Murshid: With a group of people?

Salih : No, by myself. It's better this way. I traveled to Cairo last summer too.

III. VOCABULARY

ruxṣa	(ruxaṣ) leave, vacation; permission
saafar	(ysaafir) he traveled
'aw	(conj.) or (syn. walla)
twannas	(yitwannas) he had a good time
gaddam	(ygaddim) he presented, submitted
ṭalab	(–aat) application, request
'ijaaza	(–aat) vacation
waafag	(ywaafig) he approved; he agreed
xooš	(with foll. n.) good, nice
saa9ad	(ysaa9id) he helped, assisted
mit'akkid	(–iin) certain, sure
mit'akkid 'inna	I am certain that he ...
maani9	(mawaani9) objection
jamaa9a	(group of) people

bruuHi	by myself; myself; alone
čiđi	like this, in this manner
'aHsan	(elative) best; better

IV. ADDITIONAL VOCABULARY

gaabal (ygaabil) he met s.o., had an interview with s.o.

jaawab (yjaawib) he answered (e.g., letter, phone)

xaabar (yxaabir) he telephoned

V. GRAMMAR

Perfect Tense

The verbs **gaabal** 'he met s.o.', **jaawab** 'he answered, (e.g., a letter, the phone, etc.)', and **xaabar** 'he telephoned' are regular verbs. The full conjugation of **gaabal** is given below as an example :

huwa	gaabal		'intum	________	tu
hum	________	aw	'inti	________	ti
hiya	________	at	'intin	________	tin
hin	________	an	'aana	________	t
'inta	________	t	niHin	________	na

VI. DRILLS

Drill 1 *Chain – Cued*

T : mariiđ̣ 'sick'

S_1 : weeš fiik ya ...? mariiđ̣? 'What's wrong with you, ...? Sick? '

S_2: 'ii wal̤l̤a. mariiđ̣ waajid. 'Yes, I am very sick.'

1. mṣaxxan
2. juu9aan
3. 9aṭšaan
4. mariiđ̣
5. mxabbal̤
6. ta9baan
7. muub ṣaaHi
8. muub zeen
9. ta9baan
10. mxabbal̤
11. muub zeen
12. mariiđ̣
13. muub zeen
14. mṣaxxan
15. juu9aan
16. 9aṭšaan

Drill 2 *Repetition*

huwa 'axađ ruxṣa w saafar. 'He took leave and traveled.'

hum 'axđaw ruxṣa w saafaraw.

hiya 'axđat ruxṣa w saafarat

hin 'axđin ruxṣa w saafarin.

'aana 'axađt ruxṣa w saafart.

'inta 'axađt ruxṣa w saafart.

'intum 'axađtu ruxṣa w saafartu.

'inti 'axađti ruxṣa w saafarti.

'intin 'axađtan ruxṣa w saafartan.

niHin 'axađna ruxṣa w saafarna.

Drill 3 *Variable Substitution*

ruuH twannas! 'Go have a good time!'

1. 'inti	9. 'intin
2. 'intum	10. 'inta
3. 'intin	11. 'inti
4. 'inta	12. 'intum
5. 'inta	13. 'inti
6. 'intum	14. 'intum
7. 'inta	15. 'intin
8. 'inti	16. 'inta

Drill 4 *Chain — Cued*

S₁ : ruuH twannas!

S₂ : 9adil. laazim 'aruuH atwannas.
'Right! I have to go to have a good time.'

1. ruuH tzawwaj!	10. ruuH saa9id!
2. ruuHu tzawwaju!	11. ruuHi saa9di!
3. ruuH 'ixið ruxṣa!	12. ruuH twannas!
4. ruuHi 'ixði ruxṣa!	13. ruuH saafir!
5. ruuHu 'ixðu ruxṣa!	14. ruuHi bruuHič!
6. ruuH 'isbaH!	15. ruuH xaabir!
7. ruuHi sibHay!	16. ruuHu xaabru!
8. ruuHu sibHu!	17. ruuH gaabil il-waziir!
9. ruuH štaġil!	18. ruuHi gaabli š-šeex!

Drill 5 *Substitution*

haaδa xooš rayyaal. 'This is a good man.'

1. waziir	11. siinama
2. mudiir	12. šarika
3. mu9allima	13. daayra
4. rayaayiil	14. dawaayir
5. banaat	15. xaṭṭ
6. bagḷaawa	16. dijaaj
7. 'akil	17. θallaaja
8. 'awlaad	18. ġassaala
9. madrasa	19. sayyaara
10. filim	20. ṭayyaara

Drill 6 *Variable Substitution*

huwa yHibb ysaa9id. 'He likes to help.'

1. ysaafir	11. 'inti
2. yištaġil	12. hin
3. yitwannas	13. statement
4. yišrab biira	14. 'intum
5. ysaafir	15. huwa
6. hiya	16. negative
7. 'aana	17. ydarris
8. niHin	18. yitzawwaj
9. question	19. yisbaH
10. 'inta	20. hiya

Drill 7 *Double Substitution*

huwa saa9adni l-9aam il-maaḏ̣i. 'He helped me last year.'

Example : 'inta huwa 'you – he'

'inta saa9adta l-9aam il-maaḏ̣i.
'You helped him last year.

1. 'aana – huwa
2. 'inta – huwa
3. huwa – 'aana
4. huwa – hiya
5. huwa – hum
6. huwa – 'inta
7. hiya – 'inti
8. hiya – hin
9. hiya – hum
10. hum – 'aana
11. hum – niHin
12. niHin – 'intin
13. niHin – 'intum
14. 'inta – 'aana
15. 'inta – niHin

Drill 8 *Substitution*

'aana mit'akkid 'inna raayiH ywaafig.
'I am sure that he is going to agree.'

1. that they (m.) are going to travel to America.
2. that he is going to approve my request for vacation.
3. that they (f.) are going to study at this University.
4. that we are going to travel by ourselves to London.
5. that you (m.s.) are going to get an increment (raise) this year.

6. that you (f.s.) are going to get an answer from the Ministry.
7. that you (m.p.) are going to have a good time in Bahrain.
8. that you (f.p.) are going to get permission to travel.
9. that I am going to get an answer from my friend (m.).
10. that she is going to say, "I have no objection."

Drill 9 *Double Substitution*

huwa gaal li ma 9inda maani9.
'He told me (lit: 'said to me') that he had no objection.'

Example: hiya – hum 'she – they (m.)'

hiya gaalat li ma 9indahum maani9.
'She told me that they (m.) had no objection.'

1. 'aana – hiya
2. 'aana – 'intum
3. hiya – hum
4. hiya – huwa
5. huwa – hiya
6. huwa – hin
7. 'inta – hum
8. 'inta – hum
9. 'inti – 'inti
10. 'inti – 'intin
11. 'intum – 'intum
12. 'intum – hiya
13. 'intin – niHin
14. 'intin – huwa
15. huwa – huwa

Drill 10 *Chain – Cued*

Example: T : hiya 'she'

S_1 : raayHa tsaafir wiyya jamaa9a?
'Is she going to travel with (some) people?'

S_2: la bruuHha. čiðī 'aHsan.
'No, by herself. It's better this way.'

1. huwa
2. hum
3. hin
4. 'inta
5. 'inti
6. 'intum
7. 'intin
8. hiya
9. hin
10. huwa
11. hiya
12. 'inti

UNIT 33

I. TEXT

Hasan : ʼis-salaamu 9aleekum!

xamiis : wa 9aleekum is-salaam.

Hasan : mumkin ʼasʼalak suʼaal?

xamiis : tfaḏ̣ḏ̣al.

Hasan : mumkin tguul li ween maktab il-bariid?

xamiis : ʼinta tabi tamši walla tabi truuH bi s-sayyaara?

Hasan : ʼabi ʼaruuH bi s-sayyaara.

xamiis : zeen. haaḏ̣a šaari9 zaayid. reewis ihni w ba9deen ruuH siida leen tooṣal id-dawwaar il-ʼawwal u ba9deen liff 9ala š-šimaal. ʼimši šwayy tHaṣṣil binaayteen: ʼil-binaaya lli 9ala yimiinak is-safaara l-ʼamrikaaniyya. xa̤l̤lha. dišš il-binaaya lli 9ala šimaalak. maktab il-bariid fi ṭ-ṭaabig iθ-θaani.

Hasan : maškuur!

xamiis : ʼa̤l̤la wiyyaak!

II. TRANSLATION

Hasan : Peace be upon you!

Khamis: And peace be upon you.

Hasan : May I ask you a question?

Khamis: Go ahead!

Hasan : Will you please tell me where the Post Office is?

Khamis: Do you want to walk or do you want to go by car?

Hasan : I want to go by car.

Khamis: Fine. This is (Shaikh) Zaayid Street. Back up here and then go straight to the end of the street. Turn right there and go straight until you get to the First Roundabout (circle), and then turn left. Go a little farther, and you will find two buildings: the building on your right is the American Embassy. Leave it. Enter the building on your left. The Post Office is on the Second Floor.

Hasan : Thank you!

Khamis: God be with you!

III. VOCABULARY

mumkin	(with foll. imp.) May ...?
si'al	(yis'al) he asked
su'aal	('as'ila) question
reewas	(yreewis) he backed up, reversed
'ihni	(adv.) here (var. **hini**)
'aaxir	('awaaxir) end; last (adj.)
laff	(yliff) he turned
'iid	('iideen) hand (f.)
yimiin	right (e.g., hand, side of street)
'iidak il-yimiin	your (m.s.) right hand
leen	(conj.) until, till (syn. **lamma**)
dawwaar	(–aat) roundabout, traffic circle

šimaal	left (e.g., hand, side of street)
miša	(yimši) he walked, marched
binaaya	(–aat) building
'illi	(rel. pron.) who(m), that, which
safaara	(–aat) embassy
dašš	(ydišš) he entered (e.g., house, building, etc.)
ṭaabig	(ṭuwaabig) floor, flat

IV. GRAMMAR

1. Perfect Tense

Verbs of the **miša** 'he walked' type (those that end in a vowel) are known as defective verbs. Such verbs have two stems: **miš–** with the third-person endings and **mišee–** with the other endings. Below is the full conjugation:

huwa	miš–a		'intum	————	eetu
hum	————	aw	'inti	————	eeti
hiya	————	at	'intin	————	eetin
hin	————	an	'aana	————	eet
'inta	————	eet	niHin	————	eena

Verbs which end with a doubled consonant, e.g., dašš 'he entered' are known as doubled verbs. Doubled verbs and defective verbs are similar in their conjugation.

huwa	dašš–		'intum	————	eetu
hum	————	aw	'inti	————	eeti
hiya	————	at	'intin	————	eetin
hin	————	an	'aana	————	eet
'inta	————	eet	niHin	————	eena

2. The Relative Pronoun 'illi 'who(m), that, which'

'illi introduces a relative clause which modifies a definite noun. Examples:

'il-binaaya lli 9ala yimiinak. 'the building (which is) on your (m.s.) right'

'il-walad illi ja 'the boy who came'

'il-banaat illi raaHan 'the girls who went'

If the noun which the relative clause modifies is indefinite, the relative **'illi** should not be used:

binaaya 9ala yimiinak 'a building (which is) on your (m.s.) right'

haaða rayyaal ja hni 'This is a man who came here.'

haðeel banaat drisan ihni. 'These are girls who studied here.'

Note that in the examples cited above the relative **'illi** refers to a definite noun (masculine, feminine, singular, or plural), which is the subject of the verb in the relative clause.

V. DRILLS

Drill 1 *Chain*

S_1: mumkin 'as'alak su'aal? 'May I ask you (m.s.) a question?'

S_2: tfaḏ̣ḏ̣al! 'Go ahead!'

Drill 2 *Substitution*

mumkin tguul li ween **maktab il-bariid**?
'Will you (m.s.) tell me where the Post Office is?'

1. Training Center
2. Teacher Training Center
3. fish market
4. Hamdan Building
5. American Embassy
6. Egyptian Consulate
7. you (f.)
8. you (m.p.)
9. British Consulate
10. French Embassy
11. you (m.s.)
12. Electric Department
13. Ministry of Education
14. Foreign Ministry
15. you (f.s.)
16. Broadcasting Station
17. cinema
18. Minister's Office

Drill 3 *Substitution*

haaḏa šaari9 **čibiir**. 'This is a big street.'

1. long
2. short
3. new
4. old
5. good
6. big

7. necessary
8. clean
9. dirty
10. excellent
11. beautiful
12. not good
13. not old
14. not long
15. old
16. very good
17. very big
18. very clean
19. dirty
20. excellent

Drill 4 *Variable Substitution*

reewis ihni w ba9deen ruuH siida.
'Reverse (m.s.) here and then go straight.'

1. 'ihnaak
2. 9ala l-yimiin
3. 'inti
4. ihni
5. 'intum
6. 9ala š-šimaal
7. 'intin
8. 'ihnaak
9. 'ihni
10. 'inta
11. 9ala yimiinak
12. 'inti
13. 9ala šimaalič
14. 'ihnaak
15. liffi
16. 9ala l-yimiin

Drill 5 *Variable Substitution*

liff 9ala š-šimaal! 'Turn left!'

1. right
2. your left
3. 'inti
4. your right

5. left	11. 'inta
6. right	12. your right
7. 'intum	13. your left
8. right	14. positive
9. left	15. 'inti
10. negative command	16. 'intin

Drill 6 *Chain – Cued*

S_1: 'ay dawwaar haaða? 'Which roundabout (circle) is this?

T : θalaaθa 'three'

S_2: haaða d-dawwaar iθ-θaaliθ. 'This is the Third Roundabout.'

1. 'aθneen	11. θamaanya
2. waaHid	12. 'aθneen
3. xamsa	13. waaHid
4. sitta	14. θalaaθa
5. sab9a	15. 'arba9a
6. θamaanya	16. sitta
7. tis9a	17. 'aθneen
8. 9ašara	18. θamaanya
9. waaHid	19. xamsa
10. xamsa	20. waaHid

Drill 7 *Combination*

haaða rayyaal. 'ir-rayyaal dašš il-binaaya. → haaða r-rayyaal illi dašš il-binaaya.

'This is a man. The man entered the building. → This is the man who entered the building.'

1. haaða šaari9. 'iš-šaari9 9ala l-yimiin.

2. haaði binaaya. 'il-binaaya 9ala š-šimaal.

3. haaða dawwaar. 'id-dawwaar 9ala yimiinak.

4. haaða maktab. 'il-maktab 9ala ṭ-ṭaabig iθ-θ aani.

5. haaði ṭariig. iṭ-ṭariig truuH 'ila l-9een.

6. haaði Hurma. 'il-Hurma jat 'ams.

7. haaði mara. 'il-mara raaHat is-suug.

8. haaða ṭaalib. 'iṭ-ṭaalib si'al su'aal.

9. haaði sikirteera. 'is-sikirteera tištaġil fi l-bank.

10. haaðeel 'awlaad. 'il-'awlaad daššaw il-binaaya.

11. haðeel banaat. 'il-banaat darasan ihni.

12. haaða mudiir. 'il-mudiir yisaa9id kill waaHid.

13. haaði mu9allima. 'il-mu9allima Haṣṣalat ziyaada.

14. haaða kaatib. 'il-kaatib gaddam ṭalab Hagg 'ijaaza.

15. haaði daxtoora. 'id-daxtoora saafarat il-qaahira.

Drill 8   *Question — Answer*

T : America

S₁ : min faḍlak ween is-safaara l-'amrikaaniyya?
     'Where is the American Embassy, please?'

S₂ : fi 'aaxir iš-šaari9.   'At the end of the street.'

1. Kuwait	4. bu ḍabi
2. Saudi Arabia	5. Qatar
3. Lebanon	6. France

7. America
8. Britain
9. Syria
10. India
11. Egypt
12. Pakistan
13. Canada
14. Iran
15. Jordan
16. Iraq

Drill 9 *Substitution*

'is-safaara l-'amrikaaniyya **9ala yimiinak.**
'The American Embassy is on your (m.s.) right.'

1. on your (f.s.) right
2. on your (m.p.) right
3. on your (m.s.) left
4. on the left
5. on the right
6. at the end of the street
7. on the Fourth Floor
8. on the Second Floor
9. at the end of the road
10. over there
11. at the end of the street
12. on the First Floor

Drill 10 *Double Substitution*

maktab **il-bariiḍ** fi ṭ-ṭaabig **iθ-θaaliθ.**
'The Post Office is on the Third Floor.'

1. minister – 2
2. Shaikh – 5
3. director – 2
4. secretary – 4
5. engineer – 3
6. clerk – 1
7. doctor – 7
8. nurse – 2
9. employee – 3
10. office – 1

11. company – 6
12. education – 4
13. school – 1
14. teacher – 2
15. university – 5

Drill 11 *Transformation:* imperfect → perfect

1. huwa yis'al su'aal.
2. 'aana 'areewis ihni.
3. huwa yreewis is-sayyaara.
4. hum yis'aluun 'as'ila waajid.
5. hiya tliff 9ala l-yimiin.
6. niHin nliff 9ala š-šimaal.
7. 'aana 'amši ṣoob il-baHar.
8. hum yimšuun wiyyaay kill yoom.
9. lamma tooṣal dišš il-binaaya.
10. hiya ma ddišš ihni.
11. huwa yguul ma 9inda fluus.
12. hum ysaa9duun kill waaHid.
13. hin ysaafrin wiyya jamaa9a.
14. niHin ma nsaafir bruuHna.
15. 'aana ma 9indi maani9.
16. huwa yxaabrak il-yoom.

Drill 12 *Transformation:* masculine → feminine

1. mumkin 'as'alak su'aal?
2. tfaḏḏal is'al!
3. mumkin tguul li ween?

4. 'inta tabi tamši?
5. 'inta tabi truuH ihnaak?
6. ṣabbaHk aḷḷa bi l-xeer.
7. ruuH twannas!
8. 'ixiđ ruxṣa w saafir!
9. reewis u ba9deen ruuH siida!
10. liff 9ala l-yimiin ihnaak!
11. liff 9ala š-šimaal!
12. 'imši šwayy tHaṣṣil il-binaaya.
13. dišš lamma tooṣal!
14. maškuur ya 'amiin!
15. huwa ysaafir bruuHa.
16. 'il-mudiir laazim ywaafig.

Drill 13 *Translation*

1. May I ask a question?
2. Go ahead! Ask!
3. Will you tell me why?
4. By the way! Where is he from?
5. I want to go by car.
6. Did she travel by plane?
7. He likes to help everyone.
8. This is the Post Office building.
9. We entered the building.

10. This is Shaikh Issa Street.
11. I applied for work here.
12. I travel alone. It's better.
13. We're sure the minister is here.
14. She doesn't have any objection.
15. He called me on the telephone.
16. They came and met the manager.

UNIT 34

I. TEXT

jum9a : guul li ya ṭawiil il-9umur! is-safaara l-'amrikaaniyya ba9iida min ihni?

yuusif : 'ii waḷḷa ba9iida waajid. 'iḏa 'inta mista9jil 'ixiḏ taksi.

jum9a : la 9indi sayyaara, walaakin ma 'a9rif is-safaara.

yuusif : zeen. 'inta fi jinuub il-madiina. 'is-safaara l-'amrikaaniyya fi šimaal il-madiina. ya9ni jiddaamak.

jum9a : 9ayal laazim 'aruuH siida, muub čiḏi?

yuusif : 9adil! ruuH siida tagriib masaafat 'imyat mitir u ba9deen 9ind id-dawwaar iθ-θaani liff 9ala 'iidak iš-šimaal.

jum9a : maškuur.

yuusif : mamnuun.

II. TRANSLATION

Jum'a : Tell me, please! Is the American Embassy far from here?

Joseph : Yes, indeed. It's very far. If you are in a hurry, take a taxi.

Jum'a : No, I have a car, but I do not know in which direction the Embassy is.

Joseph: O.K. You are now in the South(ern) (part) of the city. The American Embassy is in the North(ern) (part) of the city, that is, in front of you.

Jum'a :	Then I will have to go straight, won't I?
Joseph :	Right. Go straight for a distance of about one hundred meters and then at the Second Roundabout (circle) turn to your left.
Jum'a :	Thanks.
Joseph :	You're welcome.

III. VOCABULARY

'iða	if
mista9jil	(–iin) in a hurry; hurried (adj.)
xað / 'axað	(yaaxið) he took
9iraf	(y9arif) he knew
jiha	(–aat) direction, side; area
jinuub	south (of); southern part of
ya9ni	that is to say, namely
jiddaam	(prep., adv.) in front of, before
9ayal	then, therefore
masaafa	(–aat) distance
mitir	(mtaar) meter
9ind	(prep.) at the place of, near
mamnuun	(–iin) grateful, thankful

IV. ADDITIONAL VOCABULARY

safiir	(sufara) ambassador
ġunṣul	(ġanaaṣil) consul

ġunṣuliyya	(–aat) consulate
ġarb	west (of); western part of
wara	(prep., adv.) behind
foog	(prep., adv.) over; above
taHat	(prep., adv.) under; below
keelumitir	(–aat) kilometer
miil	(ʼamyaal) mile
rasta	(–aat) paved road
mukaan	(ʼamaakin) place

V. GRAMMAR

1. Perfect Tense

xaϑ ʼhe tookʼhas the variant ʼ**axaϑ**. It is conjugated exactly like **kal** or ʼ**akal** ʼhe ateʼ. (See UNIT 29, GRAMMAR 1)

2. Relative Clauses

In UNIT 33 we had examples of relative clauses in which the subject of the verb was the same as the antecedent. In this UNIT we have the other two types of relative clauses. Note the following examples:

haaϑa l-walad illi šifta.	ʼThis is the boy (whom) I saw.ʼ
haaϑeel il-banaat illi šifithin.	ʼThese are the girls (whom) I saw.ʼ
haaϑi l-binaaya lli šifitha.	ʼThis is the building (Which) I saw.ʼ

In all of these sentences the antecedents of the relative clauses, i.e., **'il-walad, 'il-banaat** and **'il-binaaya** are objects of the verb **šift** 'I saw'. If this is the case, then the verb should always have attached to it a suffixed pronoun referring to the antecedent and agreeing with it: **–a, –hin,** and **–ha.**

The third and last type of relative clauses in GA is the one in which the antecedent is the object of a preposition. In this case the preposition should have attached to it a suffixed pronoun refferring to the antecedent. Examples:

huwa lli jeet wiyyaa.	'He is the one with whom I came.'
hum illi dirast wiyyaahum.	'They (m.) are the ones with whom I studied.
haaði l-jaami9a lli dirast fiiha.	'This is the university at which I studied.
haaða d-daftar illi kitabt fii.	'This is the notebook in which I wrote.'

(Drill 12)

3. **ya9ni** literally means 'it means' and it is equivalent in meaning and usage to English 'that is to say, namely, I mean, etc.'

(Drill 5)

4. In GA **muub čiði?** 'Isn't it so?' is added to a statement to signal what is known in grammar as a "tail question":

huwa hni muub čiði?	'He's here, isn't he?'
'inta riHt muub čiði?	'You went, didn't you?'

'inta ma riHt muu čiᵭi?	'You didn't go, did you?'
naji baačir muu čiᵭi?	'We will come tomorrow, won't we?'
(**muu** is a variant of **muub**	'not')

(Drill 7)

NOTE ON TEXT

ya ṭawiil il-9umur is a polite formula of address. It implies respect and a wish for a long life. **ṭawiil il-9umur** literally means 'the one who is long of age' or 'the long-lived one'. It is used in addressing either young or old men.

VI. DRILLS

Drill 1 *Completion*

T :	'iᵭa 'inta mista9jil ...	'If you are in a hurry, ...'
S :	'iᵭa 'inta mista9jil 'ixiᵭ taksi.	'If you are in a hurry, take a taxi.'

1. 'iᵭa 'inta juu9aan ...
2. 'iᵭa 'inti 9aṭšaana ...
3. 'iᵭa l-hawa zeen ilyoom...
4. 'iᵭa maa fii gahwa ...
5. 'iᵭa 'intum mista9jiliin...
6. 'iᵭa š-šeex ihni ...
7. 'iᵭa baačir 9uṭla ...
8. 'iᵭa s-safaara ba9iida ...
9. 'iᵭa 'inta mṣaxxan ...
10. 'iᵭa huwa mariiᵭ ...
11. 'iᵭa truuH siida ...
12. 'iᵭa r-rasta muub zeena ...
13. 'iᵭa l-masaafa ba9iida ...
14. 'iᵭa 9indak fluus ...

Drill 2 *Variable Substitution*

huwa y9arif il-miškila. 'He knows the problem.'

1. hiya	11. 'inta
2. 'aana	12. 'intin
3. hum	13. statement
4. perfect	14. 'aana
5. niHin	15. huwa
6. negative	16. imperfect
7. hin	17. niHin
8. 'inti	18. 'inta
9. question	19. 'inti
10. 'intum	20. 'intum

Drill 3 *Completion*

'aana ma 'a9rif ..... 'I don't know ..... '

1. in which direction the American Embassy is
2. where the ADMA Company Training Center is
3. where she comes from
4. where the office of the Minister of Education is
5. why he doesn't like to eat fish
6. why the embassy is very far from the city
7. how far Doha is from Manama
8. how many hours it is by car from here to Dubai
9. where he got this car from
10. in which direction the American Consulate is

Drill 4 *Substitution*

ʼis-safaara l-ʼamrikaaniyya **fi jinuub il-madiina.**
ʼThe American Embassy is south of the city.ʼ

1. north of the city
2. close to the Saudi Embassy
3. on your (m.) right
4. at the end of Zayid Street
5. on the left
6. about 2 kilometers from here
7. about 15 minutes from here
8. at the Second Roundabout
9. in the Electricity Street
10. south of the Palace
11. east of the Foreign Ministry
12. at the First Roundabout

Drill 5 *Transformation*

T : **9indi suʼaal.**

S : **9indi suʼaal** yaʼ9ni "I have a question" bi l-ʼingiliizi.

1. ʼii waḷḷa!
2. masaafat ʼimyat mitir
3. šarg il-madiina
4. 9ind id-dawwaar il-ʼawwal
5. ma fii šuġul

6. 'asaafir bruuHi. čiđi 'aHsan.
7. mumkin 'as'alak su'aal?
8. mumkin tguul li?
9. fi 'aaxir iš-šaari9
10. liff 9ala l-yisaar
11. ruuH siida 'ila hnaak
12. 'aḷḷa wiyyaak ya mHammad
13. ma 9indi maani9
14. ya ṭawiil il-9umur

Drill 6 *Completion*

Deduce from the statement the teacher gives what fits the meaning.

Example : T : huwa ma 'akal il-yoom.
'He has not eaten today.'
9ayal huwa juu9aan. 'Therefore, he is hungry.'

1. maryam juu9aana waajid.
2. sadiigi saalim mariiđ.
3. 'iṭ-ṭayyaara ma jat il-yoom.
4. ṣaarli hni 9ašar siniin.
5. hiya ma tigdar tamši.
6. 'aana ma dri ween.
7. 'il-ġunṣuliyya ba9iida waajid.
8. huwa yHibb ysaa9id.

9. salma fi l-mustašfa.
10. ʼil-hawa Haarr il-yoom.
11. hiya mariiḏ̣a w mṣaxxna.
12. huwa ma siʼal leeš.
13. ma Haṣṣalt ziyaada.
14. hum ʼaxḏaw ruxṣa l-yoom.
15. haaḏa l-filim zeen.
16. haaḏi š-šigga ġaalya.
17. ʼiṭ-ṭamaaṭ raxiiṣ il-yoom.
18. ma fii tiffaaH fi s-suug.
19. haaḏi s-sayyaara 9atiija.
20. ʼaana min zamaan ihni.

Drill 7 *Question – Answer*

T : ʼis-safaara l-ʼamrikaaniyya ba9iida min ihni. muub čiḏi?
'The American Embassy is far from here, isn't it?'

S : 9adil. ba9iida waajid min ihni.
'True. It's very far from here.'

1. ʼinta ʼaxaḏt taksi, muub čiḏi?
2. 9indak sayyaara jadiida, muub čiḏi?
3. haaḏa l-mudiir zeen, muu čiḏi?
4. ʼinta mista9jil, muu čiḏi?
5. ʼiṭ-ṭariig ṭawiil, muu čiḏi?
6. ʼl-ġunṣuliyya čibiira, muub čiḏi?
7. ʼil-yoom Haarr, muub čiḏi?

8. 'il-bint mitiina, muub čiði?

9. 'il-mayy baarid, muub čiði?

10. 'il-mustašfa naðiif, muub čiði

11. huwa širib biira, muu čiði?

12. 'id-daxtar illi fi haaða l-mustašfa zeen, muub čiði?

13. 'ir-rayyaal illi ja gabil šwayy mxabbaḷ, muub čiði?

14. 'il-bint illi daššat halHiin jamiila, muub čiði?

Drill 8 *Substitution*

ruuH siida tagriib masaafat 'imyat mitir.
'Go straight for a distance of about one hundred meters.'

1.	100 meters	9.	70 meters
2.	300 meters	10.	2 kilometers
3.	700 meters	11.	3 kilometers
4.	600 meters	12.	10 kilometers
5.	900 meters	13.	350 meters
6.	400 meters	14.	40 meters
7.	500 meters	15.	70 meters
8.	150 meters	16.	200 meters

Drill 9 *Double Substitution*

'is-safaara 9ind id-dawwaar il-'awwal.
'The Embassy is at the First Roundabout (circle).

1.	2nd circle	3.	4th circle
2.	3rd circle	4.	5th circle

5. 6th circle
6. 7th circle
7. Ministry of Education
8. Foreign Ministry
9. Ministry of the Interior
10. Ministry of Pub. Works
11. Ministry of Agriculture
12. Government Hospital
13. ADMA Training Center
14. ADPC Building
15. Dept. of Elec. & Water
16. Min. of Communications
17. Teacher Tr. Center
18. Doha Hospital

Drill 10 *Variable Substitution*

mumkin tguul li **ween** ya ṭawiil il-9umur?
'Will you please tell me where? '

1. how
2. you (m.p.)
3. from where
4. which direction
5. you (f.s.)
6. you (m.s.)
7. how much
8. you (f.p.)
9. which street
10. why
11. where
12. who
13. how much
14. how many
15. you (m.s.)
16. how
17. which hotel
18. which direction
19. why
20. which one

Drill 12 *Combination*

haađa ṭaalib + 'aana darrast iṭ-ṭaalib 9aṛabi. → haađa ṭ-ṭaalib illi darrasta 9aṛabi.

'This is a student. + I taught the student Arabic. → 'This is the student (whom) I taught Arabic.'

1. haaði miškila. ma 'a9rif il-miškila.
2. ruuH il-binaaya. 'il-binaaya jiddaam is-safaara.
3. haaða safiir. šift is-safiir fi beet iš-šeex.
4. haaði ġunṣuliyya. gaddamt ṭalab šuġul fi l-ġunṣuliyya.
5. haaða mukaan. daššeet il-mukaan.
6. haaðeel 9yaal. li-9yaal yruuHuun il-madrasa.
7. 'imš il-mukaan. 'il-mukaan jiddaam is-safaara.
8. haaði bint. twannast wiyya l-bint.
9. šu 'asm il-jamaa9a? 'inta sirt wiyya l-jamaa9a.
10. ween raa9i t-taksi? 9aṭeena fluus raa9i t-taksi.

UNIT 35

I. TEXT

ʹawwal ʹams bu saalim baġa yruuH is-suug. sayyaarta čaanat xarbaana. miša ʹila s-suug u štira 9eeš u laHam Hagg 9aayilta. ʹu ba9ad štira Halwa w hduum u jawaati Hagg wilda w Hurmita liʹan 9ugub baačir 9iid rumᵭaan w in-nass aḷḷa ysallimk fi 9iid rumᵭaan yilbisuun ʹaHsan šayy 9indahum u yruuHuun yšuufuun halhum u ysoolfuun u yišrabuun gahwa.... bu saalim leen rija9 min is-suug murta gaalat la "leeš ma štareet Haliib ya bu saalim? " bu saalim gaal: "waḷḷa niseet." bu saalim baġa yruuH is-suug θaani marra walaakin murta gaalat: "ma 9alee! truuH baačir. 9indana šwayy Haliib baagi min ʹams."

II. TRANSLATION

The day before yesterday Abu Salim wanted to go (felt like going) shopping. His car was out of order. He walked to the market and bought rice and meat for his family. Also, he bought candy (sweets), clothes, and shoes for his children and his wife because Ramadhan Feast is the day after tomorrow, and people wear the best thing they have during this Feast. People go to see their folks, chat and drink coffee. When Abu Salim returned from the market, his wife said to him, "Why didn't you buy milk, Abu Salim? " Abu Salim said, "By gosh, I forgot." Abu Salim decided to go to the market again, but his wife said, "Never mind! You can go tomorrow. We have some (a little) milk left from yesterday."

III. VOCABULARY

ʹawwal ʹams	(the day) before yesterday
baġa	(yibġa) he wanted, liked
xarbaana	(–aat) out of order
štira	(yištiri) he bought
Halwa	candy, sweets; dessert
hduum	(s. **hidim**) clothes
juuti	(jawaati) pair of shoes
wild	(s. **walad**) sons; children
9iid	(ʹa9yaad) feast, festival
rumđ̣aan	Ramadhan
9iid rumđ̣aan	the Ramadhan Feast
naas	people
libas	(yilbis) he wore, put on
hal	folks (syn. **ʹahil**)
soolaf	(ysoolif) he chattered; he talked
leen	(conj.) when
mara	(Hariim) wife, woman
nisa	(yinsa) he forgot
ma 9alee!	never mind, it's all right
baagi	remainder; remaining

IV. ADDITIONAL VOCABULARY

9aṭa	(ya9ṭi) he gave
gamiiṣ	(gumṣaan) shirt
banṭaluun	(banaaṭliin) trousers, pants

kuut	('akwaat) coat; jacket
θoob	(θwaab) dress (e.g., **dišdaaša**)
ġitra	(ġitar) head dress
9gaaḷ	(–aat) headband
gaHfiyya	(–aat) hat

V. GRAMMAR

1. Perfect Tense

The verbs **baġa** 'he wanted', **štira** 'he bought', **nisa** 'he forgot', and **9aṭa** 'he gave' are defective verbs, and are conjugated like **miša** 'ha walked'. (See UNIT 30.)

2. We have seen in UNIT 13 that two imperfect tense verbs can be used, one after the other, with both agreeing with the same subject to express the English meaning of 'to want (like) to do something'. Examples:

yriid yišrab.	'He wants to drink.'
'ariid 'ašrab.	'I want to drink.'
yriiduun yišrabuun	'They (m.) want to drink.'

In this UNIT we have the verb string **baġa yruuH** 'he wanted to go, felt like going' in which the first verb is in the perfect tense. The second is always imperfect. Here are some examples:

baġeet aruuH.	'I wanted to go.'
baġat truuH	'She wanted to go.'

3. The negative particle **ma** is used to negate a perfect tense verb:

ma raaH is-suug.	'He didn't go to the market.'
ma baġeet 'aruuH.	'I didn't want to go.'

NOTE ON TEXT

Ramadhan is the Muslim holy month of fasting. During this month Muslims fast every day from early morning to sunset. After Ramadhan Muslims celebrate a holiday known as The Ramadhan Feast, which usually lasts three or four days. During this holiday, especially on the first day, Muslims wear their best clothes, go to the mosque for the early morning Ramadhan Feast prayer, visit relatives and friends, and exchange gifts.

VI. DRILLS

Drill 1 *Substitution*

baġa yištiri **Haliib**. 'He wanted to buy (some)milk.'

1. sweets
2. clothes
3. shoes (pair)
4. shirt
5. pants
6. jacket
7. dress
8. hat
9. head dress
10. candy
11. shoes (pairs)
12. shirts
13. pants (pairs)
14. jackets
15. dresses
16. hats
17. car
18. house
19. meat
20. tomatoes

Drill 2 *Variable Substitution*

baġa yruuH is-suug. 'He wanted to go to the market.'

1. bu saalim
2. bu 9ali
3. 'umm 9ali
4. 'il-maṭaar
5. niHin
6. negative
7. 'inta
8. 'inti
9. 'aana
10. 'il-beet
11. statement
12. 'intum
13. 'intin
14. question
15. hum
16. hin
17. bu Hamad
18. 'umm xamiis
19. 'inti
20. 'aana

Drill 3 *a. Substitution*

huwa 9aṭaani fluus. 'He gave me (some) money.'

1. šeexa
2. maryam
3. niHin
4. 'il-'awlaad
5. 'il-banaat
6. wilda
7. murta
8. 'inta
9. 'inti
10. 'intin
11. 'intum
12. byaat
13. 'aana
14. 'inti
15. 'intum
16. niHin
17. 'inta
18. 'intin
19. hum
20. hin

b. Double Substitution

huwa 9aṭaani fluus. 'He gave me (some) money.'

1. 'aana – huwa
2. 'aana – hiya
3. 'aana – 'inta
4. 'aana – 'inti
5. 'aana – hum
6. huwa – 'aana
7. huwa – hin
8. hum – 'aana
9. hum – hiya
10. hiya – niHin
11. hiya – 'inta
12. niHin – 'intum
13. niHin – 'intum
14. 'inta – 'aana
15. 'inti – hiya
16. 'inti – niHin
17. 'intum – 'aana
18. 'intum – hiya

Drill 4 *Variable Substitution*

huwa miša s-suug. 'He walked to the market.'

1. consulate
2. embassy
3. I
4. post office
5. place
6. sea
7. they (m.)
8. she
9. office
10. home
11. we
12. apartment
13. negative
14. you (m.s.)
15. you (f.s.)
16. question
17. he
18. I
19. you (f.s.)
20. you (m.p.)

Drill 5 *Double Substitution*

huwa štira **juuti.** 'He bought (a pair of) shoes.'

1. he – clothes
2. I – shoes
3. you (m.s.) – shirt
4. you (f.s.) – shirts
5. you (m.p.) – pants
6. you (f.p.) – jacket
7. they (m.) – jackets
8. she – dress
9. they (f.) – dresses
10. I – head dress
11. niHin – headband
12. he – hat
13. they (m.) – hats
14. you (m.s.) – car
15. she – bread

Drill 6 *Transformation:* Conjugation

'aana štireet jawaati w hduum Hagg wildi.
'I bought shoes and clothes for my children.'

1. 'inta
2. 'inti
3. 'intum
4. 'intin
5. niHin
6. huwa
7. hum
8. hiya
9. hin
10. 'aana

Drill 7 *Chain – Cued*

T :	huwa – Haliib	'he – milk'
S_1 :	leeš ma štira Haliib?	'Why didn't he buy milk?'
S_2 :	walḷa nisa.	'Honestly, he forgot.'

1. huwa – juuti	10. hum – gaHfiyyaat
2. hum – hduum	11. hiya – xubiz
3. hiya – θoob	12. hin – Haliib
4. hin – θwaab	13. 'inta – ṭamaaṭ
5. 'inta – kuut	14. 'intum – šakar
6. 'intum – 'akwaat	15. 'inti – jibin
7. 'inti – juuti	16. 'intin – 9eeš
8. 'intin – jawaati	17. 'inta – biira
9. huwa – gaHfiyya	18. huwa – Halwa

Drill 8 *Substitution*

murta gaalat: "ma 9alee!"	His wife said, "Never mind!"

1. his father	9. your (f.s.) sons
2. her father	10. your (m.p.) mother
3. my mother	11. our father
4. my brother	12. our mother
5. my sister	13. their (m.) father
6. his wife	14. their (f.) mother
7. her husband	15. his brother
8. your (m.s.) father	

Drill 9 *Transformation:* masculine → feminine

1. 'uxuu gaal: "ma 9alee!"
2. bu saalim baġa yruuH is-suug.
3. huwa miša 'ila l-beet.

4. ʹinta štireet ġamiiṣ?
5. ʹintum štireetu jawaati?
6. hum štiraw Halwa.
7. huwa libas hduuma.
8. ʹinta libast il-ġitra ʹams?
9. ʹintum ma libastu gaHfiyya.
10. baġa yruuH is-suug.
11. ja ysoolif wiyyaana.
12. ʹinta niseet tištiri laHam?
13. huwa nisa li-ktaab.
14. haađa ʹaHsan šayy 9indak?
15. huwa 9aṭaani fluus.
16. huwa raaH il-ġunṣuliyya.

Drill 10 *Questions* (based on Text)

1. ween baġa yruuH bu saalim ʹawwal ʹams?
2. sayyaarta čaanat zeena?
3. raaH bi s-sayyaara?
4. šu štira?
5. šu štira ba9ad?
6. leeš štira Halwa w hduum u jawaati?
7. mata 9iid rumđ̣aan?
8. šu tilbis fi l-9iid?
9. šu yi9maluun in-naas fi 9iid rumđ̣aan?
10. štira Haliib bu saalim?

11. leeš ma štira Haliib?
12. raaH is-suug θaani marra?
13. mata yruuH is-suug?
14. 9indahum Haliib waajid?
15. min ween il-Haliib?

Drill 11 *Question – Answer*

1. riHt is-suug il-yoom?
2. čeef riHt is-suug?
3. šu štireet?
4. štireet hduum u Halwa?
5. mata 9iid rumđ̣aan?
6. weeš ti9mal fi l-9iid?
7. fii naas kaθiir fi s-suug?
8. ween is-safaara l-maṣriyya?
9. ʼil-ġunṣuliyya wara s-safaara?
10. čam wazaara fi giṭar?
11. čam il-masaafa ʼila dbayy?
12. ʼil-baHreen šarg giṭar?
13. dbayy jinuub bu đ̣abi?
14. raaṣ il-xeema ġarb 9umaan?

Drill 12 *Translation*

1. I do not know in which direction Saudi Arabia is.
2. If you (m.s.) are in a hurry, take a taxi from here.

3. You (m.p.) can find gas stations everywhere.
4. It's about 400 kilometers from here to Doha.
5. It takes about four hours from Abu Dhabi to Beirut by plane.
6. Therefore, I have to go straight from here, don't I?
7. This is the car which I bought last year.
8. This is the question which I asked in class.
9. The building which is on your right is the Post Office.
10. Turn left here, and the Post Office will be on your left.

UNIT 36

I. TEXT

wilyam : leeš fii 9uṭla baačir ya xamiis?

xamiis : baačir 9iid rumḏ̣aan ya tawiil il-9umur.

wilyam : 'ii 9adil! 9adil: 9iidak mbaarak!

xamiis : kiḷḷ 9aam w intum bxeer ya wilyam!

wilyam : fii 'a9yaad θaanya 9indakum ihni?

xamiis : 'aḷḷa ysallimk fii 9iid iḏ̣-ḏ̣iHiyya w 9iid il-'istiglaal u 9iid il-juluus. w intum f amriika weeš fii 'a9yaad 9indakum?

wilyam : 9indana 9iideen čibiireen: 9iid il-miilaad ya9ni "krismas" u 9iid raaṣ is-sana ya9ni "nyu yiir." weeš yi9maluun in-nass fi haḏeel il-'a9yaad?

xamiis : aḷḷa ysaalimk fi ṣ-ṣabaaH yruuHuun il-masyid yṣalluun u yigruun il-qur'aan u ba9deen yruuHuun y9ayyduun 9ala halhum u 'asdiqaa'hum u yruuHuun il-muntazahaat w il-Hadaayig il-9aamma.

II. TRANSLATION

William: Why is there a holiday tomorrow, Khamis?

Khamis: Tomorrow is The Ramadhan Feast.

William: Yes, true. True! Happy Feast!

Khamis: (I hope) every year you are fine, William.

William: Are there any other holidays (that) you have here?

Khamis: God protect you: There is The Sacrifice Feast, Independence Day, and Accession Day. And you in America, what holidays do you have?

William: We have two big holidays: The Birth Holiday, that is, "Christmas" and the holiday of the beginning (lit. head) of the year, that is, "New Year". What do the people do during these holidays?

Khamis: God protect you! In the morning they go to mosque to pray and read from the Quran and after that they celebrate the Feast with their folks and their friends, and they go to parks and public gardens.

III. VOCABULARY

mbaarak	(adj.) blessed
9iidak mbaarak!	Ḥappy Holiday!
ð̣iHiyya	(–aat) sacrifice; sacrificed animal
'istiglaal	independence
9iid il-'istiglaal	Independence Day
juluus	accession to the throne; sitting
9iid il-juluus	Accession Day
miilaad	birth; birthday
9iid il-miilaad	Christmas
raaṣ	(ruuṣ) head; top of s.th.
raaṣ is-sana	New Year
9iid raaṣ is-sana	New Year holiday
masyid	(masaayid) mosque
ṣalla	(yṣalli) he prayed

gara	(yigra) he read, recited
qur'aan	Quran
9ayyad 9ala	(y9ayyid) he celebrated a feast with s.o.
muntazah	(–aat) park, recreation ground
Hadiiga	(Hadaayig) garden
9aamm	(adj.) public, common

IV. ADDITIONAL VOCABULARY

ṣaam	(yṣuum) he fasted
zaar	(yzuur) he visited
jaami9	(jawaami9) mosque
ṣalaa	(ṣalawaat) prayer
kaniisa	(kanaayis) church

V. GRAMMAR

ṣalla 'he prayed' is a defective verb and is conjugated like **miša** 'he walked'. (See UNIT 30.)

NOTES ON TEXT

1. **9iidak mbaarak**! literally means 'Your (m.s.) holiday is blessed!' and it corresponds to English 'Happy Holiday!' It is used during both The Ramadhan and The Sacrifice Feasts. It is also used for 'Merry Christmas:' The feminine form is **9iidič mbaarak**!

(Drill 3)

2. **9iid raaṣ is-sana** (lit. 'the feast of the head of the year') is equivalent to 'New Year holiday'. The same formula is also applied to the Hijra year of the Muslim calendar.

3. **kill 9aam w intum bxeer** (lit. 'every year and you (m.p.) are fine, well') corresponds to English 'Happy New Year'. It is used for a male, a female, or a group of people.

VI. DRILLS

Drill 1 *Substitution*

9ugub **baačir** 9iid iđ̣-đ̣iHiyya.

1. two days
2. five days
3. twenty days
4. one week
5. two weeks
6. three weeks
7. one month
8. two months
9. three months
10. five months
11. twelve days
12. 25 days
13. $2\frac{1}{2}$ weeks
14. tomorrow
15. ten days
16. five weeks
17. $5\frac{1}{2}$ months
18. $1\frac{1}{2}$ weeks

Drill 2 *Substitution*

9iid iđ̣-đ̣iHiyya 9ugub baačir.

1. Ramadhan Feast
2. Christmas
3. New Year
4. Independence Day
5. Accession Day
6. New Year

7. New Year
8. Christmas
9. Ramadhan Feast
10. Independence Day
11. Sacrifice Feast
12. Accession Day

Drill 3 *Repetition*

a. 9iidak mbaarak! 9iidkum mbaarak!

9iidič mbaarak! 9iidkin mbaarak!

b. kill 9aam w inta bxeer! kill 9aam w intum bxeer!

kill 9aam w inti bxeer! kill 9aam w intin bxeer!

Drill 4 *Repetition*

1. huwa ṣalla fi l-jaami9.
2. hiya ṣallat fi l-jaami9.
3. hum ṣallaw fi l-jaami9.
4. hin ṣallan fi l-jaami9.
5. 'aana ṣaleet fi l-jaami9.
6. 'inta ṣalleet fi l-jaami9.
7. 'inti ṣalleeti fi l-jaami9.
8. 'intum ṣalleetu fi l-jaami9.
9. 'intin ṣaleetin fi l-jaami9.
10. niHin ṣalleena fi l-jaami9.

Drill 5 *Variable Substitution*

huwa gara qur'aan fi l-masyiḍ. 'He read Quran in the mosque.'

1. hiya
2. hum
3. ṣallaw
4. hin
5. 'inta
6. fi l-beet
7. huwa
8. negative
9. 'intum
10. 'aana

11. fi l-jaami9
12. niHin
13. 'inti
14. riHti
15. 'intin
16. 'aana
17. niHin
18. il-beet
19. huwa
20. hiya

Drill 6 *Double Substitution*

huwa 9ayyad 9aleena. 'He celebrated a merry feast with us.'

1. huwa – hum
2. huwa – 'intum
3. hiya – niHin
4. hiya – hiya
5. hum – 'inta
6. hum – 'inti
7. hin – 'intin
8. 'inta – huwa
9. 'inta – hin
10. 'intum – niHin
11. 'intum – hum
12. huwa – 'aana
13. hiya – 'inti
14. hum – 'intum
15. hin – 'inti
16. 'aana – hum
17. 'inta – hiya
18. 'inti – niHin

Drill 7 *Variable Substitution*

huwa zaar saalim fi l-mustašfa.
'He visited Salim in the hospital.'

1. hiya
2. hum
3. hin
4. 'aana
5. 'inta
6. šift

7. 'inti
8. 'intum
9. niHin
10. zurna
11. sadiigna
12. 'uxutna
13. 'ummana
14. 'aana
15. 'inta
16. 'inti
17. 'intum
18. huwa
19. 'uxta
20. hiya

Drill 8 *Chain – Cued*

T :	'inta	'you (m.s.)'
S_1 :	ween ṣalleet?	'Where did you pray?'
T :	masyid	'mosque'
S_2 :	ṣallee fi l-masyid.	'I prayed in the mosque.'

1. 'inti – jaami9
2. huwa – masyid
3. hiya – beet
4. 'intum – madrasa
5. 'intin – muntazah
6. hum Hadiiga
7. hin – kaniisa
8. 'inta – jaami9
9. maryam – beet
10. šeexa – masyid
11. byaat – maylis
12. 'iš-šeex – jaami9
13. 'il-mara – jaami9
14. 'il-Hurma – masyid
15. 'inta – ṭariig
16. 'inti – beet
17. hum – suug
18. hiya – kaniisa

Drill 9 *Transformation:* singular → plural

1. 9iidak mbaarak!
2. kill 9aam w inti bxeer!
3. haaḏi Hadiiga 9aamma.
4. huwa yi9mal gahwa.
5. 'aana 9amalt gahwa 'ams.
6. hiya truuH il-masyid.
7. 'inta tigra qur'aan?
8. huwa y9ayyid 9aleeha.
9. 'aana 'a9ayyid 9aleek.
10. 'inta truuH il-muntazah?
11. hiya tṣuum rumḏ̣aan kill sana.
12. huwa yṣuum ba9ad.
13. 'aana ma gdar 'aṣuum.
14. 'inta ṣumt il-9aam il-maaḏ̣i?
15. 'abġa 'azuur il-mariiḏ̣.
16. 'inti tigdariin tṣalliin ihni.

Drill 10 *Transformation:* perfect → imperfect

1. baġeet 'azuur hali.
2. huwa ma gadar yṣuum.
3. 'aana ma ṣumt ba9ad.
4. hum ṣallaw fi l-jaami9.
5. hiya ṣallat fi l-kaniisa.
6. huwa baġa y9ayyid 9aleena.
7. 'inta mišeet 'ila s-suug?

8. ʹinti štireeti Halwa?
9. hum štiraw jawaati.
10. ʹaana libast ġitra w 9gaaḷ.
11. huwa soolaf wiyyaana.
12. ʹaana ma niseet li-fluus.
13. baġa yruuH θaani marra.
14. huwa ʹaxað taksi ʹams.

Drill 11 *Translation*

1. May I ask you (m.s.) a question? Go ahead! Ask!
2. Will you (f.s.) please tell ma where the Post Office is?
3. Do you want to walk or go by car?
4. Abu Salim's car was out of order the day before yesterday.
5. He bought candy, clothes, and shoes for his children and wife.
6. He returned from the market and his wife asked him why he had not bought milk for the children.
7. He said, "Honest, I forgot!" She said, "That's all right."
8. Go (m.s.) straight to the end of this street and then turn right.
9. The building on your left is the American Embassy.
10. Turn left at the Second Roundabout and the Post Office will be in front of you.
11. The distance from here to there is very far; so, you will have to go by car.
12. I wanted to come and celebrate The Ramadhan Feast with you last night.

UNIT 37

I. TEXT

mHammad : ween riHt ʹams? ma šiftak.

9ali : riHna wiyya jamaa9a ʹila n-naadi.

mHammad : weeš 9imaltu hnaak?

9ali : waḷḷa ʹaxaðna jalbuut u riHna l-baHar u ṣidna simač u ba9deen rija9na n-naadi.

mHammad : ʹaana xaabartak bi l-leel. ma čaan fii ʹaHad.

9ali : fi l-leel činna fi n-naadi t9aššeena hnaak. šribna biira w ʹakalna šiiš kabaab u ba9deen šifna filim "darakoola."

mHammad : ʹa9uuðu bi llaah! haaða filim muxiif. ʹinta tHibb haaða n-noo9 min il-ʹaflaam waajid?

9ali : la ya rayyaal muub waajid. ʹaHibb il-ʹaflaam il-pooliisiyya. w ʹinta š tHibb?

mHammad : ʹaHibb il-ʹaflaam il-hazaliyya, ya9ni l-ʹaflaam illi ð̣ð̣aHHič.

9ali : zeen. baačir fii filim ʹingiliizi hazali fi siinama l-ʹamiir. ʹariid a9zimak 9ala s-siinama 9ala Hsaabi.

mHammad : maškuur. baarak aḷḷa fiik. man il-mumaθθiliin fi l-filim?

9ali : loorel u haardi.

II. TANSLATION

Muhammad : Where did you go yesterday? I didn't see you.

Ali : We went with some people to the club.

Muhammad	:	What did you do there?
Ali	:	We took a boat and went to the sea. And we caught some fish and after that we returned to the club.
Muhammad	:	I called you in the evening. There was no one.
Ali	:	In the evening we were in the club. We had dinner there. We had some beer and we ate kabob and then we saw the movie "Dracula."
Muhammad	:	God forbid! That is a scary movie. Do you like this kind of movie very much?
Ali	:	No, man! Not very much. I like detective movies. And you, what do you like?
Muhammad	:	I like funny movies, that is, movies that make you laugh.
Ali	:	Fine. Tomorrow there is a funny English movie at Al-Amir Cinema. I would like to invite you to the cinema at my expense.
Muhammad	:	Thanks. God bless you! Who are the actors in the film?
Ali	:	Laurel and Hardy.

III. VOCABULARY

naadi	(nawaadi) club, clubhouse
9imal	(yi9mal) he did, made
jalbuut	(jalaabiit) boat, motor boat
ṣaad	(yṣiid) he caught (e.g., fish, birds)
t9aššša	(yit9aššša) he had dinner

'a9uuđu bi llaah!	God forbid! God save me from that!
muxiif	(–iin) scary, frightful
Habb	(yHibb) he liked, loved
noo9	('anwaa9) kind, sort
pooliisi	(adj.) detective
hazali	(adj.) comical, funny
đ̣aHHak	(yđ̣aHHik) he made s.o. laugh
9azam 9ala	(yi9zim) he invited s.o. to s.th.
baarak	(ybaarik) he blessed
muma$\theta\theta$il	(–iin) actor

IV. ADDITIONAL VOCABULARY

daaw	(–att) dhow, small ship
safiina	(sufun) ship
siif	('asyaaf) shore, seashore
trayyag	(yitrayyag) he had breakfast
tġadda	(yitġadda) he had lunch
raadu	(–waat) radio
talavizyoon	(–aat) television
ramil	(coll.) sand

V. GRAMMAR

Perfect Tense

ṣaad 'he caught', e.g., fish, birds, is a hollow verb, and is conjugated in the perfect exactly like **raaH** 'he went'. (See UNIT 29.)

(Drill 2)

Habb 'he liked, loved' is a doubled verb; it is conjugated like **dašš** 'he entered' in UNIT 30. The two verbs **t9aššša** 'he had dinner' and **tġadda** 'he had lunch' are doubled, but they are also defective. Such verbs are conjugated like defective verbs:

huwa t9ašša	'He had dinner.'
'aana t9aššeet	'I had dinner.'
hum tġaddaw	'They (m.) had lunch.'
'anna tġaddeet	'I had lunch.'

VI. DRILLS

Drill 1 *Chain – Cued*

T :	'inti	'you (f.s.)'
S_1 :	ween riHti 'ams? ma šiftič.	'Where did you (f.s.) go yesterday? I didn't see you.'
T :	club	
S_2 :	riHt in-naadi.	'I went to the club.'

1. 'inti – sea
2. 'intum – work
3. huwa – mosque
4. hum – church
5. 'inta – park
6. 9ali – public garden
7. šeexa – market
8. saalim – consulate
9. xamiis – Embassy
10. 'inta – Post Office
11. 'inti – restaurant
12. 'intin – department
13. 'intum – movies
14. 9eeša – sea shore
15. hum – Training Cen.
16. hin – home
17. 'inta – school
18. huwa – Dep. of Ed.

Drill 2 *Variable Substitution*

huwa ṣaad simač. 'He caught (some) fish.'

1. hiya
2. hum
3. hin
4. 'aana
5. 'ams
6. gabl ams
7. 'inta
8. question
9. 'intum
10. 'intin
11. 'inti
12. štireeti
13. statement
14. negative
15. huwa
16. Haṣṣal
17. hiya
18. niHin
19. ṣidna
20. 'inti
21. 'intum
22. huwa
23. 'inti
24. hum

Drill 3 *Substitution*

ma čaan fii **'aHad.** 'There wasn't anybody.'

1. people
2. movie
3. boat
4. ship
5. class
6. telephone
7. dhow
8. TV
9. policeman
10. soldier
11. radio
12. line

13. holiday
14. feast
15. prayer
16. mail
17. operator
18. bread
19. answer
20. message
21. money
22. school
23. chicken
24. meat

Drill 4 *Double Substitution*

'aana : tġaddeet u t9aššeet **simač.**
' I had fish for lunch and dinner.'

1. niHin – 9eeš
2. 'inta – kubba
3. 'inti – kabaab
4. 'intum – laHam
5. 'intin – dijaaj
6. huwa – 9eeš
7. hiya – simač
8. hum – Hummoṣ
9. hin – beeḏ̣
10. 'aana – dijaaj
11. niHin – laHam
12. 'inta – kubba
13. 'inti – kabaab
14. mooza – 9eeš
15. ṣaaliH – simač
16. niHin – beeḏ̣
17. hum – Hummoṣ
18. niHin simač

Drill 5 *Addition*

Example : T : haaḏa filim hindi.
'This is an Indian movie.'

S_1 : 'aana 'aHibb il-'aflaam il-hindiyya.
'I like Indian movies.'

1. haaða filim 'amrikaani.
2. haaða balad 9aṛabi.
3. haaða filim 'ingiliizi.
4. haaða filim faṛansi.
5. haaða filim 9aṛabi.
6. haaði Hadiiga 9aamma.
7. haaði sayyaara čibiira.
8. haaða kuut 'ingiliizi.
9. haaði šigga čibiira.
10. haaða beet jadiid.
11. haaði janṭa maṣriyya.
12. haaði jigaara 'ingiliiziyya.
13. haaði tiffaaHa libnaaniyya.
14. haaða filim hazali.
15. haaða filim pooliisi.
16. haaða filim muxiif.

Drill 6 *Statement – Comment*

Example : T : haaða l-filim muxiif waajid
'This movie is very scary.'

S_1 : la ya rayyal muub waajid:
'No, man! Not very much.'

S_2 : haaða l-filim muub muxiif waajid.
'This movie is not very scary.'

1. haaði l-bint jamiila waajiid.
2. haaðeel il-jamaa9a zeeniin waajid.
3. haaði s-sayyaara xarbaana killiš:
4. haaða l-mukaan ba9iid killiš.
5. haaði l-Hurma mitiina waajid.
6. haaða l-beet 9atiij waajid.
7. haaði ṭ-ṭariig ṭawiila waajid.
8. haðeel in-naas zeeniin waajid.
9. haaði l-ġitra saġiira waajid.

10. haaða l-juuti zeen killiš.
11. haaða l-muntazah naðiif waajid.
12. haaði l-9uṭla ṭawiila waajid.

Drill 7 *Substitution*

'ariid a9zimak. 'I would like to invite you (m.s.).'

1. 'inti
2. 'intum
3. 'intin
4. huwa
5. hum
6. hin
7. hiya
8. 'inta
9. mooza
10. kalθam
11. 9ali
12. 'ibraahiim
13. 'intum
14. 'intin
15. hum
16. 'il-mu9allimiin
17. 'iš-šyuux
18. 'il-banaat
19. hin
20. 'il-waziir

Drill 8 *Transformation:* feminine → masculine

1. ween riHti? ma šiftič ams.
2. raaHin wiyya jamaa9a.
3. xaðat jalbuut u raaHat.
4. raaHan yṣiidin simač.
5. ba9deen rij9an in-naadi.
6. 'aana xaabartič fi l-leel.

7. fi l-leel čint fi s-siinama.
8. tHibb il-'aflaam.
9. 'is-sikirteera foog.
10. t9arfiin il-miškila?
11. štirat θoob jadiid.
12. Haṣṣalan bi9θa.
13. haaðа 9ala Hsaabič.
14. tġaddat u t9aššat wiyyaana.

Drill 9 *Transformation:* singular → plural

1. haaða filim 'iiraani.
2. haaða filim pooliisi.
3. haaði safiina 'amrikaaniyya.
4. huwa xaabar 'ams.
5. 'aana 9iraft iṭ-ṭariig.
6. 'iða mista9jil 'ixið taksi.
7. liff 9ala š-šimaal.
8. reewis u ba9deen ruuH siida.
9. 9indi jalbuut ṣaġiir.
10. ma ṣaad simač.
11. huwa mumaθθil zeen.
12. yriid yitrayyag Hummoṣ.
13. hiya laazim truuH il-beet.
14. baġa yištiri hduum u jawaati.
15. baġeet 'ašuuf il-filim.
16. 'it-taðaakir 9ala Hsaabi.

Drill 10 *Translation*

1. I don't like this kind of movie. It is scary.
2. The actor in "Doctor Zhivago" Is Omar Sharif. He is an Arab.
3. We swam in the sea. Then we had lunch on the shore.
4. He called me last night, but I wasn't home.
5. What would you (f.s.) like to have for dinner? Fish and rice?
6. There's no work tomorrow. It's Accession Day.
7. I took my family to a park. We ate there; the children played and had a lot of fun.
8. On Independence Day we went to mosque to pray and read from the Quran; after that we went to celebrate the Feast with the Shaikhs.
9. We went to the club last night. We had dinner and saw a good movie later on.
10. We wanted to have dinner at Iwan Restaurant, but it's very expensive.

UNIT 38

I. TEXT

fi maktab il-bariid

jaasim : ween maktab il-bariid min fađ̣lak?

ṣaaliH : đaak iṣ-ṣoob.

jaasim : 'ariid aṭarriš haađa l-xaṭṭ 'ila ngiltara.

Hamad : triida 9aadi walla jawwi?

jaasim : jawwi min fađ̣lak.

Hamad : zeen. haađa ṭaabi9 bu 'imya w xamsiin fils.

jaasim : tfađ̣đ̣al! 9indi ṭard 'ariid aṭarrša 'ila l-kweet.

Hamad : ruuH id-dariiša θ-θaanya!

---

jaasim : 'abi 'aṭarriš haađa ṭ-ṭard 'ila l-kweet.

byaat : weeš fi daaxla?

jaasim : kutub u 'awraag .....

byaat : jawwi walla bi l-baHar?

jaasim : 9aadi bi l-baHar bas msajjal.

byaat : zeen. Huṭṭa 9ala l-miizaan: haađa keeluween u xamsiin ġraam. ykallif miteen u θalaaθiin fils.

jaasim : tfađ̣đ̣al! mata yooṣal?

byaat : nšaaḷḷa 9ugub šahreen walla θalaaθa.

II. TRANSLATION

At the Post Office

Jasim : Where is the Post Office, please?

Salih : That side.

Jasim : I want to send this letter to England.

Hamad : Do you want it ordinary or air mail?

Jasim : Air mail, please.

Hamad : O.K. This is a 150 - fils stamp.

Jasim : Here: I have a package which I want to send to Kuwait.

Hamad : Go to the next window!

Jasim : I want to send this package to Kuwait.

Byat : What's inside it?

Jasim : Books, papers, ...

Byat : Air mail or sea mail?

Jasim : Ordinary sea mail, but certified.

Byat : O.K. Put it on the scales! This is two kilograms and fifty grams. It costs two hundred and thirty fils.

Jasim : Here! When will it get there?

Byat : Hopefully, in two or three months.

III. VOCABULARY

ðaak	(pron.) that
ṭarraš	(yṭarriš) he sent
xaṭṭ	(xṭuuṭ) letter

jawwi	air (adj.); air mail
ṭaabi9	(ṭuwaabi9) postage stamp
ṭard	(ṭruud) package
daaxil	(prep., adv.) inside
msajjal	(–iin) registered, certified
ġraam	(–aat) gram
kallaf	(ykallif) it cost

IV. ADDITIONAL VOCABULARY

šaal	(yšiil) he carried, lifted
ṣanduug	(ṣanaadiig) box
ṣanduug bariid	mail box
9inwaan	(9anaawiin) address
mursil	(–iin) sender
bargiyya	(–aat) telegram
xafiif	(xfaaf) light (adj.)
θagiil	(θgaal) heavy

V. DRILLS

Drill 1 *Substitution*

'ariid 'aṭarriš haaða l-xaṭṭ 'ila **ngiltara.**

1. London
2. America
3. Dubai
4. Bahrain
5. Abu Dhabi
6. Kuwait

7. Sharja
8. Ajman
9. Oman
10. Ras Al-Khaima
11. Qatar
12. Iran
13. India
14. Lebanon
15. Syria
16. Iraq
17. Jordan
18. Libya
19. Tunisia
20. Saudi Arabia

Drill 2 *Variable Substitution*

ʼariid aṭarriš haaᵭa l-xaṭṭ ʼila ngiltara.

1. ṭard
2. bargiyya
3. huwa
4. Saudi Arabia
5. hiya
6. giṭar
7. hum
8. niHin
9. ṭard
10. ʼaana
11. 9ali
12. 9alya
13. bargiyya
14. ʼinta?
15. ʼinti?
16. ʼintum
17. ʼintin
18. niHin
19. ʼaana
20. hum

Drill 3 *Chain – Cued*

T : regular – air

S_1 : triida 9aadi walla jawwi? 'Do you (m.s.) want it regular or air mail?'

S_2: jawwi min faðlak! 'Air mail, please.'

1. regular – registered
2. light – heavy
3. air – regular
4. air – by sea
5. by sea – air
6. fried – baked
7. new – old
8. big – small
9. now – later
10. black – white
11. long – short
12. hot – cold
13. heavy – light
14. expensive – cheap
15. Indian – Persian

Drill 4 *Variable Substitution*

9aṭni ṭaabi9 bu 'imyat fils! 'Give (m.s.) me a 100 - fils stamp!'

1. 150 fils
2. 200 fils
3. give us
4. 300 fils
5. give her
6. $\frac{1}{2}$ rupee
7. 1 rupee
8. give them (f.)
9. $\frac{1}{4}$ dinar
10. $\frac{1}{2}$ dinar
11. give them (f.)
12. 1 riyal
13. $1\frac{1}{2}$ riyals
14. give me
15. 5 cents
16. 10 cents
17. 25 cents
18. give us
19. give her
20. give them (m.)

Drill 5 *Variable Substitution*

'ariid 'aṭarrša jawwi. 'I want to send it air mail.'

1. regular
2. registered
3. huwa
4. sulṭaan
5. mooza
6. Hiṣṣa
7. niHin
8. by sea
9. huwa
10. 'inta?
11. air mail
12. 'inti?
13. regular
14. 'intum?
15. 'intin?
16. air mail
17. hum
18. registered
19. 'aana
20. niHin

Drill 6 *Repetition*

1.	Huṭṭa 9ala l-miizaan!	'Put (m.s.) it (m.) on the scales!'
2.	Huṭṭha 9ala l-miizaan!	'Put (m.s.) it (f.) on the scales!'
3.	Huṭṭhum 9ala l-miizaan!	'Put (m.s.) them (m.) on the scales!'
4.	Huṭṭii 9ala l-miizaan!	'Put (f.s.) it (m.) on the scales!'
5.	Huṭṭiiha 9ala l-miizaan!	'Put (f.s.) it (f.) on the scales!'
6.	Huṭṭiihum 9ala l-miizaan!	'Put (f.s.) them (m.) on the scales!'
7.	Huṭṭuu 9ala l-miizaan!	'Put (m.p.) it (m.) on the scales!'
8.	Huṭṭuuha 9ala l-miizaan!	'Put (m.p.) it (f.) on the scales!'
9.	Huṭṭuuhum 9ala l-miizaan!	'Put (m.p.) them (m.) on the scales!'

Drill 7 *Substitution*

a. T : 2:50

S : keeluween u xamsiin ġraam
'two kilograms and 50 grams'

1. $1\frac{1}{2}$ kilograms
2. 2 kilograms
3. 5 kilograms
4. $1\frac{1}{4}$ kilograms
5. 1:300
6. 2:350
7. 2:700
8. 3:620
9. 3:100
10. 4:820
11. 2:750
12. 1:900
13. 10:430
14. 12:580
15. 15:240
16. 14:860

b. ykallif **miteen fils.** 'It costs 200 fils.'

1. 150 fils
2. 100 fils
3. 200 fils
4. 2 dollars
5. 5 dollars
6. 20 dollars
7. $1\frac{1}{2}$ dinars
8. 2 dinars
9. $3\frac{1}{2}$ dinars
10. $\frac{1}{4}$ dinars
11. $1\frac{1}{2}$ rupees
12. 2 rupees
13. 13 rupees
14. 100 riyals
15. 150 riyals
16. 200 riyals
17. 153 riyals
18. 500 fils
19. 4 dinars
20. 1000 dollars

Drill 8 *Question – Answer*

S_1: mata yooṣal? 'When does he (it) arrive?'

S_2: nšaal̤l̤a 9ugub šahreen walla θalaaθa.
'Hopefully, in two or three months.'

1. one or two days
2. one or two hours
3. one or two weeks
4. one or two months
5. one or two years
6. 6 or 7 days
7. 3 or 4 hours
8. 2 or 3 weeks
9. 3 or 4 months
10. 5 or 6 years
11. 4 or 5 days
12. 1 or 2 hours
13. 7 or 8 weeks
14. 5 or 6 months
15. 1 or $1\frac{1}{2}$ years

Drill 9 *Variable Substitution*

ruuH id-dariiša θ-θaanya! 'Go (m.s.) to the second window!'

1. 3rd
2. 4th
3. 5th
4. 6th
5. you (f.s.)
6. 2nd
7. you (m.p.)
8. you (f.p.)
9. 'iṭ-ṭaabig
10. you (m.s.)
11. 3rd
12. you (f.s.)
13. 'il-maktab
14. you (m.s.)
15. 'id-dariiša
16. you (f.p.)
17. 4th
18. you (m.s.)
19. 2nd
20. 'iṭ-ṭaabig

Drill 10 *Transformation*

Habb yaakil simač. 'He liked (wanted) to eat fish.' ———
huwa 'akal simač. 'He ate fish.'

1. huwa Habb yṭarrša jawwi.
2. huwa Habb ysaafir bi l-baHar.
3. hiya Habbat truuH ðaak iṣ-ṣoob.
4. hiya Habbat tšiil iṣ-ṣanduug.
5. hum Habbaw yṭarršuun bargiyya.
6. hum Habbaw yṭarršuun ṭard.
7. hin Habban yišrabin gahwa.
8. 'inta Habbeet t9arif il-9inwaan.
9. 'inta Habbeet tsaafir?
10. 'aana Habbeet 'aktib xaṭṭ.
11. 'intum Habbeetu txaabruun?
12. 'inti Habbeeti tit9aššiin?
13. 'intin Habbeetin titġaddin?
14. 'niHin Habbeena nṣalli.
15. 'aana Habbeet 'agra.
16. hiya Habbat tṣuum.

Drill 11 *Transformation:* masculine → feminine

1. huwa ṣaam rumðaan.
2. 'aana zurt sadiigi fi l-beet.
3. hum ṣallaw fi l-masyid.

4. huwa muub ihni. raaH il-kaniisa.
5. haađa mumaθθil yđ̣aHHik.
6. xamiis yriid yitrayyag.
7. 'amiin baġa ysiir is-suug.
8. hum mišaw wiyyaana.
9. bu saalim štira hduum.
10. ma 9inda juuti zeen.
11. nisa yištiri ġamiis u θoob.
12. hum yilbasuun 'aHsan šayy.
13. gaal: "ma 9alee!"
14. huwa mursil il-bargiyya.
15. trayyag beeđ̣ u xubiz.
16. t9aššeet inta?

UNIT 39

I. TEXT

'il-xaliij il-9aṛabi

saalim : leen nguul il-xaliij il-9aṛabi, weeš ya9ni?

Hamdaan : 'il-xaliij il-9aṛabi ya9ni l-bildaan il-9aṛabiyya lli 9ala l-xaliij. xaliij tidri ya9ni baHar.

saalim : weeš hiya l-bildaan? weeš fiiha?

Hamdaan : haađa weeš? dars fi l-juġraafya? 'inta tabi timtiHinni?

saalim : la waḷḷa! ṭaal 9umrak 'aana ma dri. 'abiik t9allimni.

Hamdaan : zeen. 'il-bildaan hiya l-baHreen u giṭar u bu đ̣abi w dbayy u raaṣ il-xeema w 9ajmaan w iš-šaarja w 'imm il-giween u ma dri ba9ad.

saalim : zeen. mumkin tguul li šayy 9an bu đ̣abi?

Hamdaan : 'ii na9am. bu đ̣abi, 'aḷḷa ysallimk, hiya l-9aaṣima. 'il-9aaṣima ya9ni l-madiina lli fiiha l-Haakim, ṭawiil il-9umur, u duwaayir il-Hukuuma. zeen halHiin 9indi šuġul. 'astarxiṣ. wagt θaani 'a9llmak b giṭar w il-baHreen kađaalik. fi maan illaa.

saalim : baarak aḷḷa fiik. ma9 is-salaama.

II. TRANSLATION

The Arabian Gulf

Salim : When we say The Arabian Gulf, what do we mean?

Hamdan : The Arabian Gulf means the Arab countries which are on the Gulf. Gulf, you know, means sea.

Salim : Which countries are they? What's in them?

Hamdan : What's this? A lesson in geography? You want to test me?

Salim : No, believe me. I (simply) don't know. I want you to let me know.

Hamdan : Fine. The countries are Bahrain, Qatar, Abu Dhabi, Dubai, Ras al-Khaima, Ajman, Sharja, Umm al-Qaiwain, and I don't know what else.

Salim : Fine. Will you tell me something about Abu Dhabi?

Hamdan : Certainly. Abu Dhabi, God protect you, is the capital. The capital means the city where the ruler, God prolong his life, and the government departments are. Now I have some work (to do). I take leave. I will let you know about Qatar and Bahrain some other time. Good-bye!

Salim : God bless you! Good-bye.

III. VOCABULARY

bildaan	(s. **balad**) countries, states
dars	(duruus) lesson
juġraafya	geography
mtiHan	(yimtiHin) he tested, examined
ṭaal	(yṭuul) he lasted long; he lived long
ṭaal 9umrak!	May God prolong your life!

9allam	(y9allim) he taught
9aaṣima	(9awaaṣim) capital
Haakim	(Hukkaam) ruler
daayra	(duwaayir) department
starxaṣ	(yistarxiṣ) has asked permission to leave
wagt	('awgaat) time
kaðaalik	too, also

IV. ADDITIONAL VOCABULARY

ftiham	(yiftihim) he understood
'imaara	(–aat) emirate, shaikhdom
mittaHid	(–iin) united (adj.)
ṣa9b	difficult, hard
'ittiHaad	union
rayyis	(–iin) boss, head
taariix	(tawaariix) history
Hsaab	arithmetic; (bank) account
handasa	engineering; geometry
9umri ma ...	I have never ...

V. GRAMMAR

9umr– ma + Perfect Tense

We know that a verb in the perfect tense is negated by the use of the particle **ma.** If this construction, i.e. **ma** + perfect tense is preceded by **9umur** + suffixed pronoun, we get the equivalent of (I, he, etc.) have never .....

9umri ma šribt biira. 'I have never drunk any beer.'

9umraha ma raHat il-madrasa. 'She has never been to school.'

The question 'Have (you) ever...' is expressed by **9umur** + suffixed pronoun + perfect tense:

9umrak šribt biira? 'Have you ever drunk any beer?'

(Drill 11)

NOTE ON TEXT

The term Arabian Gulf is usually limited to Qatar, Bahrain, and the United Arab Emirates, which are Abu Dhabi, Dubai, Sharja, Ajman, Umm Al-Qaiwain, Ras Al-Khaima, and Fujaira.

VI. DRILLS

Drill 1 *Combination*

haaða filim. 'aana šift il-filim 'ams. ——— haaða l-filim illi šifta 'ams.
'This is a movie. I saw this movie yesterday.' → 'This is the movie which I saw yesterday.'

1. haaða dars. 'aana dirast id-dars il-yoom.
2. haaða mudarris. 'il-mudarris mtiHanni.
3. haaða ktaab juġraafya. 'il-'awlaad dirsaw li-ktaab.
4. haaði daayra. niHin štaġalna fi d-daayra.
5. haaði blaad. huwa 9allamni bi li-blaad.
6. haaði sayyaara. 'is-sayyaara kallafat 'alfeen diinaar.

7. haaða ṭard. 'uxuuy ṭarraš iṭ-ṭard.
8. haaða xaṭṭ. sadiigi kitab il-xaṭṭ.
9. haaða rayyaal. 'ir-rayyaal raaH ðaak iṣ-ṣoob.
10. haðeel Hamaamiil. 'il-Hamaamiil šaalaw iṣ-ṣanaadiig.
11. haaði bargiyya. 'il-waziir ṭarraš il-bargiyya.
12. haaða 9inwaan. 'aana kitabt il-9inwaan 9ala l-xaṭṭ.
13. haðeel jamaa9a. niHin šifna l-jamaa9a fi gaṣr iš-šeex.
14. haaða naadi. hum li9baw fi n-naadi.
15. haaða jalbuut. hum 'axðaw il-jalbuut.
16. haaði bint. 'aana tġaddeet wiyya l-bint.

Drill 2 *Substitution*

haaða dars fi l-juġraafya. 'This is a lesson in geography.'

1. English
2. Arabic
3. French
4. history
5. arithmetic
6. geometry
7. engineering
8. Quran
9. education
10. broadcasting
11. food
12. training
13. petroleum
14. geography
15. history
16. Arabic

Drill 3 *Repetition*

1. huwa yabi yimtiHinni.
'He wants to examine (test) me.'

2. hiya tabi timtiHinni.
'She wants to examine me.'
3. hum yabuun yimtiHnuuni.
'They (m.) want to examine me.'
4. hin yabin yimtiHnuuni.
'They (f.p.) want to examine me.'
5. 'inta tabi timtiHinni.
'You (m.s.) want to examine me.'
6. 'inti tabiin timtiHniini.
'You (f.s.) want to examine me.'
7. 'intum tabuun timtiHnuuni.
'You (m.p.) want to examine me.'
8. 'intin tabin timtiHnuuni.
'You (f.p.) want to examine me.'

Drill 4 *Variable Substitution*

'aana ma dri ba9ad. 'I do not know what else.'

1. niHin
2. 'inta
3. 'inti
4. sulṭaan
5. nuura
6. hin
7. 'intum
8. 'aana
9. 'a9rif
10. leeš
11. statement
12. huwa
13. question
14. hiya
15. ween
16. keef

Drill 5 *Repetition*

1. 'abiik t9allimni. 'I want you (m.s.) to let me know.'
2. 'abiič t9allmiini.
3. 'abiikum t9allmuuni.
4. 'abiikin t9allimnani.
5. 'abiiha t9allimni.
6. 'abiihin y9allmuuni.
7. 'abii y9allimni.
8. 'abiihum y9allmuuni.
9. 'abiik t9allimni.

Drill 6 *Chain – Cued*

T : Qatar

S_1: ween giṭar? 'Where is Qatar?'

T : Arabian Gulf

S_2: giṭar 9ala l-xaliij il-9aṛabi. 'Qatar is on the Arabian Gulf'

1. Dubai
2. Bahrain
3. Sharja
4. Kuwait
5. Abu Dhabi
6. Ajman
7. Al-Fujaira
8. Doha
9. Qatar
10. Ras Al-Khaima
11. 'umm il-giween
12. Manama

Drill 7 *Question – Answer*

S_1: weeš 9aaṣimat giṭar?
'What is the capital of Qatar?'

S_2: 'id-dooHa 9aaṣimaṭ giṭar.
'Doha is the capital of Qatar.'

1. dbayy
2. bu ðabi
3. 'il-baHreen
4. li-kweet
5. maṣir
6. libnaan
7. 'ingiltara
8. 'amriika
9. giṭar
10. 'il-hind
11. 'il-'ardun
12. suuriyya
13. li-9raag
14. faṛansa
15. kanada
16. 'iiraan
17. 'il-baakistaan
18. liibya
19. 'is-suudaan
20. giṭar

Drill 8 *Double Substitution*

Haakim bu ðabi 'iš-šeex zaayid ṭawiil il-9umur.'
'The Ruler of Abu Dhabi is Shaikh Zayid.'

1. giṭar
2. 'il-baHreen
3. li-kweet
4. raaṣ il-xeema
5. dbayy
6. 'iš-šaarja
7. 'umm il-giween
8. 9ajmaan
9. bu ðabi
10. 'il-fijeera
11. 'il-baHreen
12. giṭar

Drill 9 *Variable Substitution*

huwa ftiham. 'He understood.'

1. 'aana
2. negative
3. hum
4. niHin

5.	positive	13.	hiya
6.	imperfect	14.	hum
7.	'inta	15.	negative
8.	'inti	16.	'inta
9.	'intum	17.	'aana
10.	'intin	18.	'intum
11.	huwa	19.	hiya
12.	question	20.	huwa

Drill 10 *Completion*

a. 9umri ma ..... 'I have never ..... '

9umri ma šribt biira. 'I have never drunk (any) beer.'

1.	been to Ajman	8.	traveled by ship
2.	eaten kubba and Hummoṣ	9.	had dinner at 5:00 p.m.
3.	studied French	10.	invited him to my house
4.	worked in the evening	11.	prayed in this mosque
5.	written a letter in Arabic	12.	visited this family
6.	caught any fish	13.	bought an old car
7.	seen a French movie	14.	had (gotten) any increase

b. Change the sentences in a. to: **9umraha ma ...** 'She has never ...'

c. Change the sentences in a. to: **9umrak ma ...** 'You (m.s.) have never ...'

Drill 11 *Translation*

1. This box is very heavy. I can't lift it.
2. Where is the Gulf of Oman?
3. How do you say the United Arab Emirates in Arabic?
4. Saudi Arabia is south of the U.A.E.
5. There are very good fish in the Arabian Gulf.
6. Gee, I forgot to go to the market today.
7. I will see you at some other time and tell you the problem.
8. Will you tell me something about Fujaira?
9. I'm afraid I do not know very much about Fujaira.
10. How long does it take by plane from Abu Dhabi to Beirut?

UNIT 40

I. TEXT

gitar w il-baHreen

Hamdaan : giṭar w il-baHreen gariibiin min bu ḏ̣abi. min bu ḏ̣abi ʼila giṭar Hawaali nuṣṣ saa9a b iṭ-ṭayyaara w nafs iš-šayy min giṭar la l-baHreen. 9aaṣimat giṭar id-dooHa. ʼid-dooHa madiina jamiila fiiha basaatiin u šijar u manaaḏ̣ir Hilwa. Haḏ̣iigat il-Hayawaanaat fi d-dooHa fiiha ʼasad u nimir u fiil u ġuzlaan u sa9aadiin u Hayawaanaat θaanya. ʼil-hawa fi d-dooHa yaabis fi l-geeḏ̣, ʼaybas min bu ḏ̣abi walla l-baHreen. ʼil-Harr nafs iš-šayy.

saalim : w il-baHreen jiziira walla čiḏ̣i?

Hamdaan : ʼil-baHreen ṭaal 9umrak jiziira 9ooda. fi l-Hagiiga l-baHreen Hda9šar jiziira lo ʼakθar lo ʼagall, waḷḷa ma dri. ʼil-manaama 9aaṣimat il-baHreen w il-manaama ʼakbar jiziira. li-mHarrag ʼaṣġar min il-manaama. ʼil-baHreen winsa winsa killiš. ʼil-jaww fi l-baHreen fii ruṭuuba waajid fi l-geeḏ̣. ʼaana halHiin ʼaštaġil dreewil fi šarikat baabko. gabil čint aštaġil mikaniiki fi jiziirat daas wiyya ʼadma fi bu ḏ̣abi.

saalim : weeš ʼanwaa9 is-simač fi l-xaliij ?

Hamdaan : simač il-xaliij aḷḷa ysallimk killiš zeen. ṭayyib. fi ṣbeeṭi w ṣaafi w hamuur u čan9ad u ribyaan... haaḏ̣i ʼasmaač il-xaliij.

II. TRANSLATION

Qatar and Bahrain

Hamdan : Qatar and Bahrain are close to Abu Dhabi. It is about half an hour from Abu Dhabi to Qatar by plane, and it is the same thing from Qatar to Bahrain. The capital of Qatar is Doha. Doha is a beautiful city. There are gardens, trees, and beautiful views in it. In the zoo in Doha there are a lion, a tiger, an elephant, deer, and other animals. The weather is dry in Doha in the summer; it is drier than in Abu Dhabi or Bahrain. The heat is the same.

Salim : And is Bahrain an island or what?

Hamdan : Bahrain, may you live long, is a very big island. In fact, Bahrain is eleven islands, may be more or less. I really don't know. Manama is the capital of Bahrain and it (Manama) is the biggest island. Muharraq is smaller than Manama. Bahrain is fun—— a lot of fun. The weather in Bahrain is very humid is the summer. I am now working as a driver for BAPCO. Before, I was working as a mechanic on Das Island with ADMA in Abu Dhabi.

Salim : What are the kinds of fish in the Gulf?

Hamdan : The fish of the Gulf, God protect you, are very good. (They're) delicious. There are subeiti, safi, hamur, can'ad, and shrimp. These are the fishes of the Gulf.

III. VOCABULARY

nafs	(with foll. def. n.) same
nafs iš-šayy	the same (thing)
bustaan	(basaatiin) orchard; garden
šjara	(šijar) tree (coll.)
manđ̣ar	(manaađ̣ir) view, scene, sight
Hilu	(f. **Hilwa**) beautiful, sweet
Hayawaan	(–aat) animal
Hadiigat Hayawaanaat	zoo
nimir	(nmuura) tiger, leopard
fiil	(fyaal) elephant
ġazaal	(ġuzlaan) deer; gazelle
sa9daan	(sa9aadiin) monkey; ape
yaabis	dry
Harr	heat
walla čiđi?	or what?
jiziira	(jazaayir) island
lo ... lo	either ... or
9ood	big, large
Hagiiga	(Hagaayig) truth; fact
fi l-Hagiiga	in fact
winsa	fun
winsa killiš	a lot of fun
jaww	atmosphere; weather

ruṭuuba	humidity
dreewil	(dreewliyya) driver
mikaniiki	(n.) mechanic; (adj.) mechanical
jiziirat daas	Das Island
ṣbeeṭi	kind of fish
hamuur	kind of fish
čan9ad	kind of fish
ribyaan	shrimp

IV. GRAMMAR

čaan (kaan) + Imperfect

The past continuous tense in English is expressed by **čaan (kaan)** plus the imperfect tense of the verb. Both parts of the verbs, i.e., **čaan (kaan)** and the imperfect verb, agree with the subject. Examples:

čint 'adris.	'I was studying.'
čaanat tidris.	'She was studying.'

(Drill 10)

V. DRILLS

Drill 1 *Double Substitution*

bu ḏ̣abi 9ind dbayy. gariiba minha waajid.
'Abu Dhabi is by Dubai. It is very close to it.'

1. Qatar – Bahrain
2. Syria – Lebanon
3. Abu Dhabi – Qatar
4. Syria – Iraq

5.	Iran – Iraq	11.	Kuwait – Iraq
6.	Arizona – California	12.	Ajman – Sharja
7.	Jordan – Syria	13.	England – France
8.	Michigan – Illinois	14.	Ajman – Umm Al-Q.
9.	Bahrain – Saudi Arabia	15.	Iran – Kuwait
10.	Dubai – Sharja		

Drill 2 *Substitution – Cues*

T : bu ð̣abi – giṭar – ½ hour

S : min bu ð̣abi la giṭar Hawaali nuṣṣ saa9a bi ṭ-ṭayyaara.
'It's about half an hour by plane from Abu Dhabi to Qatar.'

1. landan – beruut – 5 hours
2. bu ð̣abi – beruut – 3 hours
3. li-kweet – giṭar – 1 hour
4. dbayy – bu ð̣abi – ¼ hour
5. nyuu yoork – landan – 8 hours
6. 'il-baHreen – beruut – 2½ hours
7. 'id-dooHa – landan – 6 hours
8. 9ammaan – beruut – 1 hour
9. landan – li-kweet – 6 hours
10. dbayy – 9umaan – 1 hour

Drill 3 *Combination*

haaða walad. 'aana šift il-walad fi s-suug ––
haaða nafs il-walad illi šifta fi s-suug.

'This is a boy. I saw the boy in the market.——
This is the same boy I saw in the market.'

1. haaðа manḍ̣ar. šift il-manḍ̣ar.
2. haaða maṭ9am. sadiigi 'akal fi l-maṭ9am.
3. haaði bint. riHt wiyya l-bint.
4. haaði Hadiigat Hayawaanaat. zurt il-Hadiiga.
5. haaða mukaan. 'akalt simač fi l-mukaan.
6. haaða Hayawaan. 'il-Hayawaan čaan ihnaak.
7. haaða dreewil. 'id-dreewil yištaġil wiyya š-šarika.
8. haðeel 9yaal. šift li-9yaal fi š-šaari9.
9. haðeel rayaayiil. 'ir-rayaayill štaġlaw 'ams.
10. haðeel banaat. 'il-banaat raadin ysaafrin.

Drill 4 *Combination*

'id-dooHa madiina jamiila. fii basaatiin waajid fi d-dooHa.———
'id-dooHa madiina jamiila fiiha basaatiin waajid.

1. 'il-Hadiiga čibiira. fii Hayawaanaat waajid fi l-Hadiiga.
2. 'il-madrasa ṣaġiira. fii xamsiin walad fi l-madrasa.
3. 'il-bustaan jamiil. fii šijar waajid fi l-bustaan.
4. 'il-beet jadiid. fii xams Hijar fi l-beet.
5. 'it-taanki čibiir. fii malyoon galan mayy fi t-taanki.
6. 'il-9aaṣima čibiira. fii naas waajid fi l-9aaṣima.
7. li-kweet ġaniyya. fii batrool waajid fi li-kweet.

8. 'il-balad fagiira. ma fii batrool waajid fi l-balad.
9. 'id-daayra čibiira. fii miyat muwaḏ̣ḏ̣af fi d-daayra.
10. 'iš-šigga jadiida. fii kill šayy fi š-šigga.

Drill 5 *Transformation:* positive → elative

Example : T : 9indi ktaab jadiid. 'I have a new book.'
S : mHammad 9inda ktaab 'ajdad.
'Muhammad has a newer book.'

1. 9indi sayyaara jadiida.
2. 9indi šigga naḏ̣iifa.
3. 9indi manḏ̣ar jamiil.
4. 9indi su'aal ṣa9b.
5. 9indi muwaḏ̣ḏ̣af fagiir.
6. 9indi rayyis zeen.
7. 9indi ṭamaaṭ raxiiṣ.
8. 9inda walad mariiḏ̣.
9. 9indahum mudiir mumtaaz.
10. 9inda fluus kaθiir.
11. 9indana beet 9atiij.
12. 9inda biira baarda.
13. 9indaha miškila ṣa9ba.
14. 9inda filfil Haarr.

Drill 6 *Transformation:* adjective — elative

T : haaḏa l-walad ṭawiil. 'This boy is tall.'

S_1 : haaḏa l-walad 'aṭwal min haḏaak il-walad.
'This boy is taller than that boy.'

S_2 : haaḏa 'aṭwal walad. 'This is the tallest boy.'

1. haaḏi s-sayyaara jadiida.
2. haaḏa l-walad gaṣiir.
3. haaḏi l-miškila ṣa9ba.
4. haaḏa l-filfil Haarr.
5. haaḏa l-xass raxiiṣ.
6. haaḏi l-bint jamiila

7. haađa l-batrool ġaali.
8. haađi l-Hijra Haarra.
9. haađa l-hawa Haaff.
10. haađa š-šeex ġani.
11. haađi l-Hurma čibiira.
12. haađa r-rayyis ṭawiil.
13. haađi l-bint 9aagla.
14. haađi l-Hijra waṣxa.
15. haađa l-gaṣir zeen.
16. haađa ṭ-ṭariig gaṣiir.

Drill 7 *Chain – Cued*

S_1: čeef il-jaww il-yoom? 'How is the weather today?'

T : hot

S_2: 'il-jaww Haarr il-yoom. 'The weather is hot today.'

1. cold
2. cold and nice
3. very cold
4. very dry
5. a little dry
6. very hot
7. hot and humid
8. very humid
9. a little humid
10. hot but dry
11. very good
12. not hot
13. not humid
14. a little cold
15. cold and humid

Drill 8 *Translation*

1. I work as a driver for BAPCO Company.
2. Before, I was working as a mechanic for ADMA on Das Island.
3. This car is very good. It's very heavy.

4. This tea is very light. I can't drink it.
5. There are lots of kinds of fish in the Gulf.
6. It's about 500 kilometers from here to Al-Ain.
7. It's about the same distance to Dubai.
8. Kuwait is very far. You can't drive there by yourself.
9. In fact, tomatoes are cheaper and better over there.
10. This coffee is very strong. I can't drink it.

Drill 9 *Translation*

1. Bahrain is a large island. It is, in fact, eleven islands or more.
2. Are you (f.s.) busy today? I'm not very busy. In fact, I'm busy for three hours only.
3. If you want the truth, the fish of the Gulf are the best.
4. You can't say that the fish of the Gulf of Oman are the same.
5. Das Island is a very big island. It's in Abu Dhabi.
6. The truth is that this is the richest country.
7. The zoo in Doha has a lot of animals.
8. I do not know what to say. This is not the truth.
9. God bless you! This is the best thing.
10. When I was studying last night, my friend came.

Drill 10 *Variable Substitution*

čint ʹaštaġil ʹams.

1. saalim
2. mooza
3. Hiṣṣa
4. byaat
5. niHin
6. nṣiid simač
7. ʹaana
8. hin
9. niHin
10. huwa
11. yištiri laHam
12. ʹaana w ʹubuuy
13. hiya w rifiijatha
14. ʹintum
15. niHin

UNIT 41

I. TEXT

'amθaal

1. nuṣṣ il-miya xamsiin.
2. li-fluus tjiib il-9ruus.
3. gaṭu maṭaabix.
4. 'iđa šift rifiijak Hilu lạ taakla killa.
5. 9aṭi il xabbaaz xubzak walaw baag nuṣṣa.
6. 'illi ma y9arif iṣ-ṣagir yišwii.
7. 'il-9awar been il-9imyaan baaša.
8. yoom ṣaxxanna l-mayy širad id-diič.
9. 'iṭ-ṭuul ṭuul nxaḷa w il-9agil 9agl sxaḷa.
10. 'igđ̣ab maynuunak la yiik 'ayann minna.

II. TRANSLATION

Proverbs

1. Take it easy! ("Half a hundred is fifty.")
2. Money talks. ("Money brings the bride.")
3. He eats like a pig. ("A cat of kitchens.")
4. Don't use up your credit all at once. ("If you think your friend is nice, don't eat him all up at once.")
5. ("Give your bread to the baker although he might steal half of it.")

6. Don't kill the goose that lays the golden egg. ("He who does not know the falcon, will roast it.")
7. In the land of the blind, the one-eyed man is king. ("The one-eyed among the blind is a pasha.")
8. Forewarned is forearmed. ("When we heated the water, the rooster ran away.")
9. The mind of a child and the body of a man. ("The length is that of a palm tree and the mind is that of a young goat.")
10. A bird in the hand is worth two in the bush. ("Hold on to your crazy man, in case a crazier one comes along.")

III. VOCABULARY

maθal	('amθaal) proverb, saying
jaab	(yjiib) he brought, fetched
9aruus	(9araayis) bride
gaṭu	(gṭaawa) cat
xabbaaz	(–iin) baker
walaw	(conj.) although, even though
baag	(ybuug) he stole, robbed
ṣagir	(ṣguur) falcon; hawk
šawa	(yišwi) he grilled, roasted
9awar	(9iwraan) one-eyed (man)
'a9ma	(9imyaan) blind (man)
baaša	Pasha (title)
ṣaxxan	(yṣaxxin) he heated, warmed

širad	(yišrid) he ran away, escaped
diič	(dyuuč) rooster, cock
ṭuul	length, height, tallness
nxaḷa	(naxaḷ) palm tree (coll.)
9agil	(9guul) mind, brain
sxaḷa	(sxuuḷ) young goat, lamb
giđ̣ab	(yigđ̣ab) he grabbed
maynuun	(mayaaniin) insane, crazy (man)
'aya, ya	(yaji) he came (var. 'aja, ja)
'ayann	(elative) more, most insane

IV. ADDITIONAL VOCABULARY

9ariis	(9irsaan) bridegroom
9irs	(9raas) wedding
Hafla	(–aat) party
Haflat 9irs	wedding party, ceremony
kalb	(klaab) dog (var. čalb)
xaṛuuf	(xirfaan) lamb
bgara	(bagar) cow (coll.)
Hṣaan	(xeel) horses
bi9iir	(ba9aariin) camel (syn. jamal)
Hmaar	(Hamiir) donkey
sammaač	(simaamiič) fish dealer; fisherman
gaṣṣaab	(gaṣaaṣiib) butcher

Haddaad	(–iin) blacksmith
xayyaaṭ	(–iin) tailor
najjaar	(nijaajiir) carpenter
mHassin	(–iin) barber
dikkaan	(dikaakiin) shop, store

V. GRAMMAR

1. Conditionals

A conditional sentence in GA is one which has an if-clause and a result or main clause. The if-clause is introduced by either **ʼiðа** or **lo**. An if-clause introduced by **ʼiðа** expresses an open or a possible condition. The verb can be either perfect or imperfect in the if-clause, depending upon the meaning; in the result clause it can be imperfect or imperative:

ʼiða šift rifiijak guul la ta9aal baačir.
ʼIf you see your friend, tell him to come tomorrow.ʼ

ʼiða tšuuf rifiijak ya9ṭiik li-fluus.
ʼIf you see your friend, he will give you the money.ʼ

The clause introduced by **lo** expresses a condition which is unlikely or unreal. The verb in the lo-clause is either perfect or imperfect, depending upon the meaning; in the main clause it is either perfect (with **kaan** or **čaan**) or imperfect:

Unlikely Conditionals

lo šifta gilt la.	ʼIf I saw him, I would tell him.ʼ
lo ʼašuufa ʼaguul la.	ʼIf I saw him, I would tell him.ʼ

Unreal Conditionals

lo šifta čaan gilt la.	'If I had seen him, I would have told him.'

lo čaan 9inda fluus čaan jaab il-9aruus.
'If he had had money, he would have brought the bride.'

2. **'illi** at the beginning of a sentence means 'he who', as in the third proverbial phrase in the TEXT. Other examples: 'illi yibġa ṣ-ṣalaa yHaṣṣilha. (lit. 'He who wants prayer, can get it.') 'Make hay while the sun shines.'

'illi ma yjiiba Haliiba ma yjiiba z-zuur. (lit. 'He who is not brought by his own milk, will not be brought by force.') 'You can lead a horse to water, but you cannot make him drink.'

3. Note that **yoom** 'day' in the TEXT is followed by the verb **ṣaxxanna** 'we heated.' The resultant phrase, i.e., **yoom ṣaxxanna** means 'on the day we heated' or 'at the time we heated'. The phrase with **ma** between the adverb and the verb is also heard. Other examples:

leelat ma riHna	'the night we went'
sanat ma ya hni	'the year he came here'
yoom ma saafar	'the day he traveled'

UNIT 42

I. TEXT

daxtoor saami	:	ʼinta mitzawwij ya ʼax 9abd il-9aziiz?
9abd il-9aziiz	:	ʼii na9am. ʼil-Hamdu lillaah.
daxtoor saami	:	ʼiz-zawaaj ykallif waajid?
9abd il-9aziiz	:	waḷḷa ya daxtoor š aguul lak! ykallif waajid. ʼil-mahar il-9aadi ykallif tagriib θalaaθiin ʼalf ryaal. ʼil-9ariis yidfa9 kill šayy.
daxtoor saami	:	š da9wa! Haraam! šayy 9ajiib!
9abd il-9aziiz	:	ʼii waḷḷa šayy 9ajiib, walaakin haað̄i 9aada.
daxtoor saami	:	čeef in-naas yiHtafluun bi l-9irs?
9abd il-9aziiz	:	ṭaal 9umrak ʼawwal šayy il-9ariis yidfa9 mablaġ Hagg iṣ-ṣooġa: ð̄ahab u hduum Hagg il-9aruusa w ð̄ibaayiH Hagg iḍ̄-ḍ̄uyuuf. ba9-deen leelat il-9irs hal il-9ariis yaaxð̄uuna ʼila beet il-9aruusa w ihnaak yitgahwuun u yi9maluun raziif: yṭabbluun u yġannuun u yurguṣuun bi l-xanjar u bi s-seef u bi l-bindig u yruuHuun yimiin u yisaar ha š-šikil.
daxtoor saami	:	zeen u ba9ad?
9abd il-9aziiz	:	ba9deen fi l-yoom iθ-θaani hal il-9ariis yi9maluun Haflat ġada Hagg hal il-9aruusa w jamaa9athum. hal il-9aruusa yi9maluun Haflat 9aša Hagg hal il-9ariis u jamaa9ta w aṣHaaba. ʼil-9aruusa laazim tibga sab9 ayyaam fi beet halha wiyya l-9ariis. ma yxaḷḷuunha truuH ma9 rajilha gabil sab9 ayyaam. ba9deen il-9ariis yaaxið̄ha ʼila beeta w yi9zim halha w jamaa9athum.

II. TRANSLATION

Doctor Sami: Are you married, Brother Abdul Aziz?

Abdul Aziz : Yes. Praise be to God!

Doctor Sami: Does getting married cost a lot?

Abdul Aziz : What shall I say to you, Doctor? It costs a lot. The dowry costs about 30,000 riyals. The bridegroom pays everything.

Doctor Sami: What's wrong? Unlawful! Strange!

Abdul Aziz : Yes, indeed. It's something strange, but it's a custom.

Doctor Sami: How do people celebrate the wedding?

Abdul Aziz : God prolong your life! At first, the bridegroom pays a sum for jewelry and things: gold, clothes for the bride and slaughter animals for guests. Then, on the wedding night, the bridegroom's folks take him to the bride's home, where they drink coffee together and celebrate: they play the drums, sing, and dance with daggers, swords, and rifles, swaying left and right in this manner.

Doctor Sami: Fine. And then what?

Abdul Aziz : On the next day the bridegroom's folks give a luncheon for the bride's folks and their friends. The bride's folks give a dinner party for the bridegroom's folks and their friends. The bride has to stay for seven days with her bridegroom in the home of the bride's folks. They won't let her leave with her husband before seven days, after which the bridegroom takes her to his home and, later on, he invites her folks and their friends.

III. VOCABULARY

zawaaj	marriage, getting married
š	short for šu 'what'
mahar	dowry
da9wa	(da9aawi) matter; case
š da9wa?	What's wrong?
Haraam	unlawful; taboo
9ajiib	(–iin) strange, odd; astonishing
šayy 9ajiib	strange thing
9aada	(–aat) custom; habit
Htafal	(yiHtafil) he celebrated
mablaġ	(mabaaliġ) sum of money
sooġa	jewelry, jewels
ðahab	gold
9aruusa	(9araayis) bride (var. 9aruus)
ðibiiHa	(ðibaayiH) slaughter animal
tagahwa	(yitgahwa) he drank coffee
raziif	celebration
ṭabbal	(yṭabbil) he played, beat the drum
ġanna	(yġanni) he sang
rigaṣ	(yirguṣ) he danced
xanjar	(xanaajir) dagger
seef	(syuuf) sword
bindigiyya	(bindig) rifle

šikil	('aškaal) form, manner
ha š-šikil	in this manner
ġada	lunch
Haflat ġada	luncheon
9aša	dinner, supper
ṣaaHib	('aṣHaab) friend; fellow
baga	(yibga) he stayed
rajilha	her husband

GLOSSARY

The vocabulary items in this glossary are arranged alphabetically, according to the letters and the special symbols used in the text : ' b č d e f g ġ h H i j k l ḷ m n o q r s ṣ š t ṭ w x y z θ ð ð̣ 9.

In both glossaries nouns are entered in the masculine singular form. The plural is parenthesized in the meaning section. A few plurals that lack a singular are entered separately. Adjectives are entered in the masculine singular form, followed by the plural, if any. Feminine color adjectives are also included. Verbs are entered in the third person masculine singular form of the perfect tense, followed by the imperfect tense in parentheses in the meaning section.

GULF ARABIC – ENGLISH

'aana	I
'aaxir	('awaaxir) last, final
'aayil	oil, petroleum
'abrad	(elative) colder
'abu	(with foll. name) father of
'abu ð̣abi	Abu Dhabi
'abyað̣	(biið̣) white (f. **beeð̣a**)
'ab9ad	(elative) farther
'afgar	(elative) poorer
'agall	(elative) fewer; less
'agrab	(elative) closer
'agṣar	(elative) shorter
'aguul!	by the way!

'agwa	(elative) stronger
'aġla	(elative) more expensive
'aġna	(elative) richer
'ahil	folks; people (var. **hal**)
'aHad	someone, anyone
'aHarr	(elative) hotter
'aHsan	(elative) better
'ajdad	(elative) newer
'ajmal	(elative) more beautiful, handsome
'akal	(yaakil) he ate
'akbar	(elative) older; bigger
'akil	food
'akθar	(elative) more
'alf	('aalaaf) thousand
'al̤l̤a	God
'amraḏ̣	(elative) sicker
'amriika	America
'amriiki	('amrikaan) American
'ams	yesterday
'amten	(elative) fetter
'anḏ̣af	(elative) cleaner
'arba9a	four
'arba9iin	forty
'arba9imya	four hundred
'arba9ta9aš	fourteen
'arduni	(–yyiin) Jordanian
'arṭab	(elative) more humid
'arxaṣ	(elative) cheaper

'asad	('usuud) lion
'asim	('asaami) name
'aswad	(suud) black (f. sooda)
'aṣfar	(ṣufur) yellow (f. ṣafra)
'aṣġar	(elative) younger; smaller
'aṣHa	(elative) saner, more conscious
'aṭwal	(elative) taller
'aw	or
'awṣaṭ	middle
'awṣax	(elative) dirtier
'awwal	first
'awwal ams	(the day) before yesterday
'axað	(yaaxið) he took
'axð̣ar	(xuð̣ur) green (f. xað̣ra)
'ay?	which? what?
'ay Hazza?	what time?
'aya, ya	(yaji) he came
'ayann	(elative) crazier
'azrag	(zurg) blue (f. zarga)
'azyan	(elative) better
'aθneen	two
'að̣9af	(elative) weaker
'a9gal	(elative) wiser, saner
'a9jab	(yi9jib) he pleased
'a9ma	(9imyaan) blind
'a9taj	(elative) more ancient, older
'a9uuðu bi llaah!	God forbid!
'ibtidaa'i	elementary
'id-dooHa	Doha

ʼihnaak	there, over there
ʼihni	here (var. **hini**)
ʼii	yes
ʼii na9am	indeed, certainly
ʼiiraan	Iran
ʼiiraani	(–yyiin) Persian
ʼijaaza	(–aat) vacation, leave
ʼil-ʼaHad	Sunday
ʼil-ʼarba9a	Wednesday
ʼil-ʼardun	Jordan
ʼil-ʼaθneen	Monday
ʼil-baakistaan	Pakistan
ʼil-baHreen	Bahrain
ʼil-fijeera	Fujaira
ʼil-hind	India
ʼil-jazaaʼir	Algeria
ʼil-jum9a	Friday
ʼilla	except
ʼilli	(rel. pron.) who, that, which
ʼil-maġrib	Morocco
ʼil-manaama	Manama
ʼil-masa	(in) the evening
ʼil-qaahira	Cairo
ʼil-xaliij il-9aṛabi	Arabian Gulf
ʼil-xamiis	Thursday
ʼil-xarṭuum	Khartoum
ʼil-yoom	today
ʼil-9aam il-maaḏ̣i	last year
ʼimaara	(–aat) emirate

'imya	hundred
'ingiliizi	('ingiliiz) English (man)
'ingiltara	England
'inšaaḷḷa	God willing
'inta	you (m.s.)
'inti	you (f.s.)
'intin	you (f.p.)
'intum	you (m.p.)
'is-sabt	Saturday
'is-sabt il-maaḏ̣i	last Saturday
'is-subuu9 il-maaḏ̣i	last week
'is-suudaan	The Sudan
'is-su9uudiyya	Saudi Arabia
'istiġlaal	independence
'iṣ-ṣabaaH	(in) the morning
'iš-šaarja	Sharja
'iš-šahar il-maaḏ̣i	last month
'iš-šarg il-'awṣaṭ	Middle East
'ittaṣal	(yittaṣil) he contacted
'ittiHaad	(–aat) union, unity
'iθ-θalaaθa	Tuesday
'iḏa	if
'iḏaa9a	broadcasting (station)
'ubu	father
'ubuuy	my father
'umm il-giween	Umm al-Qaiwain
'uteel	(–aat) hotel
'uxu	('ixwaan) brother
'uxut	('axawaat) sister

baab	(biibaan) door
baačir	tomorrow
baag	(ybuug) he stole, robbed
baagi	remainder; remaining
baakistaani	(–yyiin) Pakistani
baamya	okra
baarak	(ybaarik) he blessed
baarid	(–iin) cold
baaša	(–waat) pasha
baddal	(ybaddil) he changed
baga	(yibga) he stayed, remained
bagar	(coll.) cows (f. **bgara**)
baglaawa	sweet pastry
baġa	(yibġa, yabi) he wanted
baġdaad	Baghdad
baHar	(bHuur) sea
balad	(bildaan) country: town, city
bank	(bnuuk) bank
bannad	(ybannid) he shut, closed
banṭaluun	(banaaṭliin) pants, trousers
baraz	(yabriz) he was ready
bargiyya	(–aat) telegram, cable
bariid	mail, letters
bas	(conj.) but
bas	only
batri	(bataari) battery
batrool	petroleum, gas
baṭṭiix	(coll.) cantaloupe

baxšiiš	tip, gratuity
ba9ad	too; also
ba9iid	far, far away
bdiwi	(badu) Bedouin
babsi	Pepsi Cola
beet	(byuut) house, home
beeđinjaan	(coll.) eggplant
beeđ̣	(coll.) eggs (f. **beeđ̣a**)
beruut	Beirut
biira	beer
bin	Bin, son of
binaaya	(–aat) building
bindigiyya	(bindig) rifle
bint	(banaat) girl; daughter
biṭaaqa	(–aat) card
bi9iir	(ba9aariin) camel
bi9θa	(–aat) scholarship
boṭil	(bṭaala) bottle
bruuHi	by myself; alone
bunni	(–yyiin) brown
burtaqaal	(coll.) oranges
burtaqaali	(–yyiin) orange (adj.)
bustaan	(basaatiin) garden, orchard
bxeer	well, fine
čaan	(ykuun) he was (var. **kaan**)
čaay	tea
čam?	(with foll. def. n.) how much?
	(with foll. indef. s.n.) how many?

čan9ad	kind of fish
čayyak	(yčayyik) he checked
čeef	how (var. **keef**)
čibiir	(kbaar) large; old (var. **kabiir**)
čiis	(kyaas) expense; bag
čingaaḷ	(čanaagiiḷ) fork
čiði	like this, in this manner
daar	(duur) house, home
daar il-mu9allimaat	Women's Teacher Training Center
daar il-mu9allimiin	Men's Teacher Training Center
daaw	(–aat) dhow, small ship
daaxil	(prep., adv.) inside
daayra	(dawaayir) department
daftar	(dafaatir) notebook
dagg	(ydigg) it rang
dara	(yidri) he knew, realized
darras	(ydarris) he taught
dars	(druus) lesson
darzan	(daraazin) dozen
dašš	(ydišš) he entered
dawwaar	(dawaawiir) circle, roundabout
daxtar	(daxaatir) doctor (f. **daxtoora**)
da9wa	(da9aawi) matter; case
dbayy	Dubai
difa9	(yidfa9) he paid
dihin	butter, fat
diič	(dyuuč) rooster
diinaar	(dinaaniir) dinar

dijaaj	(coll.) chicken; hens
dikkaan	(dikaakiin) shop, store
dimašq	Damascus
diras	(yidris) he studied
dirhim	dirham (unit of money)
diriiša	(diraayiš) window
dreewil	(dreewliyya) driver
duulaar	(–aat) dollar
fagiir	(–iin) poor
faransa	France
faransi	(–yyiin) French
fataH	(yiftaH) he opened
fað̣il	grace, favor
fi	in
fii	there is; there are
fiil	(fyaal) elephant
filfil	(coll.) pepper
fi l-Hagiiga	in fact
filim	(ʼaflaam) film, movie
fils	(fluus) fils
finjaan	(fanaajiin) cup; coffee cup
firn	(fraan) stove; bakery
fluus	money (f.)
foog	(prep., adv.) above; over
ftiham	(yiftihim) he understood
fundug	(fanaadig) hotel
gaabal	(ygaabil) he met, had an interview
gaal	(yguul) he said
gabil	(prep.) before; ago

gaddam	(ygaddim) he offered, submitted
gafša	(gfaaš) spoon; ladle
gahwa	coffee
gaHfiyya	(–aat) hat
galan	(–aat) gallon
galiil	(–iin) few; little
gaḷam	(gḷaama) pencil; pen
gara	(yigra) he read
garaaj	(–aat) garage
gariib	(–iin) near, close by
gaṣiir	(gṣaar) short
gaṣir	(gṣuur) castle, palace
gaṣṣaab	(gaṣaaṣiib) butcher
gaṭu	(gṭaawa) cat (f. gaṭwa)
gawi	(–yyiin) strong, powerful
geeḏ̣	summer
giṭar	Qatar
giṭari	(–yyiin) Qatari
giweeni	(–yyiin) relating to Umm al-Qaiwain
giḏ̣ab	(yigḏ̣ab) he grabbed
gḷaaṣ	(–aat) glass (for drinking)
guuṭi	(gawaaṭi) can
ġaali	(–iin) expensive
ġada	lunch
ġalaṭ	(adj.) wrong
gamiiṣ	(gumṣaan) shirt
ġanam	(coll.) sheep, goats
ġani	(–yyiin) rich
ġanna	(yġanni) he sang

ġarb	west
ġassaala	(–aat) washing machine
ġazaal	(ġuzlaan) deer; gazelle
ġitra	(ġitar) head dress
ġraam	(–aat) gram
gunṣul	(ganaaṣil) consul
gunṣuliyya	(–aat) consulate
ha š-šikil	in this manner
haaðа	this (m.) (f. **haaði**)
hal	folks (syn. **'ahil**)
hala	hi, hello
halHiin	now
haluw	hello
hamuur	kind of fish
handasa	engineering; geometry
hawa	air; weather (var. **ṭaqṣ**)
hazali	(–yyiin) comical, funny
(ha)ðaak	(haðaliik) that (f. **haðiič**)
(ha)ðeel	these
hduum	clothes, clothing
hidim	(hduum) clothes, clothing
hin	they (f.)
hindi	(hnuud) Indian
hini	here (var. **'ihni**)
hiya	she
hum	they (m.)
huwa	he
Haaff	dry
Haakim	(Hukkaam) ruler

Haal	condition
Haarr	(–iin) hot
Haawal	(yHaawil) he tried
Haaᵭ̣ir	(–iin) ready
Habb	(yHibb) he loved, liked
Habba	piece of s. th.
Hača	(yiHči) he spoke, conversed
Haddaad	(–iin) blacksmith
Hadiiga	(Hadaayig) garden
Hadiigat Hayawaanaat	zoo
Hafla	(–aat) party, celebration
Haflat ġada	luncheon
Haflat 9irs	wedding party
Hagg	belonging to
Hagiiga	(Hagaayig) fact, truth
Haliib	milk
Halwa	sweets; dessert
Hamar	(Humur) red
Hamd	praise; thanks
Hammaal	(Hamaamiil) porter
Hammaam	(–aat) bathroom
Haraam	unlawful; taboo
Harr	heat
Haṣṣal	(yHaṣṣil) he found; he obtained
Haṭṭ	(yHuṭṭ) he put
Hawaali	approximately, about
Hayawaan	(–aat) animal
Hazza	time

Hda9aš	eleven
Hijra	(Hijar) room
Hilu	(Hilwiin) sweet; beautiful (f. **Hilwa**)
Hmaar	(Hamiir) donkey
Hsaab	(–aat) bank account; bill
Hsaab	arithmetic
Hṣaan	(xeel) horse
Htaaj	(yiHtaaj) he needed
Htifal	(yiHtafil) he celebrated
Hukuuma	government
Hummoṣ	chick peas
Hurma	(Hariim) woman; wife
ja, yą	(yaji) he came
jaab	(yjiib) he brought
jaam	(–aat) glass
jaami9	(jawaami9) mosque
jaami9a	(–aat) university
jaawab	(yjaawib) he answered, replied
jadiid	(jiddad) new
jalbuut	(jalaabiit) boat
jamaa9a	people; relatives
jamiil	(–iin) beautiful; handsome
janṭa	(jinaṭ) bag; suitcase
jarrab	(yjarrib) he tried
jawaab	(–aat) answer, reply
jawaaz	(–aat) passport
jaww	atmosphere; air
jawwi	(–yyiin) airmail; atmospheric

jeeš	army
jibin	(coll.) cheese
jiddaam	in front of; in front
jigaara	(jigaayir) cigarette
jiha	(–aat) direction, side
jiHH	(coll.) watermelons
jimrig	(jamaarig) customs, duty
jindi	(jnuud) soldier
jinuub	south
jiziira	(juzur) island; peninsula
jiziirat daas	Das Island
juġraafya	geography
juluus	accession
juuti	(jawaati) pair of shoes
juu9aan	(–iin) hungry
kaan fii	there was; there were
kaatib	(kuttaab) clerk
kabaab	kabob
kalb	(klaab) dog
kallaf	(ykallif) it cost
kanaba	(–aat) sofa
kanada	Canada
kanadi	(–yyiin) Canadian
kaniisa	(kanaayis) church
kaθiir	much; many; very
kaðaalik	too, also
keelu	kilogram
keelumitir	kilometer
kill	(with foll. def. n.) all, the whole of (with foll. nondef. n.) each, every

killiš	very
kirfaaya	(–aat) bed
kirsi	(karaasi) chair
kitab	(yiktib) he wrote
ktaab	(kutub) book
kubba	kibbi
kuub	('akwaab) cup
kuuli	(kuuliyya) coolie, workman
kuut	('akwaat) coat; jacket
kweeti	(–yyiin) Kuwaiti
la	no
laazim	must, have to, should
laff	(yliff) he made a turn
laHam	(coll.) meat
laHam ġanam	mutton, lamb
lajil	in order to, so that
lamma	(conj.) when
landan	London
leel	(coll.) night, evening
leen	(conj.) when; until
leeš	why
leet	(–aat) light
li'an	because
libas	(yilbas) he wore, put on
libnaan	Lebanon
libnaani	(–yyiin) Lebanese
liibi	(–yyiin) Libyan
liibya	Libya
li-kweet	Kuwait

li-mHarrag	Muharraq
li9ab	(yil9ab) he played
li-9raag	Iraq
lo ... lo	either ... or
loon	('alwaan) color
ma	(with foll. verb) not
ma 9alee!	never mind!
maạl	belonging to
maani9	(mawaani9) objection
maað̣i	past; last
mablaġ	(mabaaliġ) sum, amount
madiina	(mudun) city
magḷi	fried
mahar	(muhuur) dowry
maHHad	nobody, no one
maktab	(makaatib) office
maktab il-bariid	Post Office
mamnuun	(–iin) grateful
man?	who?
manð̣ar	(manaað̣ir) view, scene
mara	(Hariim) woman
marag	meat broth
marHaba	hello, hi
mariið̣	(–iin) sick, ill
markaz	(maraakiz) center
markaz tadriib	training center
masa	evening, night (m.)
masaafa	(–aat) distance

masyid	(masaayid) mosque
maṣir	Egypt
maṣkat	Muscat
maṣkati	(–yyiin) relating to Muscat
maṣri	(–yyiin) Egyptian
mašġuul	(–iin) busy
maškuur	thank you
mašwi	(–yyiin) roasted, grilled
mata?	when?
maṭaar	(–aat) airport
maṭbax	(maṭaabix) kitchen
maṭ9am	(maṭaa9im) restaurant
mawjuud	(–iin) located; found
maw9id	(mawaa9iid) appointment
maylis	(mayaalis) living room
maynuun	(mayaaniin) crazy, insane
mayy	water
maθal	('amθaal) proverb, saying
ma9	with
mbaarak	(–iin) blessed
meez	(myuuz) table
mHassin	(–iin) barber
miil	('amyaal) mile
miilaad	(mawaaliid) birth
miizaan	(mawaaziin) scales, balance
mikaniiki	(–yyiin) mechanic; mechanical
min	from
min zamaan	long time ago
mistaanis	(–iin) happy

mista9jil	(–iin) urgent, in a hurry
miša	(yimši) he walked
miškila	(mašaakil) problem
mit'akkid	(–iin) certain, confident
mit'assif	(–iin) sorry
miteen	two hundred
mitiin	(–iin) fat, well built
mitir	(mtaar) meter (distance)
mittaHid	(–iin) united
mitzawwij	(–iin) married
mneen?	where from?
mooz	(coll.) bananas
msaafir	(–iin) traveler, passenger
msajjal	(–iin) registered
mṣaxxan	(–iin) running a temperature
mtaHan	(yimtiHin) he tested, examined
mudda	(mudad) period of time
mudiir	(–iin) director, manager
muhandis	(–iin) engineer
mukaan	('amaakin) place
mumarriđ̣	(–iin) male nurse
mumaθθil	(–iin) actor
mumkin	possible; possibly
mumtaaz	(–iin) excellent
muntazah	(–aat) park, recreation ground
mursil	(–iin) sender
murta	his wife
mustašfa	(–yaat) hospital (m.)
muub	(with foll. n. or adj.) not

muxiif	(–iin) scary
mu9allim	(–iin) teacher
mxabbaḷ	(–iin) crazy, insane
naadi	(nawaadi) clubhouse
naam	(ynaam) he slept
naas	people
nafs	(with foll. def. n.) same
nafs iš-šayy	the same thing
najjaar	(najaajiir) carpenter
naxaḷ	(coll.) palm tress
naϑ̣iif	(nϑ̣aaf) clean
naϑ̣ϑ̣af	(ynaϑ̣ϑ̣if) he cleaned
na9am	yes
niHin	we
nimir	(nmuura) tiger, leopard
nisa	(yinsa) he forgot
noom	(n.) sleep
noo9	('anwaa9) kind
nšaaḷḷa	God willing; yes (Sir)
numra	(numar) number
nuṣṣ	half
nxaḷa	(naxaḷ) palm tree
paaṣ	(–aat) bus; passport
pooliis	(pooliisiyya) policeman
pooliisi	detective (adj.)
qisim	('aqsaam) section
qur'aan	Quran
raabi9	fourth
raad	(yriid) he wanted, liked
raadu	(–waat) radio

raaH	(yruuH) he went
raaṣ	(ruus) head
raaṣ il-xeema	Ras al-Khaima
raayiH	(–iin) going
raa9i	(–iin) owner, proprietor
radeetar	(–aat) radiator
rajil	man; husband
ramil	(coll.) sand
raqam	('arqaam) number
rasta	(–aat) paved road
raṭib	(–iin) humid
rawwa	(yrawwi) he showed
raxiiṣ	(–iin) cheap
rayyaal	(rayaayiil) man
rayyis	(–iin) chief, boss
raziif	celebration, merry making
reewas	(yreewis) he backed up, reversed
ribyaan	shrimp
rifiij	(rifaayij) friend, companion
rigaṣ	(yirguṣ) he danced
rija9	(yirja9) he returned
risaala	(rasaayil) letter, message
rubbiteen	two rupees
rubbiyya	(–aat) rupee
rub9	(rbaa9) one-fourth
rub9a	rub'a (weight)
rumaadi	(–yyiin) grey
rumḏ̣aan	Ramadhan
ruṭuuba	humidity

ruxṣa	(ruxaṣ) permission; vacation
ryaal	('aryil) riyaal (money)
saabi9	seventh
saadis	sixth
saafar	(ysaafir) he traveled
saar	(ysiir) he left, went
saa9a	(—aat) hour; clock; watch
saa9ad	(ysaa9id) he helped
sabi9imya	seven hundred
sabi9ta9aš	seventeen
sab9a	seven
sab9iin	seventy
sadiig	('asdiga) friend
safaara	(—aat) embassy
safiina	(sufun) ship
salaam	peace
salaama	(—aat) safety, security
sallam	(ysallim) he greeted
sammaač	(simaamiič) fisherman
sana	(—waat, siniin) year
santral	telephone exchange
ṣaxxan	(yṣaxxin) he heated
sayyaara	(—aat) car
sa9daan	(sa9aadiin) ape, monkey
seef	(syuuf) sword
si'al	(yis'al) he asked
sibaH	(yisbaH) he swam
siččiin	(sičaačiin) knife
siHab	(yisHab) he withdrew (money); he pulled

siif	(syaaf) seashore
siinama	(–aat) cinema
sikan	(yiskin) he lived, dwelled
sikirteer	(–iin) secretary
simač	(coll.) fish
sima9	(yisma9) he heard
sitta	six
sitta9aš	sixteen
sittiin	sixty
sittimya	six hundred
si9ir	('as9aar) price; cost
soolaf	(ysoolif) he chattered
staanas	(yistaanis) he was happy; he had a good time
staraaH	(yistriiH) he rested
starxaṣ	(yistarxiṣ) he excused himself
su'aal	('as'ila) question
subuu9	('asaabii9) week
suudaani	(–yyiin) Sudanese
suug	('aswaag) market
suuri	(–yyiin) Syrian
suuriyya	Syria
sxaḷa	(–aat) young goat, lamb
ṣaad	(yṣiid) he caught, hunted
ṣaafi	kind of fish
ṣaaHi	(–iin) conscious; not sick
ṣaaHib	('aṣHaab) friend
ṣaaloona	soup
ṣaam	(yṣuum) he fasted

ṣaar	(yṣiir) he became
ṣabaaH	morning
ṣabir	patience
ṣabir šwayy!	wait a minute!
ṣaff	(ṣfuuf) class
ṣagir	(ṣguur) falcon, hawk
ṣaġiir	(ṣġaar) young, small
ṣaHin	(ṣHuun) plate, dish
ṣalaa	(–waat) prayer
ṣalla	(yṣalli) he prayed
ṣanduug	(ṣanaadiig) box
ṣanduug bariid	mail box
ṣa9b	(–iin) difficult, hard
ṣbeeṭi	kind of fish
ṣeef	summer
ṣiHHa	health
ṣoob	toward, in the direction of; by
ṣooġa	jewelry
š da9wa?	what's wrong?
šaaf	(yšuuf) he saw
šaal	(yšiil) he lifted, carried
šaari9	(šawaari9) street
šaarji	(–yyiin) relating to Sharja
šahaada	(–aat) certificate, degree
šahar	('ašhir) month
šakar	sugar
šarg	east
šarika	(–aat) company
šawa	(yišwi) he roasted, grilled

šayy	('ašyaa') thing; something
šigga	(šigag) apartment
šiiša	('išyaš) (gas) station
šiišt il-batrool	gas station
šikil	('aškaal) kind, part
šimaal	left (hand)
širad	(yišrid) he ran away
širib	(yišrab) he drank
širṭi	(širṭa) policeman
šita	winter (m.)
šjara	(šijar) tree
šloonak?	how are you?
štaġal	(yištaġil) he worked
štira	(yištiri) he bought
šu?	what?
šuġul	('ašġaal) work, job
šwayy	little; few
taanki	(tawaanki) tank, reservoir
taariix	(tawaariix) history
taasi9	ninth
taayir	(–aat) tire
tadriib	training
tagahwa	(yitgahwa) he drank coffee
tagriib	about, approximately
taHat	under; beneath
taksi	(takaasi) taxi
talafoon	(–aat) telephone
talavizyoon	(–aat) television
tarbiya	education

tasallaf	(yitsallaf) he borrowed
taðkara	(taðaakir) ticket
ta9aal!	(imp.) come! come here!
teebil	(tawaabil) table; desk
tfaḍḍal!	please!
tġadda	(yitġadda) he ate lunch
tiffaaH	(coll.) apples
tirak	(yitrik) he left
tiras	(yitris) he filled
tisi9imya	nine hundred
tisi9ta9aš	nineteen
tis9a	nine
tis9iin	ninety
tkallam	(yitkallam) he talked, spoke
trayyag	(yitrayyag) he ate breakfast
tuunis	Tunisia
tuunisi	(–yyiin) Tunisian
twannas	(yitwannas) he had a good time, enjoyed himself
t9allam	(yit9allam) he learned
t9ašša	(yit9ašša) he ate supper
ṭaabiġ	(ṭuwaabig) floor, flat
ṭaabi9	(ṭuwaabi9) postage stamp
ṭaal	(yṭuul) it lasted long
ṭaal 9umrak!	God prolong your life!
ṭaalib	(ṭullaab) student
ṭabbal	(yṭabbil) he beat the drum
ṭalab	(yiṭlub) he asked, requested
ṭalab	(–aat) application

ṭamaaṭ	(coll.) tomatoes
ṭaqs	weather (var. **hawa**)
ṭard	(ṭruud) package
ṭariig	(ṭurug) road, way
ṭarraš	(yṭarriš) he sent, mailed
ṭawiil	(ṭwaal) tall, long
ṭawiil il-9umur	the long-lived one
ṭayaraan	aviation, flight
ṭayyaara	(–aat) airplane
ṭayyib	(–iin) good; well
ṭa9aam	food
ṭibax	(yiṭbax) he cooked
ṭuul	length
w	and
waafag	(ywaafig) he agreed
waaHid	one (f. **waHda**)
waajid	much; many; very
wagt	('awgaat) time
walaakin	but
walad	('awlaad) boy; son
walad	(wild) son
walaw	even though
walla	or
waḷḷa	honestly; by golly
wara	(prep., adv.) behind
warag	(coll.) paper; cards
waṣix	(–iin) dirty
wazaara	(–aat) ministry
wazaarat id-daaxiliyya	Min. of the Interior

wazaarat il-'aṧgaal	Min. of Public Works
wazaarat il-batrool	Min. of Petroleum
wazaarat il-maaliyya	Min. of Finance
wazaarat il-muwaaṣalaat	Ministry of Communications
wazaarat il-xaarijiyya	Min. of Foreign Affairs
wazaarat il-9adil	Min. of Justice
wazaarat iṣ-ṣiHHa	Min. of Health
wazaarat it-tarbiya	Ministry of Education
wazaarat iz-ziraa9a	Min. of Agric.
waziir	(wuzara) minister
ween?	where?
weeš?	what?
wiiza	(wiyaz) visa
wilaaya	(–aat) state
winsa	fun, good time
wiṣal	(yooṣal) he arrived
wiyya	with
xaabar	(yxaabir) he telephoned
xaamis	fifth
xaaṭir	(xuṭṭaar) guest
xabbaaz	(–iin) baker
xafiif	(xfaaf) light, not heavy
xaliij	(xiljaan) gulf
xaḷḷa	(yxaḷḷi) he left alone, let go
xaḷḷaṣ	(yxaḷḷiṣ) he finished
xamista9aš	fifteen
xamsa	five
xamsiin	fifty
xamsimya	five hundred

xanjar	(xanaajir) dagger
xarbaan	(–iin) out of order
xaruuf	(xirfaan) lamb
xass	(coll.) lettuce
xaṭṭ	(xuṭuuṭ) (telephone) line; letter
xayyaaṭ	(–iin) tailor
xeema	(xyaam) tent
xooš	fine, good
xubiz	(coll.) bread
xyaar	(coll.) cucumber
yaabis	(–iin) dry
yamkin	probably; perhaps
yamm	by, close to, near
ya9ni	that is, I mean
yimiin	right (hand)
yisaar	left (hand)
yoom	('ayyaam) day
zaar	(yzuur) he visited
zalaaṭa	salad
zamaan	time, age
zawaaj	marriage
zawj	('azwaaj) husband
zeen	fine, good
ziraa9a	agriculture
ziyaada	excess; increase; raise (in salary)
θaaliθ	third
θaamin	eighth
θaanawi	(–yyiin) secondary
θaani	second (f. **θaanya**)

θagiil	(−iin, θgaal) heavy
θalaaθa	three
θalaaθiin	thirty
θalaaθimya	three hundred
θalatta9aš	thirteen
θallaaja	(−aat) refrigerator
θamaaniin	eighty
θamaanimya	eight hundred
θamaanta9aš	eighteen
θamaanya	eight
θaman	('aθmaan) cost, price
θilθ	('aθlaaθ) one third
θinteen	two (f.)
θna9aš	twelve
θoob	(θwaab) dress
ðaak	(ðolaak) that (one)
ðahab	gold
ðahabi	(−yyiin) gold, golden
ðibiiHa	(ðibaayiH) slaughter animal
ḍ̄aHHač	(yḍ̄aHHič) he made s.o. laugh
ḍ̄ariiba	(ḍ̄araayib) tax
ḍ̄aruuri	(−yyiin) necessary
ḍ̄a9iif	(−iin) weak, skinny
ḍ̄ibyaani	(−yyiin) relating to Abu Dhabi
ḍ̄iHiyya	(−aat) sacrificed animal
ḍ̄uhur	noon, noontime
9aada	(−aat) habit, custom
9aadi	(−yyiin) ordinary, usual

9aagil	(–iin) wise, rational
9aam	('a9waam) year
9aamm	public, general
9aaṣima	(9awaaṣim) capital
9aašir	tenth
9aayla	(9awaayil) family
9adil	justice
9agil	(9guul) mind, brain
9ajiib	(–iin) strange, extraordinary
9ajmaan	Ajman
9ala	on
9ala Hsaabi	at my expense, on me
9allam	(y9allim) he taught
9ammaan	Amman
9aṛabi	(9aṛab) Arab; Arabic (language)
9ariis	(9irsaan) bridegroom
9arras	(y9arris) he got married
9aruus(a)	(9araayis) bride
9aša	dinner
9ašara	ten
9atiij	(–iin) old, ancient
9aṭa	(ya9ṭi) he gave
9aṭni!	give me!
9aṭšaan	(–iin) thirsty
9awar	(9iwraan) one-eyed
9ayal	therefore
9ayyad 9ala	(y9ayyid) he celebrated a feast with s.o.
9ayyil	(9yaal) child
9azam 9ala	(yi9zim) he invited s.o. to s.th.

9eeš	(coll.) rice
9gaaḷ	(–aat, 9ugḷa) headband
9iid	('a9yaad) feast, festival
9iid il-'istiglaal	Independence Day
9iid il-juluus	Accession Day
9iid il-miilaad	Christmas
9iid iḏ̣-ḏ̣iHiyya	Sacrifice Feast
9iid raaṣ is-sana	New Year's Day
9imal	(yi9mal) he did; he made
9ind	in the possession of; at a place; close by, near
9inwaan	(9anaawiin) address
9iraf	(y9arif) he knew
9irs	(9raas) wedding
9išriin	twenty
9ood	big, large
9ugub	(prep.) after
9umaan	Oman
9umri ma ...	I have never ...
9umur	('a9maar) age; lifetime
9uṭla	(9uṭal) vacation; holiday

ENGLISH – GULF ARABIC

he was able; he could	gadar (yigdar)
about	tagriib, Hawaali
above	See over.
Abu Dhabi	ʼabu ð̣abi
Abu Dhabi, relating to	ð̣ibyaani (–yyiin)
accession	juluus
accession day	9iid il-juluus
actor	mumaθθil (–iin)
address	9inwaan (9anaawiin)
after (prep.)	9ugub, ba9d
age	9umur (9maar)
he agreed	waafag (ywaafig)
agriculture	ziraa9a
air mail	jawwi (–yyiin)
airplane	ṭayyaara (–aat)
airport	maṭaar (–aat)
Ajman	9ajmaan
Algeria	ʼil-jazaaʼir
all	kill (+ def. N)
alone	bruuH–
also	ba9ad
although	walaw
America	ʼamriika
American	ʼamriiki (ʼamrikaan)
Amman	9ammaan
more ancient	ʼa9taj
and	w

animal	Hayawaan (–aat)
sacrificed animal	ð̣iHiyya (–aat)
slaughter animal	ð̣ibiiHa (ð̣ibaayiH)
answer	jawaab (–aat)
he answered	jaawab (yjaawib)
apartment	šigga (šigag)
ape	sa9daan (sa9aadiin)
apples	tiffaaH (coll.)
application	ṭalab (–aat)
appointment	maw9id (mawaa9iid)
approximately	tagriib, Hawaali
Arab	9aṛabi (9aṛab)
Arabian Gulf	'il-xaliij il-9aṛabi
Arabic language	9aṛabi
arithmetic	Hsaab
he arrived	wiṣal (yooṣal)
army	jeeš
he asked	si'al (yis'al)
he ate	'akal (yaakil)
he ate breakfast	trayyag (yitrayyag)
he ate lunch	tġadda (yitġadda)
he ate supper	t9ašša (yit9ašša)
atmosphere	jaww
aviation	ṭayaraan
he backed up	reewas (yreewis)
bag, suitcase	janṭa (jinaṭ)
bag	čiis (kyaas)
Baghdad	baġdaad
Bahrain	'il-baHreen

baker	xabbaaz (–iin)
bakery	firn (fraan)
bananas	mooz (coll.)
bank	bank (bnuuk)
bank account	Hsaab (–aat)
barber	mHassin (–iin)
bathroom	Hammaam (–aat)
battery	batri (bataari)
he beat (the drum)	ṭabbal (yṭabbil)
beautiful	jamiil (–iin)
more beautiful	'ajmal
he became	ṣaar (yṣiir)
because	li'an
to become long	ṭaal (yṭuul)
bed	kirfaaya (–aat)
bedroom	Hijrat noom
Bedouin	bdiwi (badu)
beer	biira
before	gabil
behind	xalf, 9ugb
Beirut	beruut
belonging to	Hagg, maal
better	'azyan, 'aHsan
big	čibiir (kbaar)
bigger	'akbar
birth	miilaad
black	'aswad (suud) (f. **sooda**)
blacksmith	Haddaad (–iin)
blessed	mbaarak (–iin)

he blessed	baarak (ybaarik)
blind	'a9ma (9imyaan)
blue	'azrag (zurg) (f. **zarga**)
boat	jalbuut (jalaabiit)
book	ktaab (kutub)
he borrowed	tasallaf (yitsallaf)
boss	rayyis, mudiiir
bottle	boṭil (bṭaala)
he bought	štara (yištiri)
box	ṣanduug (ṣanaadiig)
mailbox	ṣanduug bariid
boy	walad (wlaad)
bread	xubiz (coll.)
bride	9aruus (9araayis)
brídegroom	9ariis (9irsaan)
broadcasting (station)	'iđaa9a
meat broth	marag
brother	'uxu ('ixwaan)
he brought	jaab (yjiib)
brown	bunni (–yyiin)
building	binaaya (–aat)
bus	paaṣ (–aat)
busy	mašġuul (–iin)
but (conj.)	bas
but	walaakin, bas
butcher	gaṣṣaab (gaṣaaṣiib)
butter	dihin (coll.)
by	yamm
Cairo	'il-qaahiṛa

he came	ʹaja, ja (var. **ʹaya, ya**) (yaji)
camel	bi9iir (ba9aariin)
can	guuṭi (gawaaṭi)
Canadian	kanadi (−yyiin)
cantaloupes	baṭṭiix (coll.)
capital	9aaṣima (9awaaṣim)
car	sayyaara (−aat)
card	biṭaaga (−aat)
carpenter	najjaar (najaajiir)
case	See **matter.**
castle	See **palace.**
cat	gaṭu (gṭaawa) (f. **gaṭwa**)
he caught	ṣaad (yṣiid)
he celebrated	Htafal (yiHtafil)
he celebrated a feast with s.o.	9ayyad (y9ayyid) 9ala
celebration	9iid (ʹa9yaad)
center	markaz (maraakiz)
training center	markaz tadriib
men's teacher training center	daar mu9allimiin
women's teacher training center	daar mu9allimaat
certain, sure	mitʹakkid (−iin)
certificate	šahaada (−aat)
chair	kirsi (karaasi)
he changed	baddal (ybaddil)
he chatted	soolaf (ysoolif)
cheap	raxiiṣ (−iin)
cheaper	ʹarxaṣ
he checked	čayyak (yčayyik)

cheese	jibin (coll.)
chick peas	Hummoṣ
chicken	dijaaj (coll.)
child	9ayyil (9yaal)
Christmas	9iid il-miilaad
church	kaniisa (kanaayis)
cigarette	jigaara (jigaayir)
cinema	siinama (–aat)
circle	dawwaar (dawawiir)
city	madiina (mudun)
class	ṣaff (ṣfuuf)
clean	naθ̣iif (nθ̣aaf)
he cleaned	naθ̣θ̣af (ynaθ̣θ̣if)
cleaner	ʼanθ̣af
clerk	kaatib (kuttaab)
closer	ʼagrab
clothes	hduum
clubhouse	naadi (nawaadi)
coat	kuut (ʼakwaat)
coffee	gahwa
cold	baarid
colder	ʼabrad
color	loon (ʼalwaan)
come!	ta9aal!
comical	hazali (–yyiin)
companion	rifiij (rifaayij)
company	šarika (–aat)
condition	Haal
conscious	ṣaaHi (–yiin)

consul	gunṣul (ganaaṣil)
consulate	gunṣuliyya (–aat)
he contacted	ʼittaṣal (yittaṣil)
he cooked	ṭibax (yiṭbax)
coolie	kuuli (kuuliyya)
cost	θaman (ʼaθmaan); si9ir (ʼas9aar)
it cost	kallaf (ykallif)
country	balad (bildaan)
cows	bagar (coll.)
crazier	ʼayaan
crazy	mxabbaḷ (–iin), maynuun (mayaaniin)
cucumber	xyaar (coll.)
cup	finjaan (fanaajiin); kuub (ʼakwaab)
customs	jimrig (jamaarig)
dagger	xanjar (xanaajir)
Damascus	dimašq
he danced	rigaṣ (yirguṣ)
Das Island	jiziirat daas
daughter	bint (banaat)
day	yoom (ʼayyaam)
New Year's Day	raaṣ is-sana
deer	ġazaal (ġuzlaan)
department	daayra (dawaayir)
detective	pooliisi (adj.)
dhow	daaw
he did	9imal (yi9mal)
difficult	ṣa9b (–iin)
dinar	diinaar (danaaniir)
direction	jiha (–aat), ṣoob

director	mudiir (–iin)
dirham	dirhim (daraahim)
dirtier	ʼawṣax
dirty	waṣix (–iin)
distance	masaafa (–aat)
doctor	daxtar (daxaatra) (f. **daxtoora**)
dog	kalb (klaab)
Doha	ʼid-dooHa
dollar	duulaar (–aat)
donkey	Hmaar (Hamiir)
door	baab (biibaan)
dowry	mahar (muhuur)
dozen	darzan (daraazin)
he drank	širib (yišrab)
he drank coffee	tagahwa (yitgahwa)
dress	hidim (hduum)
driver	dreewil (dreewliyya)
dry	Haaff, yaabis (–iin)
Dubai	dbayy
east	šarg
education	tarbiya
eggplant	beeđ̄injaan (coll.)
eggs	beeđ̣̄ (coll.)
Egypt	maṣir
Egyptian	maṣri (–yyiin)
eight	θamaanya
eighteen	θamaanta9aš
eighth	θaamin
eight hundred	θamaanimya

eighty	θamaaniin
either ... or	lo ... lo ...
elementary	'ibtidaa'i
elephant	fiil (fyaal)
eleven	Hda9aš
embassy	safaara (–aat)
emirate	'imaara (–aat)
engineer	muhandis (–iin)
engineering	handasa
England	'ingiltara
English (man)	'ingiliizi ('ingiliiz)
he entered	dašš (ydišš)
evening	masa, leel
in the evening	'il-masa
excellent, super	mumtaaz (–iin)
except	'illa
excess	ziyaada (–aat)
he excused himself	starxaṣ (yistarxiṣ)
expense, at my	9ala Hsaabi
at the expense of	9ala čiis
expensive	ġaali (–yyiin)
more expensive	'aġla
fact	Hagiiga (Hagaayig)
in fact	fi l-Hagiiga
falcon	ṣagir (ṣguur)
family	9aayla
far	ba9iid
farther	'ab9ad
he fasted	ṣaam (yṣuum)

fat	miṭiin (–iin)
father	'ubu
may father	'ubuuy
father of (with foll. name)	'abu
fatter	'amtan
favor	faḏ̣il
feast	9iid ('9yaad)
Ramadhan Feast	9iid rumḏ̣an
Sacrifice Feast	9iid iḏ̣-ḏ̣iHiyya
few	galiil (–iin)
fewer	'agall
fifteen	xamista9aš
fifth	xaamis
fifty	xamsiin
he filled	tiras (yitris)
film	filim ('aflaam)
fils	fils (fluus)
final	'aaxir ('awaaxir)
fine (adv.)	bxeer
fine	zeen (–iin)
he finished	xaḷḷaṣ (yxaḷḷiṣ)
first	'awwal
fish	simač (coll.)
fisherman	sammaač (samaamiič)
five	xamsa
five hundred	xamsimya
floor, flat	ṭaabig (ṭuwaabig)
folks	hal (var. **'ahil**)
food	'akil, ṭa9aam

he forgot	nisa (yinsa)
fork	čingaal (čanaagiil)
forty	'arba9iin
he found	Haṣṣal (yHaṣṣil)
four	'arba9
four hundred	'arba9imya
fourteen	'arba9ta9aš
fourth	raabi9
one fourth	rub9
France	faṛansa
French	faṛansi (–yyiin)
Friday	'il-jum9a
fried	magḷi (–yyiin)
friend	sadiig, rifiij, ṣaaHib
from	min
in front of	jiddaam
Fujaira	'il-fijeera
fun	winsa
funny	hazali (–yyiin)
gallon	galan (–aat)
garage	garaaj (–aat)
garden	bustaan (basaatiin) Hadiiga (Hadaayig)
gas station	šiišat batrool
he gave	9aṭa (ya9ṭi)
geography	juġraafya
geometry	handasa
girl	bint (banaat)
give me!	9aṭni!
glass	jaam (–aat)

(drinking) glass	g̣laaṣ (g̣laaṣaat)
goats	ġanam (coll.)
God	'al̤l̤a
God forbid!	'a9uuđu bi llaah!
God prolong your life!	ṭaal 9umrak!
God willing	nšaal̤l̤a
going	raayiH
gold	đahab
golden	đahabi (—yyiin)
good	zeen, ṭayyib (—iin)
he had a good time	twannas (yitwannas)
government	Hukuuma (—aat)
he grabbed	giđ̣ab (yigđ̣ab)
gram	ġraam (—aat)
grateful	mamnuun, maškuur
green	'axđ̣ar (xuđ̣ur) (f. **xađ̣ra**)
he greeted	sallam (ysallim) 9ala
grey	rumaadi (—yyiin)
guest	đ̣eef (đ̣yuuf)
gulf	xaliij (xiljaan)
habit	9aada (—aat)
half	nuṣṣ
handsome	jamiil (—iin)
handsomer	'ajmal
happy	mistaanis (—iin)
he was happy	staanas (yistaanis)
hat	gaHfiyya (—aat)
he	huwa (hum)
head	raaṣ (ruuṣ)

head band	9gaaḷ (9ugḷa)
head dress	ġitra (ġitar)
health	ṣiHHa
he heard	sima9 (yisma9)
heat	Haraara
he heated	ṣaxxan (ysaxxin)
heavy	θagiil (θgaal)
not heavy	xafiif (xfaaf)
hello!	halu!
he helped	saa9ad (ysaa9id)
hens	See **chicken**
here	hini (var. **'ihni**)
history	taariix (tawaariix)
home	beet (byuut), daar (duur)
honestly!	waḷḷa!
horse	Hṣaan (xeel)
hospital	mustašfa (–yaat)
hot	Haarr (–iin)
hotel	'uteel (–aat) fundug (fanaadig)
hotter	'aHarr
hour	saa9a (–aat)
house	daar (duur), beet (byuut)
how	čeef (var. **keef**)
how many	čam (var. **kam**)
how much	čam (var. **kam**)
humid	raṭib (–iin)
more humid	'arṭab
humidity	ruṭuuba

hundred	'imya
hungry	juu9aan (–iin)
hurry, in a	mista9jil (–iin)
husband	rajil (rjaal) zawj ('azwaaj)
I	'aana
if	'iđa
in	fi
indeed	'ii na9am
independence	'istiglaal
Independence Day	9iid il-'istiglaal
India	'il-hind
Indian	hindi (hnuud)
inside	daaxil (prep., adv.)
he invited s.o. to s.th.	9azam (yi9zim) 9ala
Iran	'iiṛan
Iraq	li-9raag
island	jiziira (jazaayir, juzur)
jewelry	ṣooġa
Jordan	'il-'ardun
Jordanian	'arduni (–yyiin)
justice	9adil
kabob	kabaab
Khartoum	'il-xarṭuum
kibbi	kibbi
kilogram	keelu (–waat)
kilometer	keelumitir
kind	noo9 ('anwaa9), šikil ('aškaal)
kitchen	maṭbax (maṭaabix)
he knew	9iraf (y9arif), dara (yidri)

knife	sičiin (sičaačiin)
Kuwait	li-kweet
Kuwaiti	kweeti (–yyiin)
ladle	gafša (gfaaš)
lamb	xaruuf (xirfaan)
large	čibiir (kbaar)
he made s.o. laugh	ð̣aHHak (yð̣aHHik)
he learned	ta9allam (yit9allam)
Lebanon	libnaan
Lebanese	libnaani (–yyiin)
he left	tirak (yitrik) saar (ysiir)
left (hand)	šimaal, yisaar
he left s.th. alone	xaḷḷa (yxaḷḷi)
length	ṭuul
lesson	dars (druus)
letter	xaṭṭ (xṭuuṭ)
lettuce	xass (coll.)
Libya	liibya
Libyan	liibi (–yyiin)
lifetime	9umur (ʼa9maar)
he lifted	šaal (yšiil)
light	leet (–aat)
he liked	Habb (yHibb)
line	xaṭṭ (xṭuuṭ)
lion	ʼasad (ʼusuud)
little	galiil (–iin)
he lived	sikan (yiskin)
located	mawjuud (–iin)
London	landan

long-lived one	ṭawiil ʹil-9umur
he loved	Habb (yHibb)
lunch	ġada
luncheon	Haflat ġada
mail	bariid
man	rayyaal (rayaayiil) rajil (rjaal)
Manama	ʹil-manaama
market	suug (ʹaswaag)
marriage	zawaaj
married	mitzawwij (–iin)
he got married	tazawwaj (yitzawwaj)
matter	da9wa (da9aawi)
I mean, i.e.,	ya9ni
meat	laHam (coll.)
mechanic	mikaniiki (–yyiin)
he met	gaabal (ygaabil)
meter	mitir (mtaar)
middle	ʹawṣaṭ
Middle East	iš-šarg il-ʹawṣaṭ
mile	miil (ʹamyaal)
milk	Haliib
mind	9agil (9guul)
minister	waziir (wuzara)
ministry	wazaara (–aat)
Min. of Agriculture	wazaarat iz-ziraa9a
Min. of Communications	wazaarat il-muwaaṣalaat
Min. of Education	wazaarat it-tarbiya
Min. of Finance	wazaarat il-maaliyya

Min. of For. Affairs	wazaarat il-xaarijiyya
Min. of Health	wazaarat iṣ-ṣiHHa
Min. of Interior	wazaarat id-daaxiliyya
Min. of Justice	wazaarat il-9adil
Min. of Petroleum	wazaarat il-batrool
Min. of Public Works	wazaarat il-'ašġaal
Monday	'il-'aθneen
money	fluus (f.)
month	šahar ('ašhir)
last month	'iš-šahr il-maađ̣i
more	'akθar
morning	ṣabaaH
in the morning	iṣ-ṣabaaH
Morocco	'il-maġrib
mosque	jaami9 (jawaami9) masyid (masaayid)
movie	filim ('aflaam)
much	waajid, kaθiir
Muharraq	mHarrag
Muscat	maṣkat
relating to Muscat	maṣkati (–yyiin)
must	laazim
mutton	laHam ġanam
(by) myself	bruuHi
name	'asim ('asaami)
near	gariib (–iin), yamm
necessary	đ̣aruuri (–yyiin)
he needed	Htaaj (yiHtaaj)
never mind!	ma 9alee!
new	jadiid (jiddad)

newer	'ajdad
night	leel (coll.)
nine	tis9a
nine hundred	tisi9imya
nineteen	tisi9ta9aš
ninety	tis9iin
ninth	taasi9
no	la
nobody	maHHad
noon	ð̣uhur
not	muub (+ N), ma (+ verb), la (+ imper.)
notebook	daftar (dafaatir)
now	halHiin
number	numra (numar), raqam ('arqaam)
nurse	mumarriið̣ (–iin)
objection	maani9 (mawaani9)
he offered	gaddam (ygaddim)
office	maktab (makaatib)
post office	maktab bariid
oil	'aayil
okra	baamya (coll.)
old	9atiij (–iin), čibiir (kbaar)
older	'akbar
Oman	9umaan
on	9ala
one	waaHid
one-eyed	9awar (9iwraan)
one-third	θilθ
only	bas

he opened	fitaH (yiftaH)
or	walla, 'aw
orange (adj.)	burtaqaali (–yyiin)
oranges	burtaqaal (coll.)
orchard	bustaan (basaatiin)
in order to	lajil
out of order	xarbaan (–iin)
ordinary	9aadi (–yyiin)
over	foog (prep., adv.)
owner	raa9i (–iin)
package	ṭard (ṭruud)
package (of cigarettes)	guuṭi jigaayir
he paid	difa9 (yidfa9)
Pakistan	'il-baakistaan
Pakistani	baakistaani (–yyiin)
palace	gaṣir (gṣuur)
palm trees	naxal (coll.)
pants	banṭaluun (banaaṭliin)
paper	warag (coll.)
park	muntazah (–aat)
party	Hafla (–aat)
pasha	baaša
passport	jawaaz (–aat) paaṣ (–aat)
past	maaḍ̄i
pastry, sweet	baglaawa
patience	ṣabir
paved road	rasta (–aat)
peace	salaam
pencil	gaḷam (gḷaama)

people	'ahil, jamaa9a, naas
pepper	filfil (coll.)
Pepsi Cola	bebsi
permission	ruxṣa (ruxaṣ)
Persian	'iiraani (–yyiin)
petroleum	batrool
piece	Habba (–aat)
place	mukaan ('amaakin)
plate	ṣaHin (ṣHuun)
he played	li9ab (yil9ab)
please!	min faḏ̣lak!
he pleased	'a9jab (yi9jib)
policeman	širṭi (širṭa)
poor	fagiir (–iin)
poorer	'afgar
porter	Hammaal (Hamaamiil)
in the possession of	9ind
possible	yamkin
post office	See office.
postage stamp	ṭaabi9 (ṭuwaabi9)
praise	Hamd
he prayed	ṣalla (yṣalli)
prayer	ṣala (var. ṣalaa)
price	θaman ('aθmaan); si9ir ('as9aar)
probably	yamkin
problem	miškila (mašaakil)
proverb	maθal ('amθaal)
public (adj.)	9aamm
he put	Haṭṭ (yHuuṭṭ)

Qatar	giṭar
Qatari	giṭari (–yyiin)
one quarter	rub9 (rbaa9)
question	su'aal ('as'ila)
Quran	qur'aan
radiator	radeetar (–aat)
radio	raadu (-waat)
Ramadhan	rumđ̣aan
he ran away	širad (yišrid)
it rang	dagg (ydigg)
Ras al-Khaima	raaṣ il-xeema
he realized	dara (yidri)
he read	gara (yigra)
ready	Haađ̣ir (–iin)
he was ready	baraz (yabriz)
red	Hamar (Humur)
refrigerator	θallaaja (–aat)
registered	msajjal (–iin)
remainder, remaining	baagi
he rested	staraaH (yistariiH)
restaurant	maṭ9am (maṭaa9im)
he returned	rija9 (yirja9)
rice	9eeš (coll.)
rich	ġani (–yyiin)
richer	'aġna
rifle	bindigiyya (bindig)
right (hand)	yimiin
road	ṭariig (ṭurug)
roasted (adj.)	mašwi (–yyiin)
he roasted	šawa (yišwi)

room	Hijra (Hijar)
living room	maylis
rooster	diič (dyuuč)
ruler	Haakim (Hukkaam)
rupee	rubbiyya (–aat)
safety	salaama
he said	gaal (yguul)
salad	zalaaṭa
same	nafs (+ def. N.)
sand	ramil (coll.)
saner	'aṣHa
he sang	ġanna (yġanni)
Saturday	is-sabt
last Saturday	'is-sabt il-maaḏ̣i
Saudi Arabia	'is-su9uudiyya
he saw	šaaf (yšuuf)
scales	miizaan (mawaaziin)
scary	muxiif (–iin)
scholarship	bi9θa (–aat)
sea	baHar (bHuur)
seashore	siif (syaaf)
second (ord.)	θaani
secondary	θaanawi (–yyiin)
secretary	sikirteer
section	qisim ('aqsaam)
sender	mursil (–iin)
he sent	ṭarraš (yṭarriš)
seven	sab9a
seven hundred	sabi9imya

seventeen	sabi9ta9aš
seventh	saabi9
seventy	sab9iin
Sharja	'iš-šaarja
relating to Sharja	šaarji (—yyiin)
she	hiya (hin)
sheep	ġanam (coll.)
ship	safiina (sufun)
shirt	ġamiiṣ (ġumṣaan)
shoes (pair of)	juuti (jawaati)
shop	dikkaan (dikaakiin)
short	gaṣiir (gṣaar)
shorter	'agṣar
he showed	rawwa (yrawwi)
shrimp	ribyaan
he shut	bannad (ybannid)
sick	mariiđ̣ (—iin)
sicker	'amrađ̣
sister	'uxut ('axawaat)
six	sitta
six hundred	sittimya
sixth	saadis
sixty	sittiin
sleep	noom
he slept	naam (ynaam)
smaller	'aṣġar
sofa	kanaba (—aat)
soldier	jindi (jnuud)
son	walad (wild)

son of	bin
someone	'aHad
sorry	mit'assif (–iin)
soup	ṣaaloona
south	januub
he spoke	Hača (yiHči)
spoon	gafša (gfaaš)
state	wilaaya (–aat)
(gas) station	šiiša ('išyaš)
he stayed	baga (yibga)
he stole	baag (ybuug)
store	See **shop.**
(cooking) stove	firn (fraan)
straight	siida
strange	9ajiib (–iin)
street	šaari9 (šawaari9)
strong	gawi (–yyiin)
stronger	'agwa
student	ṭaalib (ṭullaab)
he studied	diras (yidris)
he submitted	See **offered.**
The Sudan	'is-suudaan
Sudanese	suudaani (–yyiin)
sugar	šakar (coll.)
suitcase	janṭa (jinaṭ)
summer	geeḏ̣, ṣeef
Sunday	'il-'aHad
he swam	sibaH (yisbaH)
sweet	Hilu (– wiin)

sweets	Halwa
sword	seef (syuuf)
Syria	suuriyya
Syrian	suuri (–yyiin)
table	meez, teebil
tailor	xayyaaṭ (–iin)
he talked	tkallam (yitkallam)
tall	ṭawiil (–iin, ṭwaal)
taller	'aṭwal
tank	taanki (tawaanki)
he taught	darras (ydarris)
tax	ḏ̣ariiba (ḏ̣araayib)
taxi	taksi (takaasi)
tea	čaay
teacher	mu9allim (–iin)
telegram	bargiyya (–aat)
telephone	talafoon (–aat)
he telephoned	xaabar (yxaabir)
telephone exchange	santraal
television	talavizyoon (–aat)
temperature, running a	mṣaxxan (–iin)
ten	9ašara (–aat)
tent	xeema (xyaam)
tenth (ord.)	9aašir
he tested	mtaHan (yimtiHin)
thank you	maškuur (–iin)
that	(ha)ðaak (haðoliik) (f. **haðiič**)
there	'ihnaak
there is (are)	fii

there was (were)	kaan fii, čaan fii
therefore	9ayal
thing	šayy ('ašyaa')
same thing	nafs iš-šayy
third (ord.)	θaaliθ
one third	θilθ ('aθlaaθ)
thirsty	9aṭšaan (–iin)
thirteen	θalatta9aš
thirty	θalaaθiin
this	haaðа (m.) (haðeel) haaði (f.)
thousand	'alf ('aalaaf)
three	θalaaθa
three hundred	θalaaθimya
Thursday	'il-xamiis
ticket	taðkara (taðaakir)
tiger	nimir (nmuura)
time	wagt ('awgaat), Hazza
for a long time	min zamaan
a long time ago	min zamaan
one time	marra (–att)
what time?	'ay Hazza?
tip	baxšiiš
tire	taayir (–aat)
today	'il-yoom
tomatoes	ṭamaaṭ (coll.)
tomorrow	baačir
too	ba9ad, kaðaalik
he took	'axað (yaaxið)
toward	ṣoob

town	balad (bildaan)
training	tadriib
he traveled	saafar (ysaafir)
traveler	msaafir (–iin)
trees	šijar (coll.)
he tried	Haawal (yHaawil)
Tuesday	'iθ-θalaaθa
Tunisia	tuunis
Tunisian	tuunisi (–yyiin)
he made a turn	laff (yliff)
twelve	θna9aš
twenty	9išriin
two	'aθneen (f. **θinteen**)
two hundred	miteen
Umm al-Qaiwain	'umm il-giween
relating to Umm al-Qaiwain	giweeni (–yyiin)
under	taHat
he understood	ftiham (yiftihim)
union	'ittiHaad (–aat)
united	mittaHid (–iin)
university	jaami9a (–aat)
unlawful	Haraam
until, till	leen
urgent	mista9jil
vacation	'ijaaza (–aat), 9uṭla, ruxṣa
very	waajid, kaθiir, killiš
view	manđ̣ar (manaađ̣ir)
visa	wiiza (wiyaz)
he visited	zaar (yzuur)

wait a minute!	ṣabir šwayy!
he walked	miša (yimši)
he wanted	baġa (yibġa, yabi)
he was	kaan (ykuun), čaan (yčuun)
washing machine	ġassaala (—aat)
water	mayy
watermelons	jiHH (coll.)
by the way!	'aguul!
in this way	ha š-šikil, čiđi
we	niHin
weak	đ̣a9iif (—iin)
weaker	'ađ̣9af
weather	hawa, ṭaqs
wedding	9irs (9raas)
wedding party	Haflat 9irs
Wednesday	'il-'arba9a
week	subuu9 ('asaabii9)
last week	'is-subuu9 il-maađ̣i
well (adv.)	bxeer
he went	raaH (yruuH)
west	ġarb
what	šu, weeš, š
what's wrong?	š da9wa?
when?	mata?
when	leen, lamma (conj.)
where?	ween?
which? what?	'ay?
white	'abyađ̣ (biiđ̣) (f. beeđ̣a)
who?	man?

who, that, which (rel. pron.)	ʼilli
why?	leeš?
wife	Hurma (Hariim); zawja (—aat)
window	diriiša (diraayiš)
winter	šita (m.)
wise	9aagil (—iin)
wiser	ʼa9gal
with	wiyya, ma9
he withdrew (money)	siHab (yisHab)
woman	Hurma (Hariim)
he wore	libas (yilbas)
work	šuġul (ʼašġaal)
he worked	štaġal (yištaġil)
wrong	ġalaṭ
he wrote	kitab (yiktib)
year	sana (siniin, sanawaat) 9aam (ʼa9waam)
last year	ʼil-9aam il-maaᵭi
yellow	ʼaṣfar (ṣufur) (f. ṣafra)
yes	ʼii, na9am
yesterday	ʼams
day before yesterday	ʼawwal ams
you	ʼinta (ʼintum) (m.) ʼinti (ʼintin) (f.)
young	ṣaġiir (ṣġaar)
younger	ʼaṣġar
zoo	Hadiigat Hayawaanaat

INDEX OF GRAMMATICAL TERMS

The numbers refer to units and sections.

Adjectives

— color 17 V 2, 22 V 3
— elative 22 V 3, 23 V 1
— gender 3 V 3, 18 V 3, 6 V 2,
22 V 3, 23 V 1, 25 V 2
— nisba 6 V 2, 17 V 2
— participal 23 V 4
Article Prefix 3 V 4, 4 V 2, 5 V 2, 16 V 1
Collectives (See Nouns)
Conditionals
— likely 41 V 1
— unlikely 41 V 1
— with imperative 41 V 1
— with imperfect tense 41 V 1
— with perfect tense 41 V 1

Conjunctions

— **'iða** 41 V 1
— **lajil** 29 V 2
— **leen** 23 V 2
— **li'an** 17 V 3
— **w** 1 V 4, 16 V 1, 19 V 2
Dual 13 V 2, 16 V 1, 19 V 2
Equational Sentences 1 V 2, 4 V 1
fii 16 V 4

Intensifiers

—— **killiš** 12 V 2

—— **waajid** 10 VI 3, 12 V 2

Imperatives 9 VI 1, 15 VI 1, 16 V 3, 17 V 5, 18 V 1, 20 V 3, 23 V 3

Imperfect Tense (See Verbs)

laazim 22 V 1

Names

—— of countries 6 V 1, 10 V 1

—— proper 3 V 2, 6 V 1, 10 VI 1

Negative Commands 20 V 1

Negative Particles

—— particle **la** 20 V 1

—— particle **ma** 16 V 4, 17 V 4, 22 V 1, 28 V 3, 30 V 1, 35 V 3

—— particle **muu(b)** 10 VI 2, 23 V 4

Nouns

—— collective 16 V 2, 17 V 1, 18 V 1, 25 V 1

—— construct 4 V 2

—— dual 13 V 2, 16 V 1, 19 V 2

—— gender 3 V 2, 9 VI 2, 13 V 2, 18 V 3

—— unit 16 V 2, 17 V 1, 18 V 1, 25 V 1

Participles 23 V 4

Particles

—— **čam** (kam) 13 V 4

—— future 22 V 2

— **Hagg** 20 V 2
— interrogative 13 V 4
— **maal** 24 V 2
— vocative 5 V 1

Perfect Tense (See Verbs)

phonology
— consonant ġ 4 IV 1
— consonant H 9 V i, 10 V
— consonant ḷ 3 IV 1
— consonant r 2 IV 1
— consonant ṣ 6 IV 1
— consonant ṭ 5 IV 1
— consonant x 2 IV 1, 10 V
— consonant ð̣ 4 IV 1
— consonant 9 7 V 1, 8 V 1
— consonant clusters 12 V 1, 18 V 1
— doubled consonants 3 IV 1
— helping vowel 8 VI 1, 6 V 2, 12 V 1, 13 V 1, 14 V 1
— stress 1 IV 2, 2 IV 2, 3 IV 2, 4 IV 2, 13 V 2, 28 V 1, 30 V 2
— syllable structure 1 IV 2, 3 IV 2
— velarized consonants 3 IV 1, 4 IV 1, 5 IV 1, 6 IV 1
— vowel change 24 V 3, 24 V 5, 30 V 2
— vowel elision 1 V 3, 4 V 3, 13 V 2, 17 V 1, 30 V 1
— vowels **a** –**aa** 1 IV 1
— vowels **e** – **ee** 1 IV 1
— vowels **i** – **ii** 1 IV 1
— vowels **o** – **oo** 2 IV 1
— vowels **u** – **uu** 2 IV 1

Plurals
—— broken 18 V 2, 19 V 2
—— sound 18 V 2

Prepositions 17 VI 1, 8 VI 1, 19 V 1, 22 V 3, 26 V 3, 26 V 4
—— **Hawaali** 26 V 3
—— **ṣoob** 26 V 4
—— **9ind** 8 VI 1

Pronouns
—— antecedent 34 V 2
—— demonstrative 5 V 2, 19 V 3
—— gender 3 V 2
—— object 14 V 3, 18 V 5, 34 V 1
—— personal 1 V 1, 4 V 1, 7 VI 1
—— relative 33 IV 1, 34 V 2, 41 V 2
—— suffixed 1 V 1, 3 V 1, 6 V 3, 7 VI 1, 8 VI 1, 19 V 1, 20 V 2, 24 V 1, 29 V 2, 34 V 2

Relative Clauses 33 IV 1, 34 V 2

Special Constructions
—— ʹay Hazza 26 V 2
—— ʹa9jab 14 V 3
—— čam ṣaarlak 14 V 3
—— Haaẟ̣ir 25 V 2
—— kaan fii 29 V 3
—— maHHad 18 V 4
—— min zamaan 30 V 1
—— muub čiẟi 34 V 4
—— nšaaḷḷa 14 V 3

— — ṣaarli 26 V 1
— — waaHid min 18 V 4
— — wa la waaHid 18 V 4
— — ya9ni 34 V 3
— — yoom ṣaxxanna 41 V 3
— — 9umri ma 39 V 1

Subject Markers 12 V 1, 12 V 2, 13 V 1
Telling Ages 24 V 1
Telling Time 8 VI 2, 9 VI 2, 15 VI 2

Verbs
— — affixes 12 V 1, 13 V 3, 28 V 1
— — defective verbs 28 V 1, 33 IV 1, 35 V 1, 36 V, 37 V
— — double imperfect 13 V 3, 17 V 4, 26 V 1
— — double verbs 30 V 1
— — hamzated verbs 29 V 1
— — hollow verbs 29 V 1, 37 V
— — imperatives (See Imperatives)
— — imperfect tense 12 V 1, 13 V 1, 14 V 1, 15 V 2, 17 V 4, 17 V 5, 18 V 1, 23 V 3, 23 V 4
— — inflectional forms 28 V 1
— — negative 16 V 4, 17 V 4, 20 V 1, 22 V 1, 29 V 3, 30 V 1, 35 V 3
— — perfect tense 12 V 1, 14 V 3, 28 V 1
— — sound vowels 28 V 1, 30 V 1
— — suffixes 28 V 1, 29 V 1, 30 V 1, 33 IV 1
— — verb **'akal** 29 V 1
— — verb **baġa** 35 V 1
— — verb **dašš** 33 IV 1

—— verb **diras** 28 V 1
—— verb **gaabal** 32 V
—— verb **ja** 28 V 1
—— verb **miša** 33 IV 1
—— verb **raaH** 29 V 1
—— verb **ṣaad** 37 V
—— verb **ṣalla** 36 V
—— verb **širib** 29 V 1
—— verb **štaġal** 30 V 1
—— verb **t9ašša** 37 V
—— verb **xaḷḷaṣ** 30 V 1
—— verb **xađ** 34 V 1
—— verb stems 12 V 1, 13 V 1, 23 V 3
—— verb strings 26 V 1, 35 V 2, 40 IV 1
Vowels (See Phonology)
9ind– 8 VI 1